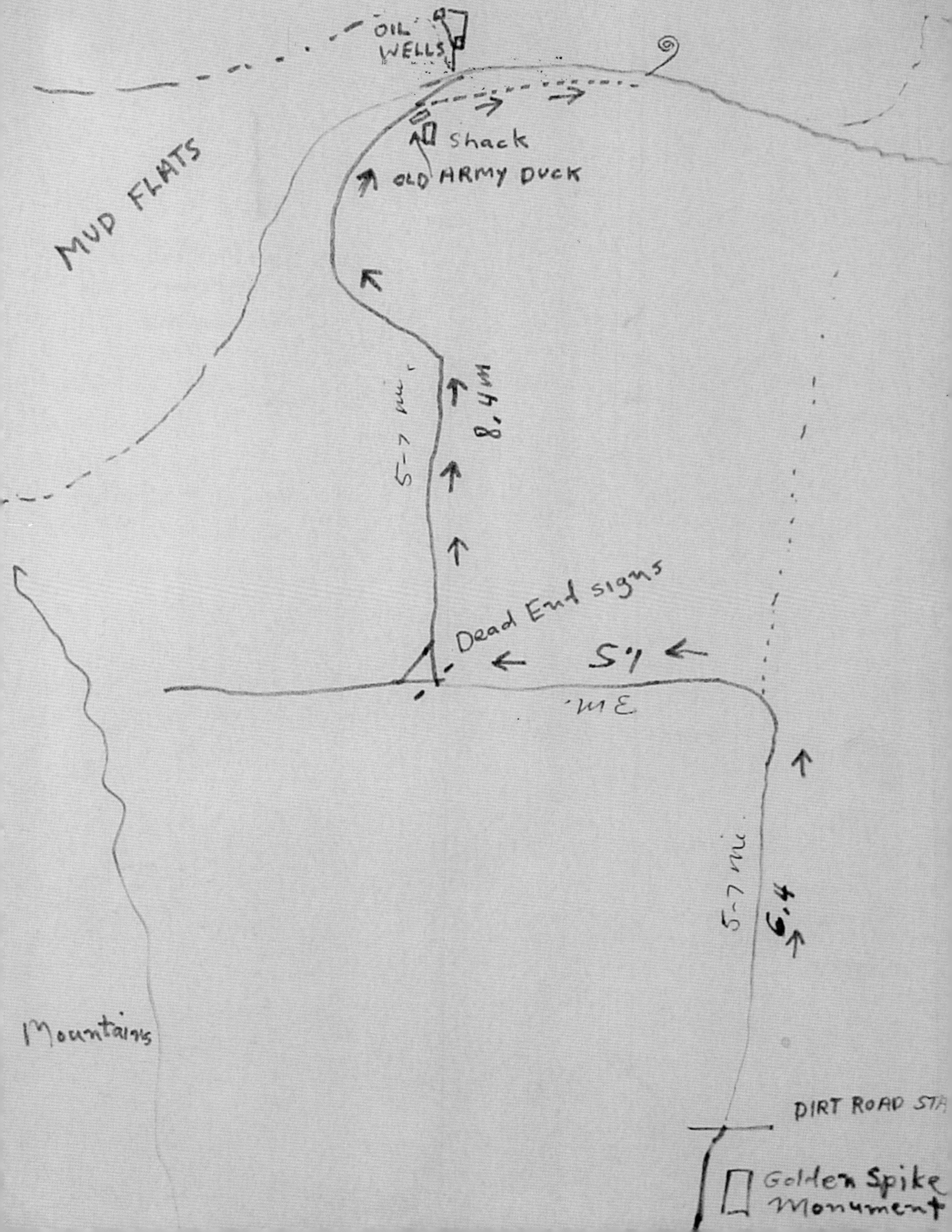

OIL
WELLS

MUD FLATS

Shack

OLD ARMY DUCK

5-7 mi.

8.4 m

Dead End signs

5.1

3 m.

5-7 mi.

6.4

Mountains

DIRT ROAD STA

Golden Spike
Monument

Mirror-Travels   Robert Smithson and History

Jennifer L. Roberts

Yale University Press *New Haven and London*

Yale Publications in the History of Art are works of critical and
historical scholarship by authors formerly or now associated with the
Department of the History of Art of Yale University. Begun in 1939,
the series embraces the field of art-historical studies in its widest and
most inclusive definition.

Series logo designed by Josef Albers and reproduced with permission
of the Josef Albers Foundation.

Designed by Daphne Geismar
Set in Scala and Scala Sans type by Amy Storm
Printed in China by World Print

Library of Congress Cataloging-in-Publication Data
Roberts, Jennifer L., 1969 –
Mirror-travels: Robert Smithson and history / Jennifer L. Roberts.
        p.   cm.
Includes bibliographical references and index.
ISBN 0-300 -09497-3 (hard cover: alk. paper)
1. Smithson, Robert—Criticism and interpretation. I. Smithson,
Robert. II. Title.
N6537.S6184R63   2004
700'.92—dc22
2003018791

Frontispiece: Robert Smithson, *Spiral Jetty*, 1971. Ink on paper,
12 x 9 in. (30.48 x 22.9 cm). The Gilbert and Lila Silverman Collection.

A catalogue record for this book is available from the British Library.
The paper in this book meets the guidelines for permanence
and durability of the Committee on Production Guidelines for Book
Longevity of the Council on Library Resources.

10 9 8 7 6 5 4 3 2 1

CONTENTS

ACKNOWLEDGMENTS

This book began, many revisions ago, as a dissertation in the Department of the History of Art at Yale University. I first thank my mentors there for giving the project the generous support, and the critical scrutiny, that allowed it to develop as it did. I am especially grateful to Jules D. Prown: not only for his encouragement of this project in particular but also for his role in building a rigorous and stimulating environment for the study of American art at Yale. The members of my dissertation committee, Thomas Crow, Bryan Jay Wolf, and Johanna Drucker, were each objects of my greatest esteem before I had the good fortune to work with them personally, and each has offered invaluable insight, advice, and debate as this project has progressed. Christopher S. Wood, although not officially a member of my committee, offered helpful commentary on the early drafts of several chapters. His profound influence as a teacher and mentor on my way of thinking and doing art history is, I hope, evident throughout this text. I'd also like to convey my appreciation to Michael Lobel and Sarah K. Rich, fellow graduate students who repeatedly intimidated me in seminars with their high standards of critical acuity, erudition, and engagement. I owe a great deal to their example.

This project has passed with me through several other institutions, each of which, in its particular constellation of colleagues and resources, has enriched it. My advisers and fellow Fellows from the Smithsonian American Art Museum, where I spent a productive year of predoctoral research and writing, contributed in innumerable ways to the final shape of this book. For their conversation and critique I thank Wendy Bellion, Kristin Schwain, Anne Collins Goodyear, Rocío Aranda-Alvarado, Jobyl Boone, Alan Braddock, Jason Weems, and William H. Truettner. I also had the good fortune to spend two years as the Carole and Alvin I. Schragis Postdoctoral Fellow in the Department of

Fine Arts at Syracuse University, where my manageable teaching schedule, along with the moral and intellectual support of my colleagues, allowed me to complete the majority of the revisions to the manuscript. I'd particularly like to thank Jonathan Massey for helping me get up to speed on the fourth dimension (no small task), and Stephen C. Meyer and Eileen Strempel for many stimulating discussions, on topics ranging from deconstruction to synaesthesia, over wine and homegrown tomatoes. My new colleagues in the Department of the History of Art and Architecture at Harvard University energized the final year of revision with fresh dialogues and perspectives; thanks especially to Eugene Wang, Jeffrey Hamburger, Yve-Alain Bois, and most of all to Robin Kelsey, a fellow connoisseur of rockpiles, who read the entire manuscript during a summer when he had better things to do. His critical insight and intellectual generosity have impacted this book at every level.

Many others have contributed to this project through their careful and generous reading of drafts of various chapters, especially Alex Nemerov, David Lubin, Sally Promey, Linda Dalrymple Henderson, Katherine Manthorne, Walter Cahn, Glenn Adamson, Carlton Evans, and Joshua Shannon. An earlier version of the material in Chapter 4 was published in *The Art Bulletin*. Thanks to Caroline A. Jones for her especially attentive reading of the article manuscript, and to Mary Miller and R. Tripp Evans, without whose patient and generous guidance in some of the most basic aspects of Pre-Columbian studies I could not have undertaken such an extensive foray into an unfamiliar subject. Thanks also to Perry Chapman and Lory Frankel, whose editorial assistance on the *Art Bulletin* version of the chapter greatly improved the current version.

Several individuals went above and beyond the call of duty to assist me with research and reproductions. I would particularly like to thank Jessica Cox and Alison Gallup at VAGA, Hannah Israel and Elyse Goldberg at the James Cohan Gallery, Mark Henderson at the Getty Research Institute, and Vicki Buchsbaum Pearse, who went to the trouble of granting me permission to reproduce an illustration from her father's invertebrate biology textbook soon after he had passed away. Rick Wilson, chief ranger at the Golden Spike National Historic Site, assisted me in working through the archives there. Like all of the rangers I met at the Site, he has cheerfully adopted the *Spiral Jetty* and its pilgrims, despite the fact that this kind of curatorship is not likely part of his official job description. Judy Throm and the entire staff at the Archives of American Art in Washington, D.C., accommodated my every request for access to the Smithson Papers and routinely hauled out heavy boxes of Smithson's books for my perusal. Anne, Robert, and Jennifer Lester graciously provided the images reproduced here from the Estate of George Lester. Genevieve Hyacinthe and Jacob Proctor, my research assistants at Harvard, offered heroic last-minute help with photographs and copyediting. Without the assistance of Nancy Holt, who made many photographs available and who graciously submitted to an interview, this project could hardly have begun. And without the expert guidance of Patricia Fidler and Michelle Komie at Yale University Press (along with the apparently boundless patience of my manuscript editor, Jeffrey Schier), it could never have come to fruition.

My work on this book would have been impossible without the financial generosity of many institutions and foundations. At the dissertation stage the project received substantial support from the American Council of Learned Societies/Henry Luce Foundation, the Patricia and Phillip Frost Fellowship at the Smithsonian American Art Museum, the Andrew W. Mellon Foundation, the John F. Enders Fellowships at Yale University, and the Charles Redd Center for Western Studies. Assistance with photographic expenses was provided by the Clark/Cooke Fund for Faculty Research at Harvard University and the Schragis Faculty Fellowship research fund at Syracuse.

For whatever insights I have been able to bring to Smithson's work, I am deeply indebted to all of those who have helped make it available to scholars in the first place. I have been fortunate to study Smithson's work during precisely the years that, for the first time, something approaching its full spectrum has been compiled, archived, and published. Most important of all was Nancy Holt's 1995 gift of Smithson's papers and library to the Smithsonian Institution's Archives of American Art. Also particularly valuable to me have been Robert Hobbs's early survey of Smithson's sculpture, Eugenie Tsai's "unearthing" of Smithson's early drawings and paintings, Robert Sobieszek's pathbreaking work on Smithson's photographs, Jack Flam's 1996 edition of Smithson's writings, and Gary Shapiro's philosophical analysis of Smithson's work. Joseph Masheck's short essays on Smithson from the seventies first raised many of the questions that this book attempts to answer. And although Ann M. Reynolds's monograph on Smithson was published too late to be considered here, her 1993 doctoral dissertation was especially important for me in its rigorous and detailed reading of some of the most difficult aspects of Smithson's work.

My deepest and most heartfelt gratitude, finally, goes to Dan Hisel. He fended off the rattlesnake at the *Spiral Jetty* site and, in every other possible way, made the joys of this project outweigh the dangers.

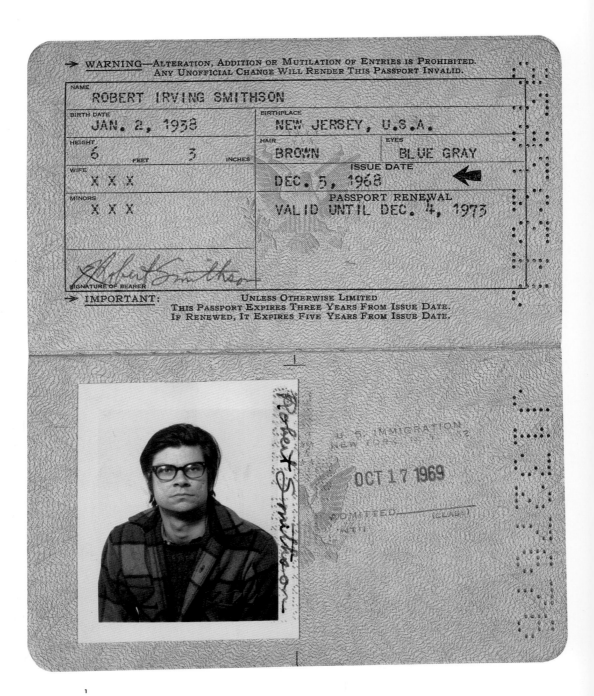

1
Robert Smithson's passport, 1968.
Robert Smithson and Nancy Holt papers, 1905–87,
Archives of American Art, Smithsonian Institution.

Robert Smithson's *Spiral Jetty* was built in the spring of 1970 along a remote portion of the northern shoreline of the Great Salt Lake (fig. 2). The *Jetty*'s physical monumentality (6,650 tons of rock and mud forming a spiral over a quarter-mile long) is matched by its art-historical renown. Widely appreciated as one of the most important and influential art projects of the twentieth century, it has been prominently illustrated in nearly every art history survey text published in the past twenty years.

Given its fame and the enormous effort required to build it, it is tempting to assume that the *Jetty*'s construction would have been the biggest thing ever to happen to this remote, sparsely populated area of Utah, where even today most of the few existing roads are unpaved, and the primary inhabitants are brine flies and scattered herds of livestock. But something big—bigger, perhaps, and illustrated even more frequently in textbooks—had already happened here. Almost exactly a century earlier, on May 10, 1869, only seventeen miles away at Promontory Summit, the last spike was driven into the last tie of the transcontinental railroad (fig. 3). This so-called wedding of the rails, vividly choreographed for posterity, hastened the close of the frontier era and furnished one of the defining images of nineteenth-century American history.

Although the existing scholarship on the *Spiral Jetty* devotes little or no attention to the Golden Spike connection, anyone who has attempted to visit the earthwork knows that the two monuments are locked in something of a lonely binary orbit. As Smithson's own route map of the area demonstrates, the only practicable way to access the *Spiral Jetty* is to pass through the Golden Spike National Historic Site (fig. 4). Even today it is from the Golden Spike site that visitors must launch their expeditions to the earthwork. It is here, after inspecting the replica locomotives and postcard displays; checking the water supply, odometer, and snake bite kit; and picking up a map to the *Jetty* from an obliging Park Ranger, that *Jetty* pilgrims leave the last stretch of pavement and set out on the bumpy journey to the lakeshore. The Golden Spike site frames the experience of the *Spiral Jetty*, and vice versa.

The connection between the *Spiral Jetty* and the Golden Spike is not simply an isolated accident of geographical contiguity. It is, rather, just one facet of

an entire complex of historical reference and reflection that structures Smithson's work. Over his brief career (cut short by his accidental death, at age 35, in 1973) Smithson worked in a remarkable array of media: painting, drawing, photography, collage, film, sculpture, and poetry among them. His work ranges in tone from the dead earnestness of his religious paintings to the cool disaffection of his gravel-mirror abstractions to the ironic wit of his travel narratives. But despite these variations, his entire career can be understood as a continuing, and constantly renegotiated, engagement with the practice and philosophy of history.

Consider, for example, the sheer volume of historical research that Smithson brought to bear upon his projects. Even a cursory glance through the Smithson papers and library (now housed, appropriately, at the Smithsonian) reveals that the artist considered the implications of his work at every possible historical scale. His project file for the *Spiral Jetty* includes, among other things, maps of the prehistoric shoreline of what is now the Great Salt Lake, several books and brochures about the construction of the transcontinental railroad, and an article on *kutsavi*, a food traditionally prepared by the Ute Indians by drying the tiny brine shrimp found in the lake (it was akin, apparently, to bacon bits). When he visited Mono Lake, a similarly brackish Western attraction, Smithson was able to discuss topics ranging from his knowledge of the deposition of calcareous tufa that marks the lake's stratigraphic history, to Mark Twain's nineteenth-century account of his visit to the area in *Roughing It*. Smithson staged frequent confrontations with his distant precedents and predecessors, ranging from the casual (as in his passing suggestion that Edgar Allan Poe was the first true earthworks artist) to the systematic (as in his *Artforum* project "Incidents of Mirror-Travel in the Yucatan," which derives its title, and a good deal else, from a nineteenth-century expedition to the same area). Such explicit references help to differentiate Smithson's work from that of many of his more properly minimalist or conceptualist colleagues, who tended to shrink from making overt historical gestures. They also provide a useful corrective to the tendency in some scholarship to interpret Smithson's art (particularly his land art) as if it occupied an empty or neutral historical space, as if his earthworks were simply oversized relocations of sculpture from

2
Robert Smithson, *Spiral Jetty*,
Great Salt Lake, Utah, April 1970.
Black rock, salt crystals, earth, and red water (algae),
3 ¹/₂ x 15 x 1,500 ft. (1.07 x 4.57 x 457.2 m).
Collection: DIA Center for the Arts, New York.
Photo: contemporary print from Smithson's 1970 negative.
Robert Smithson and Nancy Holt papers, 1905–87,
Archives of American Art, Smithsonian Institution.

3
Andrew J. Russell, *East & West Shaking Hands
at Laying [of] Last Rail*, 1869.
Yale Collection of Western Americana,
Beinecke Rare Book and Manuscript Library.

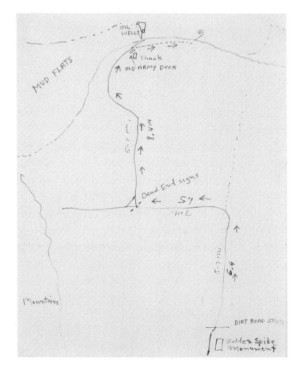

4
Robert Smithson, *Spiral Jetty*, 1971.
Ink on paper, 12 x 9 in. (30.48 x 22.9 cm).
The Gilbert and Lila Silverman Collection.

the gallery to the vast, similarly rarefied spaces of the American West. To attend to Smithson's interest in the Golden Spike, in other words, is to make it impossible to see the *Spiral Jetty*'s site as "open space" or its materials as "general conceptual matter." Smithson's spaces, however deserted they may appear visually, are thick with the histories that occupy and organize them.[1]

This book examines Smithson's encounter with these histories and with the idea of history itself. The task is not a simple one, for Smithson's operations upon history (cast as they often are in slate, mirror, or steel) are not as readily decipherable as those of a card-carrying history painter. Moreover, any historical study of Smithson's work is complicated at the outset by the fact that Smithson worked during a period of profound uncertainty about the shape and meaning of historical time. Like many of his colleagues in the postwar era, Smithson abandoned the idealist, progressive historicism that had been inherited from nineteenth-century German philosophy. Indeed, as we shall see, Smithson was given to implacably skeptical denunciations of all of our received ideas about history's course and enterprise: "History is a facsimile of events held together by flimsy biographical information." But Smithson's distrust of traditional historicism was not synonymous with a wholesale dismissal of the past. Rather it was quite the opposite: his rejection of traditional methods of historical abstraction served to open, rather than close, the pressing question of historical inheritance. Smithson's response to the failure of established historical models was not simply to discard or selectively ignore the past, but rather to become constantly, even painfully, aware of its obdurate presence. For him, history was as ponderous as so much rock and mud.[2]

Multivalent, sophisticated, and richly cross-referential, Smithson's work offers art historians a kaleidoscopic array of critical possibilities that have only begun to be explored. This book focuses closely on Smithson's historical operations; it will not attempt to provide a full survey of Smithson's work and will make only fleeting reference to many of the themes (semiotics, picturesque aesthetics, etc.) that have dominated published research on Smithson to date. Its essential gambit, of course, is that what is lost by narrowing the interpretive aperture on Smithson's work will be regained by increasing the depth and clarity of our understanding of one of its defining aspects.[3] In the first chapter I examine the religious paintings that Smithson produced during what he called his "spiritual crisis" of 1961. Wavering unsettlingly between iconography that evokes eternal revelation and modernist techniques that embrace historical entanglement, these images demonstrate that the problem of history preoccupied Smithson from the outset of his career. Chapter 2 examines the working model of history that Smithson developed between the years 1964 and 1967, after he had abandoned overtly religious motifs. Through his study of the growth of crystals, the structure of mirror reflections, and the discourse of hyperspace, Smithson posited history as an entropic process of material deposition that settles itself into a final crystalline stillness. Each of the following chapters features a critical case study that examines Smithson's historical method as it worked upon, and developed out of, a specific site. First I address Smithson's 1967 photographic travelogue "The Monuments of Passaic," then his 1969 *Artforum* project "Incidents of Mirror-Travel in the Yucatan," and finally the canonical *Spiral Jetty*. In each of these projects, Smithson worked in a place that was already doubly complex historically. Each of the sites was already marked as "historical," and each was also the subject of renewed public debate about how exactly it was to be historicized. By exploring Smithson's interventions in these debates, each chapter connects Smithson's work to a broader politics of history. And, throughout the book, I hope to demonstrate that Smithson's historical operations provide an interpretive lens through which we might gain new perspectives on other, seemingly unrelated, aspects of his career. Ultimately, this book will have as much to say about Smithson's engagement with landscape, visual perception, cross-cultural encounter, and social conflict as it will about history per se.

Historical Method and the Problem of "Continuance"
One of my key goals here—certainly the most straightforward on the face of it—is to historicize Smithson's work. This means that I will take special care to demonstrate the ways in which Smithson's work responds to specific social, ideological, and material contradictions of the sixties and early seventies. I will treat the immediate historical conditions of Smithson's famous projects as significant contributors to their form and

meaning, and ask questions accordingly: what does it mean, for example, that Smithson conducted his famous tour of the "Monuments" of Passaic, New Jersey, in the immediate wake of the passage of the National Historic Preservation Act? Does it matter that Smithson's sculptural installations on the Yucatán Peninsula coincided with a series of revolutionary discoveries about the nature and scope of Maya history? What might we learn from the fact that a series of highly publicized—and highly controversial—Golden Spike centennial celebrations had occurred at Promontory just a few months before Smithson arrived to begin building the *Spiral Jetty*?

In Smithson's case, however, one must not only take note of the synchronic structure of the artist's immediate historical context, but also account for the diachronic relationships through which Smithson understood his own moment to be connected to history. For Smithson, historical depth formations were materially continuous, not merely anamorphic projections of an absent past. Smithson understood history as a material residue, an ever-accumulating remainder of time. In developing this thoroughgoing "historical materialism," which he derived directly from the physical sciences rather than from Marxism as such, Smithson practiced a historical method that required him to wrestle physically with the histories in which he was attempting to intervene.[4]

Smithson's version of historical materialism contributed to his explicit concern with what he called "continuance," a term he used in opposition to the atomism and presentism of psychobiographical models of art criticism: "I don't go for that idea that art is personal. The personal talent might be there, but the tradition, range, extends into the past. . . . People don't know where their heads are now, they don't know where their continuance is." Smithson's work struggles at every turn to come to terms with this "continuance," a form of historical connection that he perceived as an inalienable material heritage. For Smithson, this heritage was not a catalyst for nostalgia or antiquarianism but rather a perpetual challenge to the production of form. Smithson's historical method was, like his physical production method, "worklike," a term I borrow from Dominick La Capra's notion of the productive dialogue in which the past interrogates the historian as insistently as the historian interrogates the past. Only by recognizing history's demands upon Smithson might the complexity and sophistication of his responses (whether they be echoes, rearrangements, or sublimations) begin to become apparent.[5]

Smithson's "continuance," in my view, presents a series of special challenges to historians of his work. For one thing, it asks us to confront the material, social, and political embodiment of what might otherwise appear to be Smithson's abstract experiments in "temporality." Smithson's innovative play with time and duration has been a frequent topic of discussion among art critics and historians. I will add my own analysis to this ongoing debate, and will formally analyze Smithson's cross-patterning, infolding, pulverizing, and mirroring of time. But it will be important not to dissociate Smithson's temporal experiments from their material embodiment as histories. At its most basic, this analysis amounts simply to an insistence on politicizing temporality by specifying it—and studying it—as history. What interests me most about Smithson's work is the way in which it forces us to acknowledge that time is inseparable from the history that embodies it, and that temporal models cannot be conceived without drawing upon, and in turn affecting, histories. However theoretically sophisticated Smithson's work might be, then, it is never *merely* theoretical. For it is one thing to wave away, with a flick of the poststructuralist wrist, a historical metanarrative; it is quite another to do so to an earth's worth of rocks and ruins. It is one thing to pull out the conceptual infrastructures that support traditional ideas of time, but quite another to confront the heap of deboned historical matter left behind—what Fredric Jameson calls the "sheer fact of the historicist presence" of the past. In mounting his temporal experiments, Smithson had to work through and upon preexisting historical configurations, forever altering, in the process, the histories that he encountered. In the case of a work like the *Spiral Jetty*, this means that I will read the earthwork as more than a monumental diagram of the shape of time arbitrarily installed in the Great Salt Lake. I will explore it as a historiographical intervention that gathers and redistributes the legacy of labor and progress embodied in the transcontinental railroad, and rewrites American history in the process.[6]

Inherent in this approach is my belief that in order to pursue a rigorous examination of Smithson's operations upon history, one must pay more than glancing or gratuitous attention to the history (or histories) in question. Much of this book is devoted to a close reengagement with the historical past that Smithson refigured, whether by tracking the history of race relations in the depressed textile towns along the Passaic River or tracing the path of a nineteenth-century travel writer through the Honduran jungle. This kind of analysis will require a considerable expansion of the diachronic range and sensitivity that is normally brought to bear on Smithson's work. The most rigorous and influential research on Smithson thus far has concerned itself primarily with Smithson's status within the history of modernism. The predominant approach has been to position Smithson as a key, often *the* key, figure in the transition from "modern" to "postmodern" models of art production in the United States. The resulting large body of analysis has done an excellent and necessary job of accounting for — indeed, helping to determine — Smithson's status as one of the most influential artists of the twentieth century. It has demonstrated the challenges that Smithson's work posed to the totalizing impulses associated with high modernism by detailing his unabashed contamination of idealistic aesthetics with materiality, contingency, and physical labor; his dislocation of the traditional sites of artistic production; his complication of the authorial function; and his violation of disciplinary boundaries.[7]

In principle, the various poststructuralist theories informing this criticism would allow and even encourage the reconnection of Smithson's work with its extensions in history. In practice, however, because it has tended to focus on examining Smithson's work as a disruption or displacement of a specific form of mid-century modernism, this approach has been limited by what literary critic Alan Liu calls the "historically foreshortened" quality of much postmodernist discourse.[8] Thus it routinely and productively analyzes Smithson's work as a reaction against its immediate high-modernist precedents but fails to address its pervasive dialogue with earlier precursors. The historiographical effect of this approach, if not its specific intention, is to narrow the purview of "history" to a sliver of Smithson's immediate past and to assign to it the role of hapless foil for Smithson's triumphant critiques. Although Smithson certainly did oppose elements of high-modernist thought and practice, an exclusive focus on this aspect of his work offers no way to account for the energies that he put into his encounter, as a critical practitioner and interlocutor, with a much larger body of previous historical and art-historical inheritance.

I recognize that the recent critical climate has not been particularly conducive to cross-historical study. In pursuing long historical connections, art historians today are rightly aware of the danger of reprising the triumphalism, Eurocentrism, or idealism of previous models of historical continuity. By attending so conspicuously to Smithson's juxtaposition of *Spiral Jetty* and Golden Spike, for example, I cannot help but risk venturing into methodologically objectionable territory. To an audience of Americanists, the comparison may seem suspiciously reminiscent of the nationalist-essentialist criticism that marked the early years of the field, when, in a hermeneutic of reciprocal domestication, nineteenth- and twentieth-century American art was often apposed in order to demonstrate the transhistorical persistence of core impulses of the "American Mind."[9] More generally, the *Jetty*/Spike motif may raise the specter of a threadbare brand of linear, progressive historicism, a teleological method that would seek to plot the two monuments along a timeline and show how one develops necessarily out of the other. Not only has this approach been repeatedly overruled, both in practice and in theory, by contemporary historiography and art history, but it would also seem to be particularly ill-fitted to the matter at hand. For even at the most basic formal level, the *Spiral Jetty* renounces linearity. If anything, as it swerves counterclockwise into the lake, it suggests a derailment of the linear progress that the nearby transcontinental railroad track bed once so perfectly embodied.

For these reasons, previous attempts to pursue Smithson's historical connections have generally been met with either indifference or suspicion. The common charge has been that to examine Smithson's work in terms of its historical precedents is, as Pamela M. Lee puts it, "to subscribe to the kind of enfeebled historicism . . . [that] Smithson violently rejected." To be sure, in any such analysis it is important to avoid the construction of normalizing his-

torical pedigrees. "Nothing is more damaging to theoretical knowledge of modern art," said Adorno, "than
its reduction to what it has in common with older
periods." Even so, this book begins with the proposition
that a reconsideration of the role of history in the
physical and theoretical landscape of late twentieth-
century art need not be either feeble or reductive.
Indeed, in the case of an artist like Smithson, whose
work demonstrates a persistent concern with continuity,
such rigorous reconsideration seems unavoidable.[10]

To my mind, the greatest challenge facing this
or any project that hopes to trace Smithson's historical negotiations is the imperative that it acknowledge and describe Smithson's relationship to the
past without itself resorting to the progressive or perspectival historicism that his work attempts to circumvent. How, without reflexively invoking the concepts of progress, retrospection, or influence, to
render the "continuance" between the Spiral Jetty and
the Golden Spike? One might reasonably look to
some of the alternative critical models currently populating academic historiography and art criticism:
perhaps the Spiral Jetty, coiling and recoiling around
its vortical center, performs a kind of traumatic repetition of the Golden Spike's originary puncture. Perhaps, as Smithson's dump trucks backed out over the
spiraling rubble, they stood to the Spike as Walter
Benjamin's retrospective angel stands to history. Or
perhaps the Jetty can be understood, pace Georges
Bataille, as a flume of historical expenditure escaping
the alchemical economy of the Golden Spike. I have
entertained each of these possibilities in my analysis
of the Spiral Jetty. But although these alternative critical-historical vocabularies will have much to contribute to this text (and although they have thoroughly
informed my own view of history), I have tried to
resist the temptation to apply them too neatly to
Smithson's work.[11]

There are several reasons for this hesitation.
A very simple one is that no single group of historical
theories determined Smithson's own historiographical formation. This is due more than anything to
Smithson's status as autodidact and interdisciplinar-
ian. Smithson was a voracious and sophisticated
reader who referred habitually to his intellectual
influences in his writings and interviews, yet he rarely
articulated his thoughts on history in anything resem-
bling a common historiographical shorthand. In
his writings that address temporality or history, he is
much more likely to refer to a science fiction novel by
J. G. Ballard or a poem by T. S. Eliot than to explicitly
historical meditations of Benjamin or Foucault (or,
for that matter, Hegel, Marx, or Nietzsche). Smithson
distilled his philosophy of history out of disciplines not
immediately associated with either philosophy or
history. The practice of history, for Smithson, was an
amalgamation of thermodynamics, crystallography, photography, literary criticism, and other seemingly unrelated pursuits. His historicism was built out of what
W. J. T. Mitchell calls "the turbulence and incoherence
at the inner and outer boundaries of disciplines," and
therefore both rewards and requires an interdisciplinary
analysis that reaches beyond historiography proper and
attends closely to Smithson's own diverse sources.[12]

Another reason for hesitating to translate
Smithson's work into contemporary historical theory
is that the unstinting materialism of Smithson's
"continuance" exceeds the capacities of current historiographical vocabularies. The problem of diachrony
(change over time) occupies a blind, one might more
accurately say a sore, spot in contemporary criticism.
Although abandoned in the middle of the last century
by the synchronic bias of structuralism, and then
further discredited by poststructuralist critiques of
Hegelian progress, the question of diachrony continues
to loom over critical discourse. It has now tended to
be displaced, however, into psychoanalytical models. I
am thinking of the explosion of memory discourse
in recent years and of the widespread adoption of the
spectral, the uncanny, and the traumatic as paradigms
of historical connection. Whatever considerable virtues
these models may possess, however, they rely too heavily on discontinuous explanations of diachrony to be
cleanly applied to Smithson's "continuance."[13]

Here we might pause to consider a single
example of a historical model that is potentially applicable to Smithson's work: that of Walter Benjamin.
Benjamin's theoretical esteem is so pervasive in contemporary criticism (as Peter Osborne puts it,
"Benjamin's prose breeds commentary like vaccine in
a lab") that it is worth examining as a symptomatic
phenomenon in itself. It seems to me that Benjamin's

notion of revolutionary historical constellations forming in a sudden "flash," or "blast," is attractive to us
because it provides one of the few available tools for
theorizing the continuing agency of the past in an era
profoundly hostile to traditional historicism. The
epileptic quality of Benjamin's "shock" allows us to
imagine a powerful, transformative, and even dangerous connection to the past at the same time that it
relieves us of the awesome responsibility (and the
now-impossible task) of having to specify the precise
mechanism of that connection.[14]

Smithson's work has often been connected
with Benjamin's, and for good reason: both shared an
obsession with rubble and ruin, both developed a
materialist method of citational history, both were concerned with correspondences between the archaic
and the modern, and both, as Craig Owens famously
argued, shared an essentially allegorical procedure.
Yet while I hope that this book might ultimately contribute to further discussions about Benjaminian
history, it will not itself translate Smithson's work into
Benjaminian terms. I want to avoid folding Smithson
too quickly into Benjamin: to do so would be to risk
writing a(nother) book about Benjamin rather than a
book about Smithson, and it would also serve to obscure
the ways in which Smithson's work differs from
Benjamin's. Smithson's materialist critique of opticality, for example, complicates any direct equivalences
that might be drawn to the spectacular or phantasmagor-
ical dimensions of Benjamin's imagistics of history.
And Smithson's engagement with entropy is categori-
cally incommensurable with the latent energeticism
of Benjamin's notion of the revolutionary historical
"flash." Benjamin's version of historicism relies upon
instantaneous releases across time of stored mnemonic
energies. But such discharges are essentially impossible in Smithson's historiographical universe, which
features an ever-increasing historical somnolence
marked by the slow, steady, and continuous crystallization of time. Smithson's entropy tugs and drags
against the messianic reanimation of matter that
drives Benjamin's utopian historical schemata. This
leads Smithson to take a much darker view than does
Benjamin of the prospects for revolutionary action.
Smithson dismissed as metaphysical fictions the various "forces" populating humanistic thought; the

entropic tendency of all systems, which he saw as a
material inevitability, disallows any potential (as
understood in the electrical, as well as the political
sense) for historical action. My point here is not to
discount the importance of Benjamin's work, nor
to endorse Smithson's historical model over that of
any other artist or theorist. I simply hope to delay
the process of assigning Smithson's work to any single critical discourse long enough to help recover
the complexity, variety, and contingency of the solutions
that Smithson and artists of his generation offered
to the postwar crisis of history.[15]

Smithson's Transcendentalism

There is a final critical twist to be mentioned here,
something especially strange about Smithson's entropic
historicism that reverses our usual expectations. As
I will argue, Smithson's work often attempts to define
a teleology that incorporates history yet leads *through
and out* of it into a timeless, posthistorical stasis. Thus,
if Smithson's historiography is in some ways too
stubbornly materialist to be strapped comfortably into
contemporary theoretical vehicles, it is in other ways
too stubbornly transcendentalist. This may seem an
oxymoronic assertion at best (transcendental materialism?), and a downright blasphemous one (from a
contemporary critical perspective) at worst. How could
Smithson, supposedly the anti-idealist par excellence,
have possibly subscribed to any form of transcendental system? I was certainly not expecting to find any
such thing when I began working on Smithson several
years ago; I was planning to emphasize the desublima-
tory agency of Smithson's insistence on historical
contingency and specificity. I had in mind an analysis
that would bring Smithson's entropic materialism
into alignment with something like "base materialism," the term employed by Rosalind Krauss and Yve-
Alain Bois in their groundbreaking study of Bataille's
Informe and its echoes in twentieth-century art.
Smithson's version of history, I thought, would refuse
all forms of unity, totality, or dialectical resolution,
and offer us a form of history bound and threaded to
specific places and bodies, conflicts and controversies.[16]

But when I began working in earnest on this
project, I found the task proving far more difficult—
and interesting—than I had originally imagined.

For even as he seemed to embrace the radical particularism and historical embeddedness that I had expected, Smithson seemed, puzzlingly, to make frequent gestures toward a timeless or ahistorical aesthetics, a mode of practice and reception "when you're not conscious of the time or space you are in." Smithson's own statements on time and history, sprinkled throughout the interviews and prose pieces that he left behind, seemed hopelessly self-contradictory. To be sure: in some passages Smithson sounds like a good postmodernist, as when he argues for the value of each specific moment that the artist spends in the process of working: "[a]ny critic who devalues the *time* of the artist is the enemy of art and the artist." But, far more frequently, I found Smithson seeming to wish against all odds for precisely the atemporal, ahistorical condition that I had presumed he would oppose, as when he describes one of his sculptures as "a clock that doesn't keep time, but loses it," when he praises filmmaker Roger Corman's "esthetic of atemporality," when he champions Ad Reinhardt's paintings because they assure that "[t]ime vanishes into a perpetual sameness," or when he describes his site selection process by saying that "when I get to a site that strikes the kind of timeless chord, I use it."[17]

I was in for other surprises as well. I was stunned to discover his earnest religious writings of the early sixties, in which he openly called for a reestablishment of devotional art, and even more surprised to find that motifs and structures from his early religious imagery continued to operate, thinly disguised under the rubric of crystallographic abstraction, throughout his later work. Ultimately, the most difficult aspect of Smithson's work to square with my initial assumptions was his systematic embrace of entropy. Although arguments can be made for the oppositional politics of entropy as an artistic strategy, Smithson's version seemed to me to be profoundly deterministic. For Smithson, as time passes we will eventually reach an entropic point in the future where "there can be no disorder left," all difference being obliterated in the wan stillness of posthistory.[18] This seemed to me not to resist but rather to *naturalize* the concept of a predetermined, eschatological history and to provide Smithson with a cosmic endorsement for his own aversion to activism, political or otherwise. In short: I

became more and more convinced that Smithson's convictions about the material persistence of history were counterbalanced by his need to pre-figure a transcendent, eternal condition beyond the limitations of that history. This condition was not to be metaphysical but rather, in his terms, "infraphysical," a condition to be located within rather than without the material. It was to involve, as he put it, a "transcendental state of matter."[19]

The essential claim of this book is that Smithson's confrontation with history was marked by acute ambivalence. On the one hand, Smithson had what we might call a proto-postmodern understanding of history as a force of inevitable fragmentation and loss. Yet even as he acknowledged this about history he seemed determined to overcome it, to manipulate this intransigent material into a form that might redeem its discursive essence into a greater unity. Although Smithson's work proposes the profound and unsettling historicity of all phenomena, it also attempts to produce a kind of secondhand eternity from the materials of historicity itself. His photographic projects obey a principle of infinite accumulation, in which the mnemonic power of the single image is multiplied beyond recognition into a jumbled geology of silver and paper. His crystallographic work subjects time to a lapidary process in which the alienating effects of history are ultimately cross-cancelled. Indeed, Smithson's entire production can be interpreted as a series of self-inoculating historical structures. At each point that Smithson invites history into his work, he seems to do so in order to neutralize its effects.

Perhaps inevitably, my attempts to negotiate Smithson's entropic worldview will mean that I cannot always maintain the celebratory tone of the current Smithson literature. Smithson's work is exemplary in its direct material registration of specific histories and historical conflicts, yet in its attempts to transcend those conflicts it occasionally resorts to strategies that many art historians now consider to be problematic. In some cases it appeals to a brand of primitivism informed by an ideal of primordial timelessness; in others it proposes a meticulous ethics of passivity in the face of historical injustice. Throughout his work Smithson looks forward, rather overeagerly I think, to an entropic endtime, an eternal state of cosmic sameness, in which all of history, as well as all of the clashing perspectives that embody it, will exist without conflict.

And yet one needs not necessarily agree with every detail of Smithson's eschatology in order to learn from his brilliant and remarkable work. Because Smithson engaged more seriously with the problem of history than most any other artist of his generation, his work serves as an unparalleled critical resource. His site-specific projects offer thorough and studied critiques of the dominant historical narratives that have shaped the modern American landscape. Because his experiments with new models of time and space were conducted through the medium of history, his work provides art historians with a critical opportunity to extend the practices of durational and site-specific analysis into their necessary intersection with historical politics. And finally, although Smithson's work often struggles to approximate the posthistorical, its inclusive materiality cannot help but leave traces of the historical conflicts and configurations that inform it. My task here is to retrace those traces, hoping in the process to unearth the complexity of Smithson's historical moment as well as to consider new ways of understanding Smithson's "continuance" with moments not his own.

HISTORY IN SMITHSON'S RELIGIOUS PAINTINGS

In 1961 Smithson was twenty-three years old, living in New York on Sixth Avenue in what he described as "the hinterlands between the Garment district and the Village." Having felt alienated, misunderstood, and bored by the "stifling suburban atmosphere where there was just nothing," he had left his native New Jersey soon after graduating from high school and came to New York expressly to become an artist. He had made no attempt to go to college, although he had taken several courses at the Art Students League and the Brooklyn Museum School, and he was arguably more widely read than the average college student. By this time he was beginning to establish himself as a painter; he had a solo show in 1959 at the Artists Gallery and had shown in the "New Work by New Artists" exhibition at the Alan Gallery in 1960. Smithson's work at this point combined elements of both gestural and geometric abstraction and featured tightly compacted grid compositions, scattered figurative elements, and occasional bits of overpainted collage. Smithson would later describe his work of this period in terms of the intersecting influences of Barnett Newman, Willem de Kooning, Robert Rauschenberg, and Jean Dubuffet. Irving Sandler, in a 1959 review, described Smithson's paintings as "whelped by Surrealism and primitive art" and "reared by frenzied Action Painting."[1]

Smithson was still groping for a style that suited him, but, it might be argued, so was the entire New York art world. In 1961 postpainterly abstraction was a critical favorite, but it shared space with second-generation abstract expressionism, still vital in many quarters, as well as early pop art and an entire range of new practices, including performance, happenings, and assemblage. It was the year of Morris Louis's *Unfurleds* but also Claes Oldenburg's *The Store*, Frank Stella's metallic stripe paintings but also Roy Lichtenstein's *Look Mickey*,

Clement Greenberg's *Art and Culture* but also John Cage's *Silence*.

In this heady and unstable atmosphere Smithson was as well positioned as any young painter to migrate from the fringes to the center of the downtown art world. He was certainly moving in the right circles; a regular at the Cedar Tavern and an active denizen of the Greenwich Village Beat scene, he made his way into more than one of Fred W. McDarrah's now-legendary photographs of Saturday night loft parties. He mingled with both first-generation abstract expressionists and Black Mountain artists, and he was developing a close relationship with Richard Bellamy, whose influential Green Gallery had just opened. Many of his friends and acquaintances were poets and publishers; during the late fifties he had worked at the Eighth Street Bookshop and illustrated the covers of literary magazines. He had met both Allen Ginsberg and Jack Kerouac, and he dabbled in poetry himself.[2]

In the spring of that year, Smithson was busy working on a new series of paintings in preparation for his upcoming one-man show at the Galeria George Lester in Rome. Lester had offered Smithson the show after having seen his paintings at the Alan Gallery. The Rome show was to be an enormous opportunity for Smithson: his second major solo show, his international debut, and (not least) an opportunity to spend a few weeks visiting the Eternal City itself. But Smithson was having trouble. In a series of agonized letters that he wrote to Lester as he prepared for the show, he complained of an "almost unbearable tension" in his work: "The paintings I am sending to you reveal my spiritual crisis. A crisis born out of an inner pain; a pain that has overwhelmed my entire nervous system."[3] He told Lester that he was in the process of changing his entire approach to painting: "For the most part I have abandoned the shattered image . . . the distorted image. . . . Now, I have all the Choatic deamons [*sic*] in their place. The spirit of my art is being drawn from a Pre-Renaissance mood. Nature has all, but evaporated. Divine Suffering has taken the place of Nature."[4]

It is difficult to imagine Robert Smithson, who would later become famous for his shattered glass, manneristic distortions, and almost preternatural ironic detachment, beset by this or any other spiritual crisis. But it was at about this time that he jettisoned his teenage atheism and wholeheartedly, if temporarily, embraced the Catholic faith of his upbringing. He began to produce expressly religious paintings, painted in stark color and a heavy, obsessive line, many of which featured variations on the crucifixion, stigmatization, and entombment of Christ (see figs. 5, 6, 8–10).[5]

Smithson's religious paintings were essentially unknown until 1985, when the Diane Brown Gallery in New York mounted a small exhibition of Smithson's early work (drawn primarily from George Lester's collection). Since then, there has been increasing interest, manifested most notably in the work of Eugenie Tsai and Caroline A. Jones, in the wide range of paintings, drawings, and collages that Smithson produced between 1958 and 1964. Yet critical attention to the religious paintings in particular remains scant. This is partly because many, perhaps the majority, of the religious paintings were lost or intentionally destroyed before Smithson's death. What's more, Smithson produced his overtly religious paintings for only about a year; by 1962 he had tempered his "Divine Suffering" with irony, and by the time he began producing sculptures based on the structure of crystals in 1964, all religious iconography (along with all figuration) had disappeared from his work. Because the religious paintings derive from what appears to have been a transitory religious episode in his youth, and because they seem to depart so substantially from the tenor of his mature production, they have not generally been perceived as essential to the critical analysis of his later work. But most fundamentally, I suspect, the religious paintings have failed to attract sustained scholarly attention because they raise the exceedingly thorny question of the sincerity of Smithson's religious beliefs. For to recognize religious impulses in Smithson's work, early or late, is to be confronted with an image of Smithson that is difficult to orchestrate with his reputation for skeptical irreverence.[6]

Here I will tackle the complex issue of Smithson's religious sincerity by tracing the rhetoric of mystical timelessness as Smithson attempted to deploy it pictorially in his early paintings. My comments here will only begin to address the questions that Smithson's religious work raises. Much remains to be done: a thorough foundational study of this material (one that I hope will someday be written) will require an extensive biographical background, a comprehensive iconographic analysis of the intricate imagery, and a detailed investigation of Smithson's place in the history of American Catholicism in the tumultuous era of Vatican II. My aim here will simply be to establish, through a series of close documentary and formal analyses, the centrality of Christian mysticism in Smithson's early understanding of history. Broadly defined, mysticism concerns itself with transcending the limitations of worldly historical perspectives by devising methods of evoking a timeless, eternal, all-embracing consciousness. Smithson's "ikons" (as he called his religious paintings) struggle to produce this consciousness in and against a postwar environment marked by historical fragmentation. That they fail in this attempt— victims of Smithson's own ambivalence about history as well as the internal contradictions he discovers within the formal apparatus of religious figuration— does not obviate the sincerity of their aim. Indeed, fully and painfully aware of his failures to evoke the timeless through figurative representation, Smithson would go on to pursue his mystical aims by other means. Although the specific Catholic motifs would disappear from Smithson's work, many of the structures of their articulation would not.

To interpret Smithson's early paintings, drawings, and writings in terms of their attitudes toward temporality, then, is to reveal important continuities between his religious work and his later work. Smithson's religious work inaugurated a dialectical conflict between the eternal and historical that would continue to define his practice for the rest of his career; it must not be seen as simply postponing the development of his mature work but rather enabling it. Many of the most radical aspects of Smithson's later temporal strategies were already under halting investigation in his religious work. Indeed, much of what we have come to understand as Smithson's "postmodernism," such as his concern with the interchangeability of center and periphery, his engagement with the corporeality of perception, and his sense of the reified and particulate nature of time, derives ultimately from his engagement with the lugubrious premonitions of Christian mystics bemoaning a fallen world.

"The Decaying Force of Duration": Mysticism and Smithson's Critique of Modern Art

To anyone familiar with Smithson's later writings—biting and skeptical as they are—his nineteen letters to George Lester, written primarily in 1961 as he prepared paintings for his show in Rome, prove startling. The letters, which clearly demonstrate the intensity of Smithson's religious convictions during this period, have gone unpublished and virtually unnoticed since Lester donated them to the Archives of American Art in 1987. Although the letters' anguished tone remains almost embarrassingly foreign to Smithson's later writings, they remain an indispensable guide to Smithson's artistic and philosophical struggles in the early sixties. Without consulting the letters, one may easily be left with the impression that the religious concerns evident in Smithson's early iconography are simply one of his ironic quirks or the result of a greater or lesser degree of "interest" in religion.[7]

Most of the letters feature Smithson struggling to convince a reluctant Lester to design the upcoming Rome exhibition to place more emphasis on what Smithson calls his "religious" and "spiritual" work.[8] Smithson repeatedly defines himself as a religious artist. In a short biographical statement that he submits to Lester for inclusion in the catalogue, he prominently lists his 1950 confirmation as a Roman Catholic. In another letter he mentions that he is pursuing the publication of some of his poems with Sheed & Ward, which he describes as "a very powerful avant-garde Catholic publishing house," and begs Lester to include one of them, an Eliot-inspired "Incantation," in the catalogue: "Please do not ignore the incantation, because you think it is too religious."[9] Smithson insists that "the over all effect of the show + catalog should convey a 'Dark Night of the Soul.' The paintings should make people mortified and fill their eyes with suffering. These paintings are not for arty-chatter but for the lacerated soul."[10]

Smithson argues that if Lester wants to "be in [on a] new epoch in art," he should attend to the "new concern for the spirit in N.Y.C.," which will soon overtake "the latest obscure mess of abstraction." "Don't be afraid of the word 'religion,'" he says; "the most sophisticated people in Manhatten [sic] are very much concerned with it." The magnitude of Smithson's youthful confidence on this point is worth noting. As he says later in the same letter, "After my visit to Rome, and when I return every body [sic] in New York art circles will know about the George Lester Gallery and Robert Smithson. I don't have to appeal to the art world here; they will follow."[11]

It is important to distinguish Smithson's "concern for the spirit" from the "second religiousness" that Jack Kerouac identified as typical of the Beat experience. If anything it was a reversion to a first religiousness, since it amounted to Smithson's deliberate rejection of his recent Beat experiences in favor of an earlier form of Christian art and worship. Smithson's letters and writings of this period reveal that he drew his inspiration primarily from patristic texts (by the early church fathers) and medieval mystical tracts (particularly the work of Meister Eckhardt). Although Smithson owned a few books on Eastern spirituality, his library concentrated much more heavily on Christian mysticism, the life of St. Francis, third-century desert ascetics, and the martyrs of the early church. Many of his books on these topics were written by British Catholic apologists of the twenties and thirties and have the musty air of English belletristic conservatism. T. S. Eliot was perhaps his primary influence here, but Smithson also owned at least three of G. K. Chesterton's religious books (written after Chesterton had converted from Anglicanism to Roman Catholicism in 1922) and at least five by the mystic poet and theologian Evelyn Underhill, the preeminent writer on mysticism in the first half of the twentieth century. This was all of a piece with Smithson's general interest in Anglo-American conservative modernism of the interwar period: his favorite writers at this time included Wyndham Lewis, H. G. Wells, Ezra Pound, and T. E. Hulme. Although by 1973 Smithson would renounce all of these writers as "antidemocratic intelligentsia," during his spiritual crisis of the early sixties they helped him to articulate his discomfort with contemporary art and culture. Indeed, he would later admit that he had been attempting "to reestablish traditional art work in terms of the Eliot-Pound-Wyndham Lewis situation."[12]

Creeping Jesus (fig. 5) is one product of Smithson's attempts to reestablish traditional art. Rendered in a highly linear figurative style with sporadically attached collage elements taken from advertising imagery and broad washes of bright, sometimes caustic, color, the painting draws freely upon the standard repertory of Christian iconography. Smithson's model here is clearly the crucifixion, although he reconfigures the expected scene somewhat by permeating it with contemporary consumer products. The collaged figures of three women, which appear to have been excised from a single magazine advertisement, stand below the body of Christ. They might easily be mistaken for the figures traditionally depicted at the foot of the cross, except that one of them plays a home organ, and two hold forth shiny new household appliances for our spiritual contemplation. Although these appliances recall the attributes of succor held by the saints in attendance at the crucifixion (particularly Mary Magdalene's customary jar of ointment), they also seem closely related to the Roman attributes of torture (will they scald Christ with the coffee? Brand him with the iron?). Christ's attenuated body cringes as if anticipating this; attached firmly to the cross, he can only hang helplessly as he is besieged by the symbols ("36%") and products (cars, skis, irons, coffeepots, maraschino cherries) of contemporary consumer culture. Smithson's painting forces divinity and modernity into an antagonistic, even painful, juxtaposition. The painting does not comfortably reestablish the devotional painting tradition so much as it pictures the difficulty of doing so in the modern world.

The clash of sacred and profane in *Creeping Jesus* occurs not only in space but also in time. Consider the temporal status of the consumer objects. The objects, caught up in the accelerating temporality of production and advertising, their future obsolescence prefigured in the anachronistic "historical" costumes of their bearers, harbor a kind of predatory temporality at odds with the timelessness of the divine. Smithson borrows the title *Creeping Jesus* from a phrase in a poem by William Blake, who had used it to suggest the absurdity of imagining that Christ could ever reduce himself to the level of petty human concerns. Such a Christ, as G. K. Chesterton commented in his book on Blake, would have to be "a lower and meaner Jesus" (hence the term's later adaptation as the name for a

species of creeping weed). Smithson updates this Blakean insight for the postwar era by imagining the discomfiture of the eternal when forced into juxtaposition with the ever-accelerating time cycles of a consumerist utopia of accumulation.[13]

On the right side of the picture Smithson has collaged an image of a hand ringing a bell. The ringing bell bears ritual significance; here it probably indicates the precise instant of transubstantiation in the Catholic mass. Yet the bell's traditional role as an instantaneous harbinger of divine incarnation is complicated by its fractured and replicated image, which borrows from Cubo-Futurist convention in order to suggest dynamism, change, and duration. The hacking motion implied by the echoed wrists, too, calls the bell's benevolence into question. By including an allusion to modernist painting here, among the ranks of temporal threats to the body of Christ, Smithson hints that his concerns about modernity go beyond his discomfort for the products of mass culture to an unease about modernist standards of representation.[14]

Indeed, Smithson's letters to Lester brim with invective against both Futurism and Cubism, as does an unpublished essay, called "The Iconography of Desolation," that he was writing when he painted *Creeping Jesus*. In the essay, Smithson takes particular issue with Duchamp's *Nude Descending a Staircase*, precisely because it entangles itself in duration: "Revelation has no dimensions. If it did, it would be dead in space and time. The early Christian Fathers never Fixated on dimensions in their theology. If they did, they would have developed icons something like Marcel Duchamp's *Nude Descending a Staircase*, which Duchamp calls '. . . an expression of time and space through the abstract presentation of motion.' Marcel Duchamp stopped painting early in his life, because he *wasted* his art in time and space. Duration cut him off from revelation, thus confining grace to the chessboard."[15]

Here Smithson offers *Nude Descending a Staircase* as a kind of anti-icon. Whereas the true icon aims to reveal the divine body in a way that eludes and transcends vulgar dimensionality, Duchamp makes an *expression* of dimensional extension one of his primary goals. Duchamp's anti-icon subjects the perfect divine form to inertia, decay, and distortion; it subjects it, in short, to the condition of durational extrusion that governs all other objects in the temporal world (else-

5
Robert Smithson, *Creeping Jesus*, 1961.
Photo collage and gouache, 18 x 14 in. (45.7 x 35.6 cm).
Estate of Robert Smithson.

where in the article Smithson refers to "the decaying force of duration"). Thus the quasi-Futurist bell in *Creeping Jesus*, its brassy pivotings directly recalling Duchamp's painting, joins the anti-iconic forces threatening the body of Christ. It shatters what should be an immediate, instantaneous presence into a historical extension. Like the obsolescent matter embodied in the consumer products, the bell signals the "wrath" or "waste" of time.[16]

A recurrent theme in Smithson's letters to Lester is his conviction that art had been steadily degenerating since the advent of Renaissance humanism. He saw Cubism not as a rejection of Renaissance painting, but rather as its natural declension: Cubism simply followed upon the humanist spatializing (perspective, modeling, etc.) of the Renaissance tradition. Developing his own idiosyncratic brand of Pre-Raphaelitism, Smithson argued that the traditions of Byzantine devotional painting should be revived. Writing to Lester after he had sent a group of his paintings off to Rome, Smithson stated that "the show that I sent you was born out of an inner crisis, that has it's [sic] roots in the Pre-Renassaiance [sic]. The broken icons of Byzantium inspired me more than all the insipid equine figures of the Florentines." Smithson, in fact, frequently referred to his own paintings as "ikons." Although paintings like *Creeping Jesus* seem too agonistic to function as devotional images per se, they do dramatize Smithson's efforts to exorcise "insipid" Renaissance space and revive the hieratic airlessness of the Byzantines.[17]

For Smithson, this involved rejecting not only Renaissance art but also all of its extensions in modernism. Indeed, Smithson's letters to Lester have it in for virtually all "modern 'Isms.'" In one particularly vitriolic letter, undated but most likely written in June of 1961, he makes a list of "anti-art" of the twentieth century and includes "Futurism, Dada, 'The Wild Beasts' [Fauvism], The Ash-Can School, Cubism, Brute Art, among others." This jeremiad against modernism culminates in Smithson's proposition that "Jackson Pollock . . . died of modern demonic possession," and his claim that "Happenings are simply 'the Black Mass' for the retarted [sic] and should be stopped." This comment on the happenings, which by 1961 were becoming mainstream, hints at the extent to which Smithson's relationship to the New York art world was changing during this period. It is not overstating the case to say

that in these letters to Lester he essentially secedes from the avant-garde.[18]

Although these epistolary manifestos on devotional painting may seem to reflect an insufferable overconfidence on Smithson's part, the images that he produced that year tell a different story. Like *Creeping Jesus*, which enacts the struggle to evoke a timeless devotional experience rather than successfully doing so, Smithson's religious paintings of 1961 reveal a halting and ambivalent approach to the project of producing an art of "no dimensions." A close look at two other paintings from this period demonstrates that much of Smithson's ambivalence hinged upon his awareness of the fatal contradictions inhabiting the practice of representation itself. Although Smithson claimed to want to create true devotional images—images of timeless revelation, above and beyond the chaos and ruin of human history—he found that the pictorial means he had at his disposal were inadequate to the task. He was unable to keep history out of his religious paintings, and there were two central causes of this failure: one was the historicity of line, the other the historicity of vision itself.

Lineage; Lineament; Limbo: Smithson's Use of Line

During the early sixties, Smithson practiced an almost exclusively linear form of representation; indeed most of the works he produced between 1961 and 1964 were not paintings but crisp drawings in pencil or ink on paper. Even his fully realized oil-on-canvas paintings were, as Peter Halley has pointed out, "really highly linear, colored drawings in paint." The linear bias of this work is clear, and yet its very ubiquity in Smithson's paintings puts us in danger of overlooking its significance. A close formal and historical analysis of line in Smithson's religious paintings can help us to retrieve the decisive significance that the drawing process held for the artist. I will suggest here that Smithson returned repeatedly to linear representation during these years because line was itself intimately connected to the "spiritual crisis" that he described in his letters to Lester.[19]

In reading Smithson's letters to Lester, it quickly becomes evident that what seems to have bothered Smithson most about contemporary art was its propensity for action. "All modern schools of art, that are infused with action, ultimately 'despair and die.'"[20]

"Witness, the new vogue of 'Happenings' sweeping NYC's Beatnik realm, where art is swallowed up by action."[21] Smithson's counterpoint to "action" is religious "Passion," and he develops the distinction at length in his letters. Most important here, he associates "action" with history and reification, and "Passion" with timelessness and transcendence: "Action changes with the 'spirit of the times,' whereas Passion is eternal."[22] "Action Painting is the art of Despair. . . . Action is against Passion. Action leads to dead matter, while Passion leads to the life spirit. In his last years, Pollock, tryed [sic] to find *proportions* for his tortured soul, but his [sic] wasn't artist enough to exorcise his demons. So he, rode to his death in an infernal machine."[23]

Pollock, with whom Smithson was clearly preoccupied during these years, was of course best known for his poured "skein" paintings, fields of swirling, puddling, over- and interlapping lines that recorded the trajectory of the artist's arm and body as it moved above the canvas. Michael Fried famously described these paintings as having effected a decisive break with the history of representation in the West by undermining assumptions about the mimetic role of line. In Pollock's paintings, line functions independently of delineation, since it has been released from its usual charge of securing figuration through contour. As Michael Leja has convincingly argued, this free, abstract line placed Pollock's paintings into direct dialogue with period discourses of electrodynamics, the "drive-discharge" model of the psyche, and other manifestations of an emergent pan-energism in postwar culture. Smithson, with his pronounced aversion to "action," reacted against precisely these energetic connotations of Pollock's line. Indeed, in the quote above he goes so far as to read Pollock's death by car crash (which had occurred just five years earlier, in 1956) as a consequence of the artist's failure to pull himself out of the whorling vortices of line that embodied his "tortured soul." Smithson also refers to the corpus of late paintings, in which Pollock experimented with a kind of re-figuration by translating his energetic line back into contour, as well-meaning but inadequate attempts at "proportion."[24]

What did Smithson mean by this "proportion" that, if properly executed, might have saved Pollock? According to Smithson's letters to Lester, Pollock was not alone in his failure to locate it: all modern artists "refuse to seek for the invisible *proportions*, and so they fall into the pit of despair." Smithson's understanding of proportion (a term that he nearly always underlines for emphasis in his letters to Lester) appears to have derived from his reading of William Blake; as he explains: "The 'fearful symmetry' that Blake speaks about in his poem *Tyger* is what I mean by *proportion* rather than breakdown or distortion." As this citation and the Blakean title of *Creeping Jesus* suggest, Smithson had studied Blake's work carefully. He had seen a selection of Blake's original drawings on exhibition on at least one occasion, and he owned several books on and by Blake, including Northrop Frye's famous study, *Fearful Symmetry*. Smithson's strategies for avoiding the trap of "action" and finding refuge in the eternal stillness of proportion were closely tied to his understanding of Blake, not just to Blake's poems but also his drawings and paintings, which embodied specific ideas about line that were at odds with the dynamic qualities of Pollock's arabesques.[25]

Smithson was deeply influenced by Blake's philosophy of line, which was derived partially from neoclassical strategies of producing formal precision, clarity, and stability. For Blake, line was a mystical instrument, and a linear style was necessary in the delineation of eternal proportion because it avoided the worldly caprices of perspective and modeling. Blake's line was, first and foremost, a bounding line: an instrument of delineation, taxonomical clarity, rectitude, immediacy, decision. As Blake himself put it, "How do we distinguish the oak from the beech, the horse from the ox, but by the bounding outline? . . . What is it that builds a house and plants a garden, but the definite and determinate? What is it that distinguishes honesty from knavery, but the hard and wiry line of rectitude and certainty in the actions and intentions? Leave out this line, and you leave out life itself; all is chaos again, and the line of the almighty must be drawn out upon it before man or beast can exist."[26]

In this formulation, line is not only determinate but also eternal: it functions to reveal the diagrammatical essence of Creation that exists independently of the temporary and superficial appearances of the profane world. An incisive line functions as an index of the artist's capacity, which Blake labeled "Imagination," to see *through* temporal contingency to the essentials beneath: "This world of Imagination is the world

Robert Smithson, *Christ Series: Christ in Limbo*, 1961.
Ink and gouache, 24 x 18 in. (61 x 45.7 cm).
Estate of Robert Smithson.

of Eternity; it is the divine bosom into which we shall all go after the death of the Vegetated body. This World of Imagination is Infinite & Eternal, whereas the world of Generation, or Vegetation, is Finite & Temporal. There Exist in that Eternal World the Permanent Realities of Every Thing which we see reflected in this Vegetable Glass of Nature."[27]

 I will return to this "Vegetable Glass of Nature," which Smithson would reconceive in his outdoor mirror installations of the late sixties, in later chapters. What is important to note here is that for Blake, unlike many later naturalist-romantics who saw nature as a direct revelation of divinity, the outward forms of nature are fallen and fragmentary reflections of hidden proportions accessible only to mystics and communicable only through linear depiction. He often expressed this by noting that pure linear contour, through which the artist perceives and communicates "Permanent Realities," does not exist in visible nature but only in the mystic artist's imagination. "Nature has no Outline, but Imagination has."[28]

 Smithson's drawings and paintings of 1961 can be seen to work through the collision of the two models of line under discussion here: Pollock's and Blake's. The representational content of the images, which usually features a conflict between the divine body on one hand and nature or popular culture on the other, corroborates a deeper philosophical question raised by the method of depiction. Namely: can the mystical-fixative properties of the Blakean outline hold back the dynamic, contingent, temporal-historical whips and drips of Pollock? The richly unsettling *Christ in Limbo* (fig. 6), for example, traces out an unresolved crisis of contour. In this image, which alludes to medieval manuscript illuminations showing Christ breaking souls out of their captivity in limbo, the body of Christ occupies the rough center of the composition, surrounded by a framing membrane that separates him from the teeming marginalia of the drawing. Were this an illustration by Blake, who used clean linear sections to segregate different orders of creation in his work, the bubble would guarantee the separation of Christ from the surrounding yeasty space. Yet Blake's bounding line here is a semipermeable membrane at best. A band of small creatures has managed to pass through it into Christ's territory, and the lanky extremities of the crea-

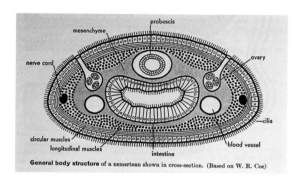

General body structure of a nemertean shown in cross-section. (Based on W. R. Coe.)

tures of limbo, generally unclassifiable structures that appear to be purely fantastical members of the lower orders of animalia, also threaten to puncture Christ's protective boundary. The overdetermined stress to which this contour is subjected hints that this painting hinges upon an acute ambivalence about the function and power of the hieratic line itself. The painting threatens to dismantle, even as it asserts, the eternal inviolability of Blakean lineament.[29]

 The creatures of limbo bear a strong resemblance to the microscopic cross-sectional diagrams of the cellular structures and segmented body plans of lower invertebrates that Smithson had been studying for years in his books on natural history (fig. 7). Thus it is not only nature but specifically microscopic nature that appears to populate Smithson's limbo. This brings Smithson's work into a particular form of conflict with the eternal outline, for it puts Blake's claim about the pure ideality of outline under microscopic scrutiny. G. K. Chesterton described Blake's linear idealism as follows: "The most important conception can be found in one sentence which he let fall as if by accident, 'Nature has no outline, but imagination has.' If a clear black line when looked at through a microscope was seen to be a ragged and confused edge like a mop or a doormat, then Blake would say, 'So

8

Robert Smithson, *Man of Ashes*, 1961.
Tempera and pencil, 18 x 11 3/4 in. (45.7 x 29.8 cm).
Estate of George B. Lester.

much the worse for the microscope.'"[30]

It is precisely this microscopic line that both populates and constitutes Smithson's painting. *Christ in Limbo* essentially interprets Christ's descent into Limbo as a descent in scale, Alice-in-Wonderland style, into the microscopic world. The profound ambivalence of the painting derives from the fact that Smithson is not so ready as is Chesterton's Blake to brush off the microscopic line as "so much the worse for the microscope." The entire situation threatens to be so much the worse for Christ as well. Squashed as if onto a microscope slide with a drop of pond water, peered at by some gigantic eye above, his fragile, mis-scaled body under threat from the liney forms, Christ is placed in immediate and uneasy juxtaposition with the "ragged and confused" origins of his own linear construction.

The lines of limbo also embody history at the level of process. The image displays quite emphatically the history of the drawing itself, its development through repetition and gradual modification. The drawing has been produced in what we might call geological fashion, each mark building upon the last in a complex array of stratification and subdivision. Smithson's use of sequential cell-like compartments, each of which is often occupied, protoplasm-style, by a nucleic dot, allows him to build up the bodies of the creatures through a process of serial or modular accumulation. In limbo, each line implies and produces another; each line provides not a firm and final boundary for the form that it circumscribes but simply a kind of platform for the reflexive addition of another line. In fact, the creatures' illegibility from an iconographical standpoint only underlines their status as pure accretional drawing. This process of linear stratigraphy, moreover, contains its own echoes of mutational evolution. Smithson seems fascinated by the way in which the simple repetition of a line or cellular unit across space tends to amplify minute distortions in the original form. Here, as in similar accretional drawings of the early sixties like *Man of Ashes* (fig. 8), Smithson develops the evolutionary potential of the doodle. There could be nothing more threatening to the eternal lineaments of the icon than this chaos of lineage.

The morphogenetic potential of Smithson's painting is closely tied to its appeal to microscopy and, by extension, to natural history. Smithson had grown up wanting to be a field naturalist or a zoologist. He had devoured books on the evolution of animals, painted a dinosaur mural in the hallway of his school at age seven, and made sure that the Smithson family vacations included visits to Ross Allen's reptile farm in Florida. He spent innumerable hours at the American Museum of Natural History, and he even developed a small natural-history museum of his own in the family basement. Thus he was early exposed to the idea of history as natural history, and to an image of the passage of time embodied in the evolving morphological diagrams of the bodies of living creatures. A favorite source of these and other natural-historical diagrams was Ralph Buchsbaum's classic textbook *Animals Without Backbones* (from which fig. 7 is taken). Smithson's aunt Julia gave him this book for his twelfth birthday; its spine eventually became so weakened from repeated opening, and its pages so thoroughly decollated for Smithson's collage projects, that it approached invertebrate status itself.[31]

Christ in Limbo draws further upon the discourse of microbiology in order to question the possibility of the eternal outline. Note the ciliated extensions extruding from the cell-like compartments in the painting. These "cilia" complicate the function of line as pure contour, not only because they visually "fuzz," through the addition of tiny perpendicular units, a clean boundary line (as in Chesterton's microscopic "doormat"), but also and especially because each individual "hair" is simply a line *as line*, freed from the function of bounding and contour, simply waving free on the page. In this regard they directly connect the drawing to Smithson's anxieties about Pollock. Pollock's roiling line, supposedly exiled through Blake's mystical/proportional draughtsmanship, sneaks in through the back door of microbiological illustration. And just as cilia function in flagellate animals as primordial instruments of propulsion and sensation in an aqueous medium, so do these ciliated lines of the drawing introduce a suggestion of current, atmosphere, and motion into the airless stillness of the Eternal Imagination. In doing so they necessarily suggest contingency; bending this way or that, having no "eternal" posture, the ciliated line encodes the immersion of Christ in specific (natural-) historical conditions, whether we want to call these the primordial soup or, following Blake, "The Sea of Time and Space."

Thus the flagellate line poses an enormous threat to the eternal body of Christ. We might even see this painting as another version of the Flagellation—a leap of interpretation that may seem improbable at first but which appears more viable if we look also at other paintings of the period. In *Jesus Mocked* (fig. 9, a kind of iconographical hybrid of the Mockery and the Flagellation), a linear Christ is beset by whiplike lines, while *Fallen Christ* (fig. 10), a stations-of-the-cross episode, features a conspicuously ciliated crucifix.[32]

Perhaps, then, the bounding line provides no mystical vision of Blake's Eternal; perhaps it is simply a trap, an endless, self-involuting whorl of history. Perhaps line, in other words, is only a kind of limbo. Limbo: from Latin "edge" or "border," in Catholic theology a place where souls must wait, excluded from the eternal beatific vision, until their rescue. Smithson's *Christ in Limbo* ultimately casts doubt on the efficacy and the possibility of that rescue; whereas most manuscript illuminations of this scene show Christ triumphantly setting free the inhabitants of Limbo, Smithson's Christ has fallen into the border, trapped by the temporal implications of his own linear representation.

Despair and the Historicity of Vision

For Blake, true art was the product of a kind of imaginative vision that transcended all merely corporeal opticality. "He who does not *imagine* in strong and better lineaments, and in stronger and better light than his perishing mortal eye can see does not *imagine* at all." The "Corporeal Vegetative Eye" is a fallen instrument, morbidly dependent upon everyday time and space. As such it can provide only fragmentary, contingent information: "The Visions of Eternity, by reason of narrowed perceptions / Are become weak Visions of Time & Space, fix'd into furrows of death." Like Blake, Smithson understood everyday vision to be a somatic operation hopelessly entangled in spatiotemporal distortions. There is Eternal Vision and there is temporal vision; Smithson was deeply concerned with the distinction during this period and would remain so for the rest of his life. As he put it, "The Great Universal Vision is caving in, and the Age of Astonishment is beginning."[33]

For Smithson, all of this had immediate ramifi-

9

Robert Smithson, *Jesus Mocked*, 1961.
Watercolor on paper, 37³/₄ x 35 in. (96 x 89 cm).
Estate of George B. Lester.

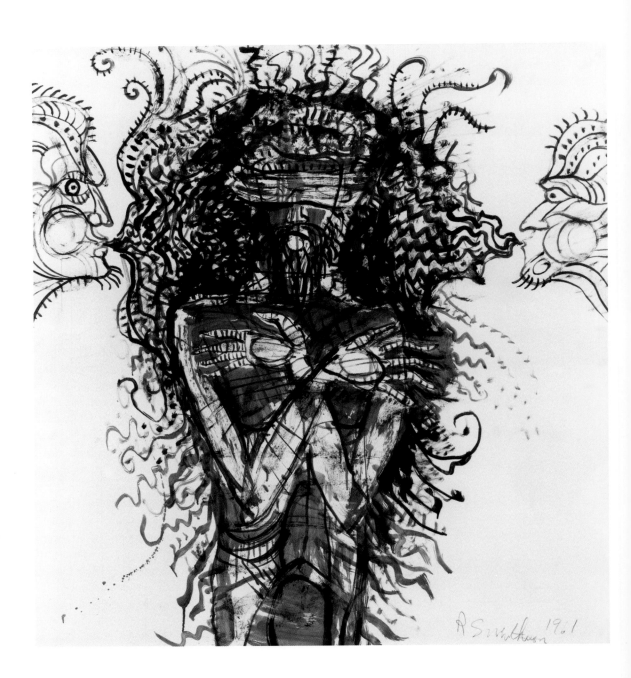

Robert Smithson, *Fallen Christ*, 1961.
Ink and gouache on paper, 18 x 24 in. (45.7 x 61 cm).
Estate of Robert Smithson.

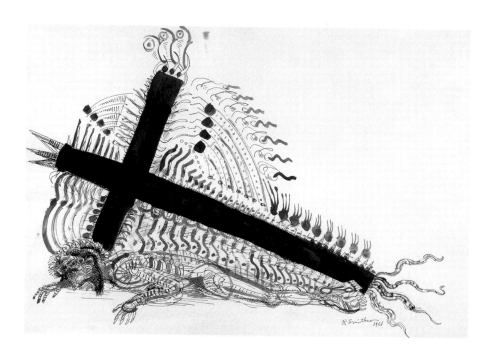

cations for his own painting. Which brand of vision would viewers bring to his work? How could he be sure that his own "ikons" would not become "weak Visions of Time & Space" in the vulgar eyes of their viewers? His anxiety about this becomes clear in a letter he wrote from Rome to Nancy Holt (whom he would later marry). In it, Smithson described his discomfort at the fact that people were looking (or, more precisely, "staring") at his paintings while his show was on view at Lester's gallery. He complained, "People want to stare with aggressive eagerness or they feel they must stare in order to grant approval. There is something indecent about such staring." Staring seemed to him blasphemous or obscene; he felt that his paintings were violated, not consummated, by the vision of tourists, "like the private parts of butterflies [pinned] against the walls of ice cubes." He found himself mus-

ing that his "ikons" would be better off in a church than an art gallery, if only because it would be harder to see them there: "The dark Roman churches appeal to me because much of the art can not be defiled by vulgar liberal eyes." In his essay "The Iconography of Desolation," Smithson specified that icons were not to be "looked at" in the same way that one looks at other objects. "Art was never objectified during the Ages of Faith; art was an 'act' of worship. Icons would never be 'looked' at like a tourist looks at an objet d'art, even if he is a 'passionate sightseer.'" The practice of "looking at" contradicts devotion for Smithson, because the spatiotemporal entanglement of the corporeal eye prevents devotional immediacy. Corporeal vision defiles the icon by historicizing it, pulling it out of the realm of the timeless.[34]

Smithson's work of this period, whether explicitly

religious or not, repeatedly imagines this historicizing visual defilement as a process of burial of the revelational presence of the artwork. In *Alive in the Grave of Machines* (fig. 11), for example, Smithson surrounds an iconic human figure with images of automobiles and automotive parts cut from what appear to be magazine advertisements. Although this painting recalls *Creeping Jesus* in its concern with the detritus of modern consumption, it goes further by neatly equating this trope of waste with the theme of vision. The "machines" in the grave of machines function simultaneously as images of waste and as proxies for vision itself. Smithson painted blobby, eyelike forms in the margins of many of his 1961 paintings (including *Creeping Jesus* [see fig. 5], in which they lurk among the household appliances). Here, in the grave of machines, the cast-off tires and hubcaps clearly evoke eyes (in case we should miss the connection, Smithson has added what is unmistakably an eye at the upper left corner of the painting). The hubcap patterns suggest the striations of the cornea or the splay of eyelashes. The eye-tires (tired eyes?) also suggest Blake's organic "Vegetative" eyes by evoking anemones, jellyfish, and other radially symmetrical invertebrates.

Yet these eyes are not merely protoplasmic; there is another, equally crucial, set of meanings condensed into their radial forms. The forms are organic, but they are also machines, suggesting photographic apertures or film reels (note the small movie camera at lower right). Smithson thus equates the organic and the mechanical, applying the pejorative associations of fallen vision to both. The organic eyeball is no better than the photographic; both are estranged from the "Great Universal Vision," and both produce distortions. Given these themes of visual distortion and displacement, it is no accident that the grave of machines is filled with collage. Note that Smithson does not use collage for the man's body (which, in fact, resembles some sort of exercise in the proportional ideal)—he uses it only to construct the population of vision-machines in the surrounding space. Collage occupies, indeed constitutes, the space of mundane accumulation.

But there is something else about Smithson's use of collage that links it even more strongly to vision: only through collage does Smithson allow perspective into this or any other painting of this period. For all his interest in the linear during these years, linear per-

spective was absolutely taboo. Smithson's drawings and paintings are resolutely flat and hieratic, except when he imports collage, which functions as a carrier of depth, distance, and point of view. I will have much more to say about perspective and point of view—as will Smithson—but for now I will point out merely that Smithson does not see perspective as an elastic operation of universal understanding but instead as a kind of machine for the production of reified "views," fixed on scraps of paperwaste. Each perspectival view becomes an artifact of a single angle of vision at a single moment in history.

These view-scraps, which participate structurally in the junkyard car-parts aesthetic of the collage as a whole, serve to link profane vision with the passage of time and the ruined accumulations of history. History is a junkyard, and each act of lowercase-v vision tosses another artifact onto the pile. Smithson's decision to link vision with a specifically automotive iconography here is deliberate and important. The car features prominently in many of Smithson's collages of this period (*Creeping Jesus* included) as a representative of history and indeed of everything that prevents access to presence and eternity. First, for Smithson, auto parts had deeply personal connections to his own history: his father had worked for Auto-Lite (an auto parts company). In an interview Smithson recalled "some interesting things that he used to bring home—like films—where they had all these car parts sort of automated, you know, like marching spark plugs and marching carburetors and that sort of thing." And Smithson's maternal grandfather had been (of all things) a wheel maker. Cars also function in Smithson's work as representatives of the accelerated pace of postwar consumer production and obsolescence, suggesting speed and "action" and thus, in Smithson's mythology of the period, reified waste ("Action leads to dead matter"). Most importantly, the car is both a historical and existential instrument of tragedy; the flipped chassis and scattered tires in the grave of machines clearly evoke the death of Jackson Pollock.[35]

The tragedy of the automobile combines here with the tragedy of collage and perspective. Thus the tire falling away into perspective space at the lower right corner of the work amounts to a kind of historical ruin. Distorted by perspective, the photographic image of the tire is embedded in time and space

Robert Smithson, *Alive in the Grave of Machines*, 1961.
Collage and ink on paper, 24 x 14 in. (61 x 35.6 cm).
Courtesy of the Collection of Andrea Rosen, New York.

and thus suggests the fossilized remnant—like some Paleozoic cephalopod—of a single moment of vision from a single point of view. The upside-down car above it is the detritus of a different moment, a different view. These wasted "views" are the fallen remnants of Blake's Eternal Imaginative Vision and, like Humpty-Dumpty, they cannot be put back together again. As Smithson wrote in one of his letters to Lester, "The vision can't pull it self [sic] together because the breakdowns and distortions are separated by despair." "Breakdown"—a term that also refers to automobiles —was just the right term to use here. Human vision, like collage and like urban junk, is scrappy, disconsolate, and disconnected, scattered across space and through time. The best that fallen humanity can hope for, without access to "the Great Universal Vision," is a junkyard of visual data.[36]

Eugenie Tsai has pointed out that 1961 was an auspicious year for collage, with the Museum of Modern Art's *Art of Assemblage* exhibition mounting a historical survey from Picasso to John Chamberlain. By 1961, collage was already an important part of the burgeoning street-junk aesthetic of the Beats and of artists like Allan Kaprow, Claes Oldenburg, Robert Rauschenberg, and Jasper Johns. Indeed, *Alive in the Grave of Machines* can be seen as Smithson's critical commentary on the emergence of these artists, especially when we consider that the painting was produced at almost precisely the same time that Kaprow held his *Yard* happening at the Martha Jackson Gallery. Kaprow's installation forced viewers to wade through hundreds of old tires piled in the courtyard of the gallery (fig. 12); Smithson's painting buries a man under a heap of hubcaps. Like Kaprow, Smithson is clearly fascinated by junk, by the ever-accelerating pace of postwar consumerism and its attendant accumulation of waste. But he resists giving in to its appeal. For Smithson in 1961, Kaprow's *Yard* would have seemed the perfect embodiment of "the pit of despair" into which he felt all modern artists were falling: "According to St. Thomas Aquinas despair is the worst sin." "The Spirit reveals itself differently in every age, provided dispair [sic] doesn't crush revelation."[37]

Smithson frequently refers to despair in his writings of this period; this usage is not offhanded. Despair is a religious term. Throughout the religious literature in Smithson's library it is identified as the inevitable result of skepticism, which is itself defined as a tendency to see things in their outward, temporary, and fragmentary lights, giving the impression of a dismantled and pulverized world, rather than in their inner essences, which maintain an eternal form and truth. As Chesterton noted in his book on Blake, "It means believing one's immediate impressions at the expense of one's more permanent and positive generalizations." Chesterton also calls skepticism "a mere flinging of facts at a great conception" and "a mere attack by masses of detail," both of which might serve as fairly accurate descriptions of the relationship of the tires to the man in Smithson's painting.[38]

Smithson was clear in his letters to Lester about the connection of despair with everyday vision: "The deadly effect of despair breaks down or distorts . . . all vision, confounding divine and worldly into a horrible mire." Another connection he made between despair, skepticism, and vision was his frequent use of the symbol of the tear. Indeed, in paintings like *Tear* (fig. 13) Smithson emphasizes the eye as an organ of excretion rather than reception; beneath the crying eyes grows a heap of archaeological waste, indistinguishable from many of Smithson's other depictions of opaque geohistorical detritus. The visual field constituted by this lachrymose looking prevents a clear view of eternal truths. The "Great Universal Vision," we might say, is refracted beyond recognition by the tear-filled skeptical-historical view. Everyday vision drowns out, rather than focuses and constitutes, its object. In the epigraph of "The Iconography of Desolation," Smithson quotes the following passage from *Alice in Wonderland*: "'I wish I hadn't cried so much!' said Alice as she swam about, trying to find her way out." The idea of being drowned by the waste products of the corporeal eye could hardly be expressed more succinctly. Smithson would explore this idea again and again in his later work, although, seeking less affective equivalents, he would come to replace "teardrops" with glass, mirrors, and similar materials as his agents of refraction.[39]

Iconoclasm

As the summer of 1961 approached, Smithson looked forward to visiting Italy for his show. He mentioned to Lester that he was especially interested in seeing early Renaissance art in Florence, the frescoes by Pietro

Cavallini in the church of Santa Cecilia in Trastevere,
the catacombs, and the paintings of Botticelli ("I like
Botticelli, because he burnt so many of his vain works
after hearing the terrifying prophecies of Savonarola.").
But if Smithson had hoped to find in Rome the timeless tranquility of pre-Renaissance tradition, the Eternal
in the Eternal City, his trip turned out to be a disappointment. His letters home to Nancy describe his experiences in the city in detail, but his observations feature
the scatological, the ornamental, and the dispropor-
tional rather than the spiritual ideal. He finds that even
the Eternal City of Rome roils in "tutti-frutti" and
"beads and fake jewels and piles of hair doos [*sic*]."
What's more, he describes all this quotidiana with
irony, humor, and even relish.[40] Smithson would later
admit that visiting Rome had only exacerbated the
tension he felt, already evident in his paintings, between
his desire for timelessness and his fascination with
history and decay. Speaking in 1972 about his trip, he
discussed the impact that the city's millennia-worth
of ruins (which he associates with the Baroque and the
grotesque) had upon him. He said: "So my trip to Rome
was sort of an encounter with European history as a
nightmare . . . my disposition was toward the Byzantine. But I was affected by the baroque in a certain
way. These two things kind of clashed." He also commented, "There was a kind of grotesqueness that
appealed to me. As I said, while I was in Rome I was
reading William Burroughs' *Naked Lunch* and the
imagery in that book corresponded in a way to a kind of
grotesque massive accumulation of all kinds of rejec-
tive rituals. There was something about the passage
of time."[41]

   With this, Smithson joined a long tradition of
American writers and artists deeply affected by what
we might call the abject materialism of Roman history,
by the experience of having seen (in Henry James's
words) "the past, the ancient world, as you stand there,
bodily turned up with the spade and transformed
from an immaterial, inaccessible fact of time into a
matter of soils and surfaces." What might earlier have
seemed to Smithson, from across the Atlantic, to be
an opportunity to access the spiritual eternity of Christian tradition, turned into an opportunity to observe
eternity operating in and through the material, in and
through the Baroque, in and through objects and
images and soils and surfaces. The acute tension that

Robert Smithson, *Tear*, 1963.
Gouache, photo, and crayon on paper, 24 x 26 in. (61 x 66 cm).
Estate of Robert Smithson.

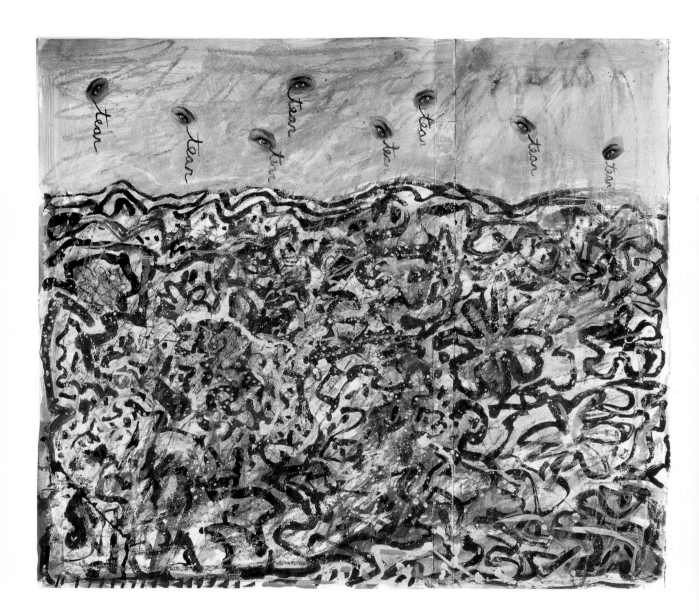

Smithson had previously felt between eternity and history began to dissolve while in Rome.[42]

He first mapped some of the procedures of this dissolution in the second half of his 1961 "Iconography of Desolation" essay. The first part of the essay, from which I have been quoting throughout this chapter, shares in the tortured and contrary tone of his springtime letters to Lester. About halfway through the essay, however, Smithson's tone shifts, as he begins to provide an ironic celebration of that which he had previously feared: the breakdown of the separation between the timeless and the temporal, between the sacred and the profane. The main transition occurs with this paragraph: "We now discover an iconoscope that shall forgive the divorce of heaven and hell while it flashes before us for our selective graces — the bits and pieces of Divine Catastrophe. Such a scope has lost all division and order. One must pick over the scattered icons the way a bum picks over the dumps. The iconoscope will now be plugged in."[43]

The first thing to note about this "iconoscope," which represents the literal "breaking point" of the essay, is that Smithson conjures it for use as an iconoclastic instrument. The device reduces divinity to "bits and pieces." After the iconoscope is "plugged in," the essay's controlled contrasts between sacred and profane break into a stuttering progression of overlapping imagery and shifting modes of address: "Here begins the canticle of Philomela, the screech owl. Itys. Itys. 'Let the insects do the suffering for us!' says the Word Dissected. Roll on! A pale man wanders off the stage and falls into a backfiring redemption fuming the germs of vice and virtue. Smashing down over the rocks goes the Virgin's coffin into the foaming contentment surrounded by progressive Christendom. THE LIGHT SHINES IN DARKNESS!"[44]

Smithson had already stated in the essay that despair distorts vision, "confounding divine and worldly into a horrible mire." This "horrible mire," of course, is exactly what we get after Smithson plugs in the iconoscope. The iconoscope represents Smithson giving in to despair, fully allowing himself (and us) to look at the icon. Whereas previously Smithson had preserved the image of the divine body lying intact, alive, and alone under a pile of visual-historical waste, now he shatters its contours and proportions. The icon, subjected like all other objects to the fragmentations and distortions of worldly vision, becomes inextricable from the general jumble of "views" taken from different angles and rendered in different media. In the following passage, for example, Smithson alludes to several different modes of representation; the divine is subjected to photography, film, painting, and engraving: "A specter of Creeping Jesus is strontiumized in the Cedar Street Tavern through the eye of a safety pin. A peal of woes. A nameless augur pronounces the benediction: 'Convert to Hoboken, and cry unto her!' The unpainted vision departs. . . . A wolf-man (geniuses know where he lives) howls on a fire escape in Chelsea. Fac me plagis vulnerari. Who can paint it steadily? In St. Patrick's Cathedral a wax pope watches Luis Buñuel's *Viridiana* in tones of crimson. The graphic needle pierces the Hairy-Heart — atrobilious acid squirts onto canvas thin as a spider's web."[45]

It is important to keep in mind, of course, that Smithson's iconoscope not only throws the icon down into a heap of imagery, but also (in the same motion) consigns it to the rubble of time. The divine has fallen into history, into the twentieth century, where it mixes absurdly with safety pins, Hoboken, and Buñuel films. The Buñuel reference is especially important here, not only because Buñuel was well known for his blasphemies, but also because the medium of film itself, for Smithson, performs the ultimate blasphemy: it draws the icon out into space and time simultaneously. It is no accident that filmic discourse frames much of the essay: "Lights! Camera! Action! Prepare for the Practical Martyrdom! A clever soul places the body into a deep-freeze on a bed of thorns, whereupon the soul proclaims, 'You'll forget ice-cream once you taste ice-blood.' Cut. Print it! Listen to the sounding brass or the tinkling cymbal: take your pick. 1-2-3-4. Forward! Footage, more footage! Dies irae, dies illa. Bring Icon-400 into the ultraviolet rays."[46]

Such spatiotemporal extension, such a drawing out into "footage," does considerable violence to the instantaneous integrity of the icon. This temporal-visual defilement of the icon, its filmic fall from grace into space, scatters it throughout the dimensional continuum, where it interpenetrates the field of mundane modernity. It might be compared, in fact, to a drawing-and-quartering of the divine body. (Indeed, Smithson would later write about film's connection to evisceration; in his 1972 essay "The Spiral Jetty" he described the way his film editor "pulled lengths of film out of the movieola with the grace of a Neanderthal pulling intestines from a slaughtered mammoth.") At any rate, in 1961 Smithson was already imagining the iconoclastic potential of film. In fact, a close examination of the typescript of "The Iconography of Desolation" essay at the Archives of American Art reveals that, rather than "iconoscope," Smithson had originally used the term "kinetoscope" (Edison's precursor of the movie projector) to identify his iconoclastic instrument. It was only at the last minute, apparently, that he added the neologism "iconoscope" over the rubbed-out "kinetoscopes" on the typescript.[47]

It might be tempting to interpret Smithson's iconoclastic breakage as a refutation of all of his previous ambitions toward transcendence. But there is a sense in which the scene seen through Smithson's iconoscope has managed to recuperate all of the timelessness that had once inhabited the intact icons. The iconoscope offers a certain cold comfort — it manages, by bringing the opposite spheres of sacred and mundane into a dedifferentiated equilibrium, to wrest a form of transcendence out of the iconoclasm itself. The pressure differential between the sacred and the mundane is released, in Smithson's words "forgiven," by the inertia of iconoscopic equilibrium. To be sure, Smithson's iconoscope produces chaos and disorder. But this is an evenly distributed disorder; the Unity previously embodied in the bounded icon is perversely regained, after the iconoclasm, by the refined, homogeneous consistency of its dispersion.

This homogeneity, this dissipation, ensures an end to the struggle between the sacred and the profane. In a classic thermodynamic transformation, the energies expended to keep the two realms apart have been exhausted, and all further tension is impossible. Smithson's iconoscope is, in this sense, an entropic instrument, and his iconoclastic maneuver is a key early manifestation of his career-long interest in entropy and the methodologies of equilibrium. In fact, the course of Smithson's essay — obsessively preserving, then despairingly breaking, the boundaries which preserve an ontological differential between the sacred and the profane, mimics the plotline of many of the stories about entropy that he was reading at the time. The final paragraph of Thomas Pynchon's 1959 story

"Entropy" provides a good comparison. Recognizing that the heat death of the universe is imminent, a man and woman seal themselves into a hothouse in order to preserve themselves from the rapid dissipation of energy occurring outside. Yet the woman realizes that to remain sealed inside the house is only to delay the inevitable, and, with a "clasm" of her own, decides to get it over with: "She moved swiftly to the window before Callisto could speak; tore away the drapes and smashed out the glass with two exquisite hands which came away bleeding and glistening with splinters; and turned to face the man on the bed and wait with him until the moment of equilibrium was reached, when 37 degrees Fahrenheit should prevail both outside and inside, and forever, and the hovering, curious dominant of their separate lives should resolve into a tonic of darkness and the final absence of all motion."[48]

Just as the final equilibrium in Pynchon's story has a "tonic" effect, so too does Smithson's iconoscope bring about a palpable sense of *relief*. Smithson's invention of the iconoscope here inaugurates his transition from a youthful horror at the inevitable ruination of the world to his later embrace of entropy as the very definition of beauty. With the iconoclasm, the icon undergoes an immediate and total transformation from a discrete, differentiated point of timelessness to an infinitely scattered, dedifferentiated, lapidary field which, in its static equilibrium, homogeneity, and glinting beauty, recuperates the very sense of eternity originally sought in the intact icon. The iconoscope provides its own view of eternity, although that eternity now weaves itself throughout an entire fractured field instead of remaining sequestered within an iconic boundary. And indeed, within a few months of "plugging in" the iconoscope, Smithson was writing to Lester that he had discovered that "the way up is the way down." Instead of reaching upward toward infinity, Smithson would from then on reach "*downward* toward infinity." He had glimpsed a way to suggest the eternal through the temporal. If Smithson had previously struggled with the tension between the eternalizing aims of mysticism and the temporal despair of skepticism, he has now developed something approaching an equilibrium between the two, a kind of skeptical mysticism or mystical skepticism. This "mystical skepticism," in fact, would go on to inform Smithson's crystallographically inspired work of the mid-to-late six-ties. As he wrote in a 1967 article about the crystalline labyrinths of thirties architecture, "Belief is not the motive behind the timeless, but rather a skepticism is the generating force."[49]

Smithson; Greenberg; Fried

I have suggested that Smithson's work of 1961 harbors a consistent impulse toward timelessness, first in its ambivalent attempt to defend an instantaneous model of "revelatory" reception against the historicizing aggressions of biological, consumerist, and visual tem-porality, and then in its construction of a broader sense of eternity from the infinite accumulations of histor-ical ruination itself. Before moving on to the next phase of Smithson's career, I would like briefly to address some of the implications of this reading for our under-standing of Smithson's position in art-historical nar-ratives about modernism in the early sixties, particularly as that position is mapped in his relationship to his two most conspicuous art-critical contemporaries, Clement Greenberg and Michael Fried. Since Smithson's relation to these figures has usually been defined as an outright opposition that marks and defines Smith-son's key role in an emergent postmodernity, it is instructive to reassess this view with an eye to the assumptions that Smithson shares with both critics.

It is true that Smithson explicitly contested Greenberg's aesthetics during these and later years. In a jab no doubt intended at Greenberg, in 1961 Smith-son referred to postpainterly painting as "the latest obscure mess of abstraction" and specifically dispar-aged Kenneth Noland's concentric paintings (Greenberg's favorites) by claiming that "those without souls can continue seeing truth in targets."[50] But the critical ani-mus Smithson demonstrates in these and other squabbles with Greenberg obscures the deeper corre-spondences between the two writers. Both Smithson and Greenberg, for example, were concerned about the problems that historical time poses to the instanta-neous, revelatory artwork. According to Greenberg in 1959, avant-garde artwork can succeed only to the degree that it separates itself from duration. In lan-guage similar to Smithson's assertion that revelation must eclipse the decaying force of duration, Green-berg argues that "pictorial art in its highest definition

is static; it tries to overcome movement in space or time. . . . [T]he whole of a picture should be taken in at a glance; its unity should be immediately evident, and the supreme quality of a picture, the highest mea-sure of its power to move and control the visual imag-ination, should reside in its unity. And this is some-thing to be grasped only in an indivisible instant of time. No expectancy is involved in the true and pertinent experience of a painting; a picture, I repeat, does not 'come out' the way a story, or a poem, or a piece of music does, It's all there at once, like a sudden revela-tion. . . . You are summoned and gathered into one point in the continuum of duration."[51]

We might well wonder at this point why Smith-son was bothering to argue with Greenberg. He clearly shared Greenberg's interest in "sudden revelation" and understood along with Greenberg that in order to procure it one needed to define a mode of reception that would factor out the temporal and material exten-sion of the work. The sticking point for Smithson was not Greenberg's aim but rather his method. Greenberg claimed that great art revealed itself to the viewer in a purely optical fashion, defining the optical as that which could transcend matter and time. For Greenberg, the experience of the work should involve the impression "that matter is incorporeal, weightless, and exists only optically like a mirage."[52]

Smithson, of course, could not subscribe to this optical transcendence. It went against everything he knew about the limitations of the "Corporeal Veg-etative Eye" and its temporal and material complica-tions. He recognized that Greenberg was essentially attempting to use opticality to perform a dualistic sep-aration of Spirit from Matter. What is crucial to under-stand here is that Smithson faults Greenberg not because he aims at transcendence, but because (with his invalid "optical" method based on the very corporeal space that it aims to transcend) he is destined to fail to attain it.[53]

Several years later, Greenberg's brilliant protégé Michael Fried would also come to struggle with the threat that temporal, spatial, and phenomenal extension pose to the "at-onceness" of the artwork. Fried's semi-nal 1967 article "Art and Objecthood" framed this strug-gle as the menace of "literalism" (by which he meant, essentially, minimalism's activation of everyday space and time) to the very survival of art itself. Smithson quarreled publicly, and famously, with Fried over the article. In the narrative of postwar art criticism, the Smithson/Fried bout is usually interpreted as a collision of personalities that had been theretofore following wholly incommensurate philosophical trajectories. Fried's article is seen as the swan song of a retroguard transcendent modernism—a song that galvanized Smithson (who seemingly swooped in from his own bizarre world of science fiction and geology) to propose a new paradigm for an art of the concrete, the durational, and the entropic.[54] But Fried's passionate defenses of art from objecthood employed many of the same strategies that Smithson had earlier used to defend icons from objecthood. Note, for example, the uncanny resemblance between Smithson's thoughts on duration in 1961 and Fried's in 1967. Smithson, 1961: "Revelation is eclipsed by the decaying force of duration." "Soon there will be nothing to stand on except the webs of manufactured time warped among throbbing galaxies of space, space, and more space."[55] Fried, 1967: "The literalist preoccupation with time—more precisely, with the *duration of the experience* . . . confronts the beholder . . . with the endlessness not just of objecthood but of time; or as though the sense which, at bottom, theatre addresses is a sense of temporality, of time both passing and to come, *simultaneously approaching and receding*, as if apprehended in an infinite perspective."[56]

Such resemblances show how an understanding of Smithson's religious paintings forces us to reconsider his relationship to high modernist criticism. Fried's discomfort in the face of everyday duration had once been Smithson's own. Smithson, like Fried, had attempted to focus the confusion and horrible "endlessness" of time. Smithson's writings and iconic paintings of 1961 had already worked through what Fried saw as the mortal challenge of literalism to the modernist artwork. In many ways, Fried's "Art and Objecthood" can be interpreted as a secularized reiteration of Smithson's "Iconography of Desolation."

Smithson's celebrated arguments with Fried in the late sixties, therefore, must be reexamined. Consider the letter to the editor that Smithson published in *Artforum* magazine in October of 1967, attacking "Art and Objecthood." In the letter, Smithson lampoons Fried for quixotically "cling[ing] for dear life" to the intimacies of modernist conviction in the face of the infinities of phenomenological space and durational time. He is careful to expose and to ridicule the spiritualist overtones of Fried's position, painting Fried as a religious fanatic who attempts, "in a manner worthy of the most fanatical puritan," to ward off the terrors of worldly space and time by ritualistically employing "Seven Deadly Isms, verbose diatribes, scandalous refutations, a vindication of Stanley Cavell, shrill but brilliant disputes on 'shapehood' vs. 'objecthood,' dark curses, infamous claims, etc." But we can now say that the acuity of Smithson's criticism (Fried himself has recently described it as "brilliant" and Smithson as "by far the most powerful and interesting" critic of his work in general) was due largely to his intimate familiarity with the nature of Fried's own struggle. Perhaps Smithson's sarcasm and condescension were attempts to deflect attention from his own previous affinities with Fried's quasi-religious aims at revelation.[57]

The ferocious wit of Smithson's letter has also tended to obscure the fact that, even as late as 1967, Smithson had not rescinded his own claims to eternity. His approach to Fried was similar to his earlier approach to Greenberg inasmuch as he attacked Fried not for aiming at the eternal but for going about it the wrong way. Near the end of the letter, in a passage often overlooked, Smithson comments that "eternal time is the result of skepticism, not belief."[58] This phrase nicely encapsulates Smithson's own transition from a model of eternity based on belief to one based on skepticism. His tone toward Fried is condescending because he knows that he has already tried Fried's eternalizing strategy, has found it wanting, and has developed a better one. In a postlapsarian world it is useless to attempt to stuff the reified accumulations of history back into a single point or "instant." Instead it is better to adopt a strategy of infinite skepticism, infinite fragmentation, infinite duration, in order to arrive at eternal time. Smithson's historical transcendence was inclusionary while Fried's was exclusionary, but it was a brand of transcendence nonetheless. Chapter 2 will explore Smithson's inclusionary transcendence of the late sixties, and the crystalline strategies of its achievement, in more detail.

Smithson's religious period, therefore, should not be understood as a detour of misguided mysticism that postponed the launch of a properly postmodern career. Smithson's aversion to "action," his hopes for historical transcendence, and his dalliance with the comforts of absolute stillness would not be "corrected" in his later work; rather they would be instrumental in establishing the dialectical tensions that have made his work so influential in the first place. After all, Smithson would still be quoting Chesterton as late as 1972 in the epigraph to his "Spiral Jetty" essay; phrases pulled intact from his "Iconography of Desolation" essay would pop up again in a series of 1970 preliminary sketches for a film called *Tropical Cargo*; his understanding of vision as a machine for the production of oblique perspectival artifacts would underlie all of his later work with sculpture, photography, and film; and his investigation of the volatility of contour when examined microscopically would have a profound effect on his later experiments with the instability of boundary and scale.[59] In short, Smithson's religious paintings introduced a permanent inflection toward tranquility into a body of work that might otherwise have participated unhesitatingly in the aesthetics of "action" of the early sixties. The vehicle of that tranquility would change from Christian revelation to crystallography and four-dimensional geometry, to a rhetoric of exhaustion or acedia, and to a fractal aesthetics locked in recursive symmetries. But the stillness itself would remain. The essential aims of Smithson's dalliance with religion—his struggle to imagine a totalizing perspective outside of human time and history—would remain operative in his work for the rest of his career. His challenge would now be to transcend history not by eluding it but by working through and upon it.

THE DEPOSITION OF TIME

One of the canonical specimens of Italian Mannerist painting, known for the audacity with which it challenges the conventions of its high Renaissance predecessors, is Pontormo's *Deposition* altarpiece (1525–28) in the Capponi Chapel at Santa Felicità in Florence (fig. 14). Scholars of Renaissance art have long noted the painting's cryptic, even disturbing, qualities. John Shearman has described the unusual rotational effect of the composition, which derives from the orthogonal separation of Mary and Christ along with the spiraling contours traced by the limbs and drapery of the figures: "As the body of Christ is lowered forward it also pivots, it seems, on the crouching figure in the center beneath the knees, while the movements around the Virgin flow reciprocally back to the center-line at the top." And yet any suggestion of dynamism that might be implied by the screwlike composition is immediately retracted by other aspects of the painting. Irrational shifts in scale and color seem to fracture the very space in which the image is constructed, preventing the buildup of pictorial momentum. The absence of atmospheric effects, the icy, jarring colors, and the evacuation of the central axis of the composition plot the figures in a frozen vacuum. As Arnold Hauser has observed, a feeling of aftermath, a "sense of resolved tension," exists in Pontormo's work, as if the choreographic energy of high Renaissance painting had been petrified, decentered, and redistributed across a series of attenuated forms. The result, to borrow a phrase from Daniel B. Rowland, is "a world where action is impossible."[1]

The Capponi altarpiece has traditionally been labeled a *Depozitione*, although some have argued that it should instead be considered a Lamentation, Entombment, or Pietà. The confusion as to its intended subject matter is due to the absence of either a crucifix or a tomb in the painting, and to the enigmatic disposition of the figures, whose poses are not firmly associable

14

Jacopo Pontormo, *The Descent from the Cross*, 1525–28.
10.3 x 6.4 ft. (3.1 x 2 m).
Capponi Chapel, S. Felicità, Florence, Italy.

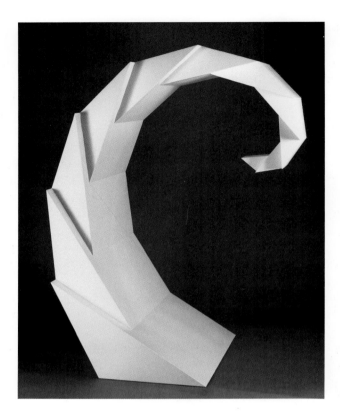

15
Robert Smithson, *Gyrostasis*, 1968.
Painted steel, 73 5/8 x 54 1/8 x 39 1/4 in. (187 x 137.5 x 99.7 cm).
Hirshhorn Museum and Sculpture Garden,
Smithsonian Institution. Gift of Joseph H. Hirshhorn, 1972.

16
Robert Smithson, *Untitled*, 1964. Blue metal frame and
orange plastic mirrors, 81 x 35 x 10 in. (205.7 x 89 x 25.4 cm).
Estate of Robert Smithson.

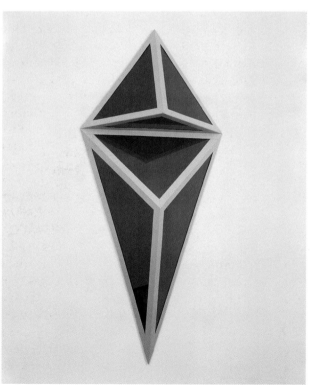

with any specific iconographic program. This confusion serves as a further insinuation of stasis: severed from particular narrative references in the scripture, the painting is able to explore a more abstract and radically atemporal postdepositional condition. Leo Steinberg calls Pontormo's image "visionary and ahistorical" for this reason. Indeed, by eliminating dynamism and abjuring the certainties of narrative, Pontormo seems to suggest that the meaning of Christ's post-Crucifixion departure from the human historical world can be expressed only by performing the exhaustion of time itself.[2]

Some commentators have interpreted this exhaustion as an abdication of religious faith; Giuliano Brigante, perhaps trading on the traditional association of sloth with sin, notes that there is "surely no expression of religious feeling . . . in the tired beauty of the forms here. The twining bodies, gliding into the spiral of the perspective against a cold, glittering sky convey only a sense of painful languor . . . their sadness is really so desperate and languishing that it can scarcely be called Christian grief." Others, however, see the painting's renunciation of humanist dynamism as a new way of evoking a "higher" spiritual realm free from the futile gyrations of worldly space and time. The languor of the figures, in this sense, is itself transcendent. The painting suggests the winding-down of time and motion and amounts, in Steinberg's words, to an "eternal presentiment of redemption."[3]

Smithson scrutinized Pontormo's altarpiece carefully. Although his letters from Italy in 1961 do not mention any visits to the Capponi Chapel, it is clear that by the mid-sixties he had, at the very least, closely examined the painting in reproduction. Along with several other books on Mannerism, he had a copy of Daniel B. Rowland's 1964 *Mannerism: Style and Mood*, which prominently features Pontormo's painting in a chapter called "Two Depositions: An Introduction to

Mannerism in Art History." Smithson annotated short phrases throughout the chapter and seems to have been especially interested in Rowland's references to what we might call the *depositional temporality* of Pontormo's painting, its suggestion of a "timeless frozen world completely foreign to the full daylight and the pleasant landscapes of Perugino and Raphael."[4]

The aftereffects of Smithson's encounter with Pontormo can be surmised throughout his work of the mid- and late sixties. In a piece like his 1968 *Gyrostasis* (fig. 15), a fabrication of painted steel composed of triangular solids proceeding in a diminishing series to form a rigid spiral, Smithson produced his own winding-down of time. His description of this and other of his "gyrostatic" sculptures might just as well be used as a wall label for Pontormo's painting: "All rotational progressions are brought to a static state. The rotation is non-dynamical, inactive, and stopped. Movement is impossible. Temporal duration is excluded. . . . All turning is hung in suspension. Everything exists in a state of rigid equilibrium, as in crystallographic systems at the point of least action."[5]

Gyrostasis is one of many sculptural installations of the mid- and late sixties through which Smithson explored what he called "the crystalline structure of *time*."[6] Resolutely abstract, with hard, cool surfaces and quasi-mathematical logics of construction and arrangement, this work could not seem to depart more substantially from the religious painting that preceded it. But as the connection to Pontormo's *Deposition* suggests, Smithson's new work did not represent nearly so radical a departure from his earlier mystical priorities as one might conclude. Pontormo's painting is reprised in Smithson's sculpture: both works use a crystalline rhetoric of aftermath to evoke a "timeless frozen world." Even so, Smithson's adaptation of Pontormo (as opposed to some other religious painter) can tell us a great deal about the way Smithson's idea of mystical timelessness had changed by the time he produced *Gyrostasis*. Rather than attempting to revitalize a Byzantine formula of devotional immediacy by returning to the state of affairs prior to the malignant spatio-temporal "action" of Renaissance and modern art, Smithson has now adopted a Mannerist model of transcendence, in which Renaissance dynamism, fragmented, reified, and calcified at the brittle entropic end of its existence, adopts its own form of crystalline eternity.

Because the transfer of Smithson's allegiance from pre- to post-Renaissance sensibility was accompanied by his transition from representation to abstraction, it is sometimes difficult to trace the thematic continuities between his religious paintings and the sculptural work that followed it. Yet just as we can see *Gyrostasis* as a conversion of Pontormo's Mannerist passion into the syntax of crystallography, so can we understand other aspects of Smithson's sculpture in terms of its translation from iconography to crystallography. In some cases, such as the shared concern with asymmetry lurking behind the spiral structure of both Pontormo's *Deposition* and Smithson's *Gyrostasis*, unlocking these connections requires extensive digression into the crystallographic literature that Smithson was reading. In others, however, little translation will be necessary. The "crystallographic systems" that Smithson mentions in his statement above, for example, are systems of growth that occur through molecular accretion. The name of this growth process, in crystallographic parlance, is *deposition*.

From Icon to Crystal: "Non-Dynamic Time"

From approximately 1962 to 1964, Smithson refrained from exhibiting his work, undergoing instead an intense program of reading and reflection. When he emerged from this self-imposed exile, he began exhibiting a new series of sculptures that he would later describe as his first mature work. The new work signaled an acute stylistic shift; whereas in 1961 he had been filling page after page with writhing, metamorphic figure drawings, by 1965 he was having disaffected sculptures of plastic, mirrors, and steel fabricated for him by local professionals. The structure of these sculptures originated in Smithson's study of crystallography and included pieces such as *Cryosphere* (derived from the structure of ice crystals) and a series of untitled polygonal wall structures (fig. 16) that suggested crystalline forms and facets. Many of these sculptures incorporated mirrored surfaces, and several, though not themselves shaped like crystals, used mirrors to "crystallize" either the rooms in which they were installed or objects brought near them. Describing his *Four-Sided Vortex*, for example, Smithson called it "a well of triangular mirrors — any object may be placed in here — it reveals all kinds of delicate polyhedra."[7]

At this point Smithson also began to publish essays in exhibition catalogues and major art periodicals. In his writing, too, he borrowed liberally from crystallographic concepts and terminology. In his critical essays on Donald Judd (1965) and on minimal sculpture (1966), he made frequent comparisons between minimalist form and crystal morphology, and equated the new methods of seriality with the processes of crystal growth. In other essays of this period, such as "The Crystal Land" (1966) and "Towards the Development of an Air Terminal Site" (1967), he discussed the landscape itself as if it were undergoing a process of crystallization. Although his writings after 1968 were rarely as explicit in their crystallographic reference (largely because by then he had toned down much of the science-fictional tenor of his first writings), certain motifs borrowed from crystallography would remain operative in his work throughout his career. Crystallography became an important discourse through which Smithson would develop his philosophies of vision, language, and (most importantly for the purposes of this book) history.[8]

In a 1972 interview with Paul Cummings for the Archives of American Art, Smithson acknowledged the importance of crystallography in his work, and he described it as the breakthrough that allowed him to resolve the struggles of his early paintings and launch his mature career. After telling Cummings about his 1961 trip to Rome and the simultaneous fascination and repulsion that he had felt toward the jumble of history, he went on to describe his next step: "Well, gradually I recognized an area of abstraction that was really rooted in crystal structure. In fact, I guess the first piece of this sort that I did was in 1964. It was called the *Enantiomorphic Chambers*. And I think that was the piece that really freed me from all these preoccupations with history."[9]

What was it about crystal structure that delivered Smithson from his "preoccupations with history"? Crystallography provided Smithson with a new understanding of time itself, one that resembled his earlier ideal of a timeless state but that suggested a way of incorporating and neutralizing history rather than attempting to evade it through spiritual appeals. In crystallography, Smithson found a way of placing history, with something of Pontormo's cryogenic intuition, "in suspension." Through his abortive attempts

at hieratic, revelatory drawing in the early sixties, Smithson had already concluded that a wholesale rejection of history was impossible. His crystallographic sculptures, while carrying forward his earlier aversion to action, allowed Smithson to incorporate time and movement in a static form. It suggested a way of fracturing and freezing the movement of time, converting it from a dynamic to a depositional state. In addition, by avoiding the taint of the organic, crystallography permitted Smithson to bypass his earlier discomfort with the creeping historicity of nature: as he wrote in a letter to Martin Friedman, "The Natural world is ruled by the temporal (dynamic history), whereas the crystalline world is ruled by the atemporal (non-dynamic time)."[10] Crystallography also served, in a way that would have major implications for his career, to translate his transcendent leanings into a vocabulary more palatable to the emerging "cool" sensibility of the sixties.

I should caution that Smithson's work of these years should be understood as loosely, rather than precisely, "crystallographic." Smithson based aspects of his work on a few essential principles of crystal structure; he was not interested in producing replicas of actual crystals or a body of installations whose forms would derive, with the predictability required of scientific accuracy, from laws of crystal formation. Nor did his ideas about the relationship between temporality and crystallography develop into a single, internally coherent model of history. There is no empirical crystal to which we can point that might serve as a perfect illustrational microcosm of Smithson's historical universe. Smithson seems instead to have borrowed isolated motifs from various areas of crystallography in order to model different features of his ideas about the structure of historical time. He drew upon a form of growth defect in crystals, the screw dislocation, to articulate the nature of temporal progression; he borrowed a concept from crystal symmetry, *enantiomorphism*, to model the relationship between past and future; and he appealed to the thermodynamic stability of crystal structure to evoke the all-embracing terminal equilibrium that, he felt, subtended all worldly historical conflict. And yet if Smithson's engagement with crystallography was improvised and even occasionally haphazard, this is precisely why it is so useful to any analysis of his work during this period. Not only does

17
From Charles William Bunn, *Crystals:
Their Role in Nature and Science*, 1964.

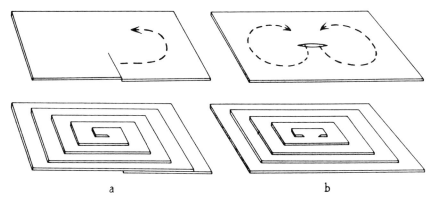

a   b

Thin crystals of paraffin hydrocarbons which have grown by continuous deposition on dislocated layer edges. (a) Spiral growth from a single dislocation. (b) Two opposite dislocations can give concentric layers.

his opportunism in this regard allow us to better identify the ideological niches that he enlisted crystallography to fill, but it also serves as a constant reminder that Smithson was loathe to borrow prepackaged ideational templates from other disciplines. His engagement with crystallography, like his work as a whole, was experimental and revisionary at every step.

**Deposition, Dislocation, and History
as "Spiral Wreckage"**
The process of crystal deposition (formation) often involves molecular misalignments; indeed there is an entire taxonomy of structural imperfections in crystallography, with tantalizingly deconstructive names like *slips*, *glide planes*, *vacancies*, and *displacements*. Smithson, considering the annotations in his books and the screw/spiral motifs throughout his work, was most interested in the "screw dislocation." This kind of misalignment does not, properly speaking, mar or

destroy the crystal, rather it allows it to grow; it does not prevent but rather *compels* the deposition of a solid crystal structure. Misaligned molecules provide the step edges upon which the addition of further molecules may occur. Imperfections facilitate accretion. As described in Charles Bunn's *Crystals: Their Role in Nature and Science*, one of Smithson's favorite books, this form of dislocation (fig. 17) produces a spiral pattern of growth: "There is one type of imperfection which is self-perpetuating; this is the type of imperfection known as a screw dislocation. . . . Molecules readily add onto the edges of layers, and if this happens on the edge of the step formed by a screw dislocation, it can go on happening indefinitely; the layer is never completed, and the crystal, so to speak, grows 'up a spiral staircase.'"[11]

Figure 17, from Bunn's book, diagrams this depositional strategy. Another of Smithson's textbooks used an explicitly temporal metaphor for this process,

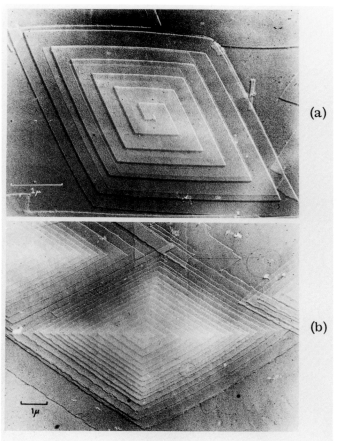

18

I. M. Dawson, electron micrographs, reproduced in Charles William Bunn, *Crystals: Their Role in Nature and Science*, 1964.

PLATE 5. Crystals of the paraffin hydrocarbon hectane, showing (a) spiral layer formation originating from a single screw dislocation, (b) concentric layer growth originating from a pair of opposite (left- and right-hand) dislocations. Electron microscope photographs by I.M. Dawson. Magnifications 15,000 and 7,500, respectively.

suggesting (in a sentence Smithson underlined) that "when growth takes place the step can advance only by rotating round the dislocation point somewhat like the hands of a clock." A particularly vivid electron micrograph of the process occurring in paraffin hydrocarbon hectane crystals (fig. 18) must have seemed to Smithson a picture of the microscopic accumulation of time itself. Smithson carefully excised this entire page from his copy of Bunn's *Crystals*. Its ghostly images of temporal buildup stand behind the sculptural stacks and spirals that Smithson produced throughout his career, even as late as 1972, the year before his death. In the essay he wrote about the *Spiral Jetty* that year, he described the earthwork as "advanc[ing] around a dislocation point, in the manner of a screw."[12]

Perhaps the most direct echoes of Smithson's engagement with screw deposition are to be found in a series of stacked-mirror installations that he produced in 1966–67. *Mirrored Ziggurat* of 1966 (fig. 19), which bears an unmistakable resemblance to the electron micrograph of the double-dislocated structure in figure 18, is a case in point. While the sculpture does not (and of course could not) precisely replicate the molecular structure of a screw-dislocated crystal, it is interesting to note that Smithson has preserved in the piece the essential principle of dislocated accumulation that most interested him. The mirrors are the key element here, because they serve as the material to be deposited on the stack while also serving as the instruments of dislocation. Each mirror reflects the base of the mirror above it and the top of the mirror below it; this has the effect of doubling and distancing the junctions between the mirrors and introducing the impression that there is space between them, as if they were floating or hovering one above the other. This illusionistic repulsion between the material parts of the sculpture helps to refute any impression of organic connection or development from one mirror to the next. The sculpture reads, like a crystal, as a stack of separate, deposited parts, fissured by dislocations.

Smithson, in his 1972 interview with Paul Cummings, explicitly discussed his stacked sculptures in terms of both history and crystallography. After mentioning the interest in ancient history that he developed during the mid-sixties, he claimed that "I became more and more interested in the stratifications and the layerings. I think it had something to do with the

19

Robert Smithson, *Mirrored Ziggurat*, 1966.
Mirrors, 11 x 25 $^1/_2$ x 25 $^1/_2$ in. (30 x 65 x 65 cm).
The Metropolitan Museum of Art.
Gift of Barbaralee Diamonstein-Spielvogel, 1986 (1986.272a-e).

way crystals build up too." Indeed, *Mirrored Ziggurat*, with the Mesopotamian overtones of its flat-topped pyramidal structure, evokes an entire complex of historical and monumental themes. If we are to take Smithson's claim about the "crystalline structure of time" seriously, we might begin by asking what it might mean to interpret the dislocation-deposition model of crystal growth as a model of time. This is a useful exercise because it immediately runs up against intractable vocabulary failures that help to convey the extent of Smithson's departures from prevailing conceptions. Reading *Mirrored Ziggurat* as a model or maquette of time and history disturbs many of the essential metaphors that have been commonsensically used to understand temporality.[13]

First, the *Ziggurat* does not imagine time as an internally driven organic development. The dislocations between the units ensure this. Although the *Ziggurat* derives its structure from what is commonly referred to as crystal "growth," growth, with its organic connotations, is not an entirely accurate way to describe the cumulative logic of either the crystal or the sculpture. Instead, in the process of crystal deposition, Smithson had found in nature what we might call a Manneristic model of progression. Time here is not an organic development emanating from a living "seed" or origin, but an inert encrustation precessing around a "slip," a "fault," or a "dislocation." Time is a static, indifferent accretion obeying a crystalline matrix. It loses any connection to an animate origin or center and becomes something superficial, uninspired, belated, supplemental. There is a sense of decadent ornamentalism about the entire affair.

Although Smithson's depositional time does suggest some sort of progression, it is impossible to equate this progression with movement in the usual sense. Time does not "fly" or "pass"; these terms imply that time is capable of arriving and departing, whereas Smithson's sculpture imagines it as a material sediment that remains on hand indefinitely. Time merely accretes in prepackaged quanta. This form of depositional progression relates directly to Smithson's longstanding ambivalence about dynamics and his predilection for works of art (like Pontormo's) that convert motion to stasis. In this case, for example, we might consider *Mirrored Ziggurat* in terms of its relation to cinema. The sculpture, with its thin sheets of mirror-coated glass, has a strikingly pellicular quality about it. It recalls a stack of film frames, and suggests that Smithson's interest in cinema (see discussion of Smithson's "iconoscope" in Chapter 1) informs his interest in crystallographic time as well. As film theorists have long agreed, a central paradox of cinema is its treatment of motion as an illusion created by a succession of still frames separated by interstitial gaps. The dislocation-deposition model of crystal formation is suggestively analogous with cinema, which, according to film theorist Mary Ann Doane, evokes "the impossibility of movement and change given the reducibility of all movement to an accumulation of static states."[14]

Nor does the depositional model of time allow us to consider time as a "space." Although the matrix of temporal particles in Smithson's time-crystal is gridded and essentially regular, it is not tabular. What I mean by this is that the grid units are not to be understood as empty spaces that crystal molecules may or may not occupy. The units can only exist in a state of fullness. This has important implications because it dissolves the commonsensical distinctions between time and history. Time is not an empty container in which historic events occur. Rather, time is itself a historical plenum. Time and its historical content are coterminous, and no temporal model exists independently of the material history that constitutes it.

Finally and most importantly, the *Ziggurat* and the depositional model informing it imagine time as entropic. It may seem odd that a sculpture as geometrically precise, regular, and rectilinear as *Mirrored Ziggurat* could be described as entropic. But the lay association of entropy with irregularity, abjection, or formlessness is not altogether accurate. For Smithson, in fact, the governing characteristic of entropic systems is their equilibrium, or, in other words, their absolute regularity. In an unpublished essay called "Spiral Wreckage" Smithson makes this clear: "When final equilibrium takes place we get relatively stable or rigid divisions of matter, as in crystals which are divided into lattice or grid parts." History, understood in this way, is not a triumphant progress but rather an inevitable deposition of time into a condition of "final equilibrium."[15]

Enantiomorphism and the Play of Mirrors
The mirrors of *Mirrored Ziggurat* play a complex but crucial role in Smithson's time-crystal. As mentioned

above, the mirrors serve as dislocative agents, introducing illusionistic space between the parts of the sculpture. At the same time, however, they also unify the sculpture. Because it is impossible to determine the precise point at which one mirror meets another, the illusionistic fissuring of the mirrors also knits the pieces together in an indeterminate embrace. Each mirror both repels and transfixes the mirrors adjoining it, producing the illusion of a structure that is riven throughout yet is, on the whole, whole. In this sense, the mirrors allow the sculpture to evoke the paradoxes of entropic finality, which Smithson understood as a condition characterized simultaneously by unity and fragmentation: "the configuration of maximum wholeness [is] at the same time that of maximum division or entropy."[16]

Smithson's other mirror installations often have the same double effect. *Chalk-Mirror Displacement* (1969) is a good example (fig. 20). A heap of particulate chalk is sliced into eight segments by eight mirrors placed in an asterisk pattern. From a purely physical standpoint, the mirrors function as agents of fragmentation, interrupting the gestalt of the heap and preventing the viewer from experiencing any unified apprehension of its conical geometry. But the fact that these are mirrors (and not otherwise identical slabs of steel or aluminum) immediately complicates that reading. For even as the mirrored surfaces clearly divide the pile of chalk, the optical effects of that partitioning oddly reinforce the overall impression of wholeness. An experiment: lie on the floor next to this piece (attempting not to alarm the museum guard) so that your eyes are below the upper edge of the mirrors and you are able to see into only one of the chalk wedges. What you will see is not a single wedge-shaped slice of the cone. The mirrors instead produce illusions that recuperate the image of the whole—you are presented with the image of the entire cone. The whole is immanent in the part. The sculpture is actually quite aggressive and even alarming in its unity; it looks the same from every angle (and in this sense performs its own neutralization of motion by eliminating the phenomenological narrative of the moving viewer). The mirrors refuse any kind of partial view. The only thing that saves the sculpture from becoming a horrifying über gestalt is the faint visual wobble or perturbation along the edges of the mirrors, which indicate the severance of the parts. The mirrors divide on one level and unify on the other. They simultaneously fragment the piece and introduce a specter (one is not sure whether it is a ghost or a premonition) of wholeness.

The ambiguous effects of the mirrors in *Mirrored Ziggurat* and *Chalk-Mirror Displacement* relate directly to crystallography, which treats mirror relationships in a similarly paradoxical fashion. Perhaps the most pervasive motif to be found in Smithson's work and writings is that of *enantiomorphism*, a term that denotes the relationship between two solid forms that are mirror images of each other. The term is common to crystallographers because many crystals adopt enantiomorphic forms (meaning that one can find both "right-handed" and "left-handed" crystals of the same substance). Such crystals include quartz, the most common mineral, and certain crystals formed from stereoisometric molecules like tartaric acid. Common examples of enantiomorphic forms in the everyday world, often offered in crystallography texts as a way to help readers visualize the relationships going on at the molecular level, include the human left and right hands, and screws with left- and right-handed (clockwise and counterclockwise) threads. Indeed the enantiomorphic relation is often called "screw asymmetry," because all helical forms are enantiomorphic. Smithson's interest in spirals is directly connected to their enantiomorphic character, as we shall see.[17]

Although the mirror relation of enantiomorphic forms may seem to imply a straightforward symmetry or bilateralism, enantiomorphism actually involves a special class of symmetry so mind-bogglingly complex that it is often described in crystallography texts as a species of dissymmetry. This is because enantiomorphs, although identical in all respects save their differential "handedness," are totally irreducible to each other. One cannot be superimposed upon the other—just as the glove for the left hand cannot fit on the right and a lightbulb with a clockwise thread cannot be inserted into a socket made for a light bulb with a counterclockwise thread. We get little sense of this superimposition problem by looking at the diagram of enantiomorphic quartz crystals in Bunn's *Crystals* (fig. 21). After all, it would seem to be easy enough simply to flip one image over onto the other to make the two images coincide. True enough. But this

Robert Smithson, *Chalk-Mirror Displacement*,
1987 version of a 1969 work.
Double-sided mirrors and chalk, 10 x 120 x 120 in.
(25.4 x 304.8 x 304.8 cm). Art Institute of Chicago.
Through prior gift of Mr. and Mrs. Edward Morris, 1987.277.

flipping operation that we have just mentally performed is imaginable only because we are looking at two-dimensional representations, not the three-dimensional crystals themselves. To make the two forms in the diagram coincide we actually need to transport one of them up and off the page through another dimension — the third. The same would be true of any mirrored two-dimensional forms. For example, there is no way to turn a sheet of paper cut into the shape of a lower-case *e* into its mirror image by simply scooting it around on the surface of a table. One must resort to a maneuver that occurs outside of the two-dimensional plane of the form itself, that is, flipping the *e* up and over in three-dimensional space. One always needs an extra dimension to bring such mirrored forms into alignment.

The utter strangeness of *three*-dimensional enantiomorphs might now become apparent. Where is the extra space that might allow us to rotate a left-handed chunk of crystal into alignment with its right-handed counterpart? Nowhere in the three-dimensional world that we are equipped to comprehend. Using the extra-dimensional rule of coincidence, we must conclude that if enantiomorphic crystals can be aligned, it can occur only in some four-dimensional space, a space outside of all Euclidean comprehension. As explained in one of Smithson's books on physics: "The left side of a straight line can be interchanged with its right side by rotating the line in a plane, the clockwise direction on a surface can be interchanged with an anticlockwise direction by moving the surface in three-dimensional space (turning over), a left-hand screw with a right-hand screw — or the left hand with the right hand — by 'moving' the object in four-dimensional space."[18]

Setting aside the fourth dimension for now, we can perhaps begin to understand why previous research has implicitly associated Smithson's use of enantiomorphism with a deconstructive agenda.[19] The two sides of an enantiomorph cannot, by definition, be resolved or synthesized in a moment of rational gestalt. Enantiomorphs imply, indeed require, a radically empty center — there is no worldly space between them where both forms can coexist. A pair of enantiomorphs is essentially an empty set of spatiocognitive parentheses, made all the more frustrating by the tantalizing resemblance between the two forms. They seem to be derived from some common root form, but

they cannot be reduced back to it. The maddening strangeness of the enantiomorphic relation was bothering philosophers long before the crystallography books in Smithson's library were written. Kant labored over the problem in his *Prolegomena to Any Future Metaphysics*: "What can be more similar in every respect and in every part more alike to my hand and to my ear than their images in the mirror? And yet I cannot put such a hand as is seen in the glass in the place of its original; for this is a right hand, that in the glass is a left one, and the image or reflection of the right ear is a left one, which can never take the place of the other. . . . [N]otwithstanding their complete equality and similarity, the left hand cannot be enclosed in the same bounds as the right one (they are not congruent); the glove of one hand cannot be used for the other."[20]

Smithson's most conspicuous deployment of the enantiomorphic concept was his 1964 piece *Enantiomorphic Chambers* (fig. 22), which comprised two wall-hung steel supports holding mirrors set at oblique angles. The two chambers, themselves enantiomorphs, held the mirrors at an angle precisely calculated to provide the viewer with a visceral demonstration of the incommensurability of enantiomorphic forms. According to Smithson, when viewers stood between the two chambers, their mirrored images canceled themselves out, "abolish[ing] the central fused image," and causing the viewer, essentially, to disappear. The installation invited the viewer to occupy the space of convergence of the two enantiomorphic self-images, but then evacuated the very space in which that convergence might occur. The *Chambers*, which also constitute a withering critique of perspective representation, will be discussed in greater detail in Chapter 4. For now it is enough to point out that enantiomorphism offered Smithson a way of thinking about mirroring that emphasized the irreconcilable difference, as well as the similarity, between a form and its reflection, a way of viewing the mirror as a tool of cutting or splitting rather than strict unification. Enantiomorphism served as the primary metaphor through which he imagined the function of the mirrors that he consistently used in his work between 1964 and 1969, in series such as the mirror strata (see fig. 19) and mirror displacements (see figs. 56, 57, 59–61). When Smithson says that mirrors function to "generate incapacity," when he speaks of "a mirror looking for its reflection

From Charles William Bunn,
Crystals: Their Role in Nature and Science, 1964.

Robert Smithson, *Enantiomorphic Chambers*, 1964.
Painted steel and mirrors. Location unknown.

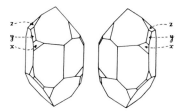

Left- and right-handed quartz crystals, with hemihedral facets x, y, and z.

but never quite finding it," or of something being "extinguished by reflections," he is referring to the enantiomorphic quality of mirroring. The essential dissymmetry of the mirror, its inability to recuperate that which it reflects, became his general model of reflection and a hallmark of his entire body of work as he defined it: "A lot of people are disturbed by my work because it is not within their grasp; it isn't a simple symmetry." The fragmentary action of the mirror has wide currency today, of course, in our post-Lacanian, post-Derridean theoretical landscape, but in the mid-sixties it was primarily through a crystallographically inflected sculptural practice that Smithson was able to develop the broader implications of dissymmetry for himself.[21]

The Mirror in the Moment: Enantiomorphism and the Deconstruction of the Now

Smithson was not, of course, content to consider enantiomorphism—with its powerful tropes of incompletion and interstitial vacancy—as a purely spatial phenomenon. The temporal implications of the concept, while not immediately obvious in the installations themselves, find clear renditions in Smithson's writings. In many of his essays of the mid-sixties, Smithson makes reference to an empty or nonexistent present flanked by the equilateral projections of past and future. In one essay he writes that "the future crisscrosses the past as an unobtainable present." In another he speaks of "a double perspective of past and future that follows a projection that vanishes into a nonexistent present." Smithson's understanding of this temporal "double perspective" was derived from enantiomorphism and was bolstered by supporting material from his usual interdisciplinary brew of sources, including a generous helping of science-fictional time-play and certain temporal motifs in Nabokov. In each case Smithson imagines time as a mirrored double-projection of future and past. The failure of the two halves of time to coincide leaves the space between them—the present—as "unobtainable." As he noted in 1969, "If one wishes to be ingenious enough to erase time one requires mirrors."[22]

Smithson's model of the unobtainable present is, I think, the aspect of his work that most fully approximates the poststructuralist worldview. Although I will complicate this reading in a moment, it is worth pointing out that enantiomorphism offers a passable

approximation of *différance* (Derrida's keyword for the difference which evades, precedes, and constitutes all presence—a difference which operates both spatially and temporally, which both *differs* and *defers*). Enantiomorphism provides a model of resemblance, repetition, and reflection but offers no ground upon which a metaphysics of presence or adequation can take hold; it constitutes an identity riven by alterity. Indeed, the fault line, central axis, or hinge of the enantiomorphic relation seems to encapsulate perfectly the empty center of postmodern subjectivity.[23]

This enantiomorphic evacuation of the present is quite similar to the dismantling of the "Now" that became one of the major tasks of the deconstructive project. By the "Now" I mean the key philosophical concept that goes by many other names—Presence, Being, *eidos*, Unity—all of which convey traditional Western philosophy's aim to define subjectivity as an unmediated (immediate) presence of the self to itself. Self-consciousness must occur instantaneously, in the Now—"I must know myself and know myself to be knowing myself at the moment that I know"—because otherwise a delay or deferral is introduced into consciousness that immediately proscribes the fullness of self-knowledge and splinters the self into a string of re-collection and re-presentation. Durational time, the enemy of the Now, is also the enemy of the self; as Mark C. Taylor puts it, time "threatens to fault the identity of the subject and to interrupt the presence of the present."[24]

In the previous chapter I discussed the centrality of this Now for the modernist aesthetics prevailing in Smithson's formative years in New York. In the postwar world, with its fragmentation and disillusionment of subjectivity, the avant-garde work of art was given the urgent task of collecting or compelling the embattled modern subject into unified coherence. In Greenberg's "at-onceness" and Fried's "Presentness" (as in Smithson's early aims at "Revelation"), the distinctive value of the work of art was to be its capacity to stabilize liberal-humanist subjectivity by producing immediacy. But even as Fried and Greenberg were institutionalizing the Now, much of continental philosophy was busy deconstructing it. Drawing upon the work of Husserl and Kierkegaard earlier in the twentieth century, thinkers such as Martin Heidegger, Maurice Merleau-Ponty, Emmanuel Levinas, and Derrida were ques-

tioning the logical tenability of this Now. The models of time developed in their work suggest the impossibility of self-present consciousness and challenge the foundations of Western metaphysics.

Smithson's access to this debate on the level of properly "philosophical" discourse was oblique but significant. His crystallographic image of the present being perpetually evacuated by its flanking extensions of past and future was supplemented by his reading in Husserl's *The Phenomenology of Internal Time Consciousness.* Husserl explained the "present" as a point that was always diverging forward into protention and backward into retention. Smithson owned a copy of *The Phenomenology*—its influence is clear when he claims, for example, that in one of his traveling projects "the present fell forward and backward into a tumult of 'de-differentiation.'"[25] In each attempt to grasp at the present, one will encounter only a void, a gap suspended by the reflective ligatures of protention and retention.

"Total Crystalline Consciousness": Smithson's Fourth Dimension

By evacuating the present, Smithson also performs a radical deconstruction of the notions of immanence and subjectivity that rely upon it. Smithson's enantiomorphic model reduces the centered and cohesive humanist worldview to a crystalline rubble of irreconcilable halves. Considering this splitting of the immanent self, we might return briefly here to Smithson's earlier career and note that his engagement with enantiomorphism in the mid-sixties functions as a direct (if disaffected) continuation of the obsessive concern with handedness that he had displayed in his religious paintings. A survey of Smithson's "ikons" reveals that the problem of corporeal symmetry was very much on Smithson's mind in 1961. At that point, it seems to have been related to his exploration of the mystery— and the tragedy—of Incarnation. How is divinity— which transcends time and space—to occupy quotidian dimension? In the diptych *Man of Sorrow 1* and *Man of Sorrow 2* (both 1961), Smithson presents a pair of disembodied hands whose prominent stigmata identify them as the hands of the incarnate and crucified Christ (figs. 23, 24). He revisits this compositional device in painting after painting of the early sixties: *Feet of Christ, Blind Angel, Green Chimera with Stigmata* (fig. 25), and others. In each case, the theatrical display of the stigmata accompanies an exaggeratedly bilateral composition and a conspicuous failure of the center (the "blindness" of the angel, the eyeless face and gaping void of the mouth of the Chimera, etc.). The "stigma" here seems to be related to symmetry itself, as if the crucifixion were merely an allegory for a more essential geometrical tragedy in which divine transcendence is forced into the humiliation of bilateral symmetry. The self-identical body of the divine, subject to the indignities of the enantiomorphic paradox on earth, unfolds into a mirror world that cannot locate the transcendent identity of the split beings that populate it. It seems that in these and other works of the early sixties (including several that refer to the iconography of St. Francis receiving the stigmata), Smithson struggles with what he sees as the inherently peripheral operation of revelation in the physical world. The central anxiety of these paintings is that direct contact with transcendence is simply not possible; it can manifest itself only as a series of dissymmetrical

25

Robert Smithson, *Green Chimera with Stigmata*, 1961.
Oil on canvas, 47.2 x 56.7 in. (120 x 144 cm).
Estate of George B. Lester.

From Charles William Bunn,
Crystals: Their Role in Nature and Science, 1964.

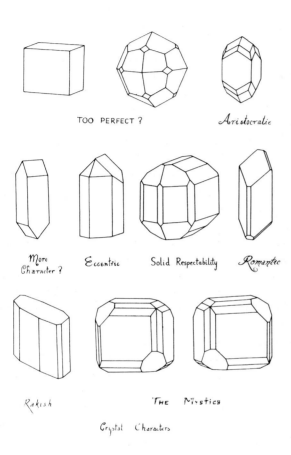

TOO PERFECT ?   *Aristocratic*

More Character ?   *Eccentric*   Solid Respectability   *Romantic*

Rakish   THE Mystics

Crystal Characters

traces on the isolated extremities of worldly forms. One hopes for the ecstasy of St. Teresa, but ends up with the delayed, diluted, rerouted—one might even say suburban—scars of St. Francis.

Despite the tormented posture of these paintings, however, it is important to remember their essential presumption: namely, that the unified condition from which these figures have fallen does (or did) in fact exist. In this sense, the enantiomorphic splitting of the embodied figures indicates the possibility of transcendence even as it admits its terrestrial intermission. This possibility, I believe, remained latent for Smithson

in his later pieces, like the *Enantiomorphic Chambers*, as well. This is why I will now attempt to overturn, even while acknowledging, the deconstructive interpretation of Smithson's use of mirroring.

A transcendental connotation has accompanied the concept of enantiomorphism from the outset, not only in Christian discourse but also in certain pseudo-mystical strains of science and mathematics. As mentioned earlier, the puzzle of enantiomorphism has remained vivid for centuries; this is largely because its "solution" does not exist in the everyday three-dimensional universe that we are equipped to observe with our senses. Yet it is precisely this worldly incompatibility that has historically inspired contemplation about the possibility of a "higher" dimension in which such a solution might be feasible. It seems impossible that a mirror and its reflection or a right hand and a left hand could be completely unrelated; thus they encourage the spectator to infer or imagine another dimension in which these reflected forms might be reconciled. In fact, mirrored forms have long begged—and have often been used to answer—the question of a four-dimensional, radically unified condition. In 1827 Möbius made precisely this argument, claiming that the existence of solid mirrored forms implies, compels, and virtually maps out the existence of a fourth dimension, unavailable to our own sensory apparatus, through which enantiomorphs can be brought into alignment. Throughout the literature on four-dimensional geometry since that time, enantiomorphism has often been offered as an argument or even as proof of the empirical existence of a higher dimension, or hyperspace. Thus the deconstructive potential of enantiomorphism is, perhaps appropriately, only half of the story. Enantiomorphs, in proper deconstructive fashion, evacuate the possibility of adequation in the everyday three-dimensional world, but they also imply, even require, a higher unity in another kind of space, another dimension.[26]

Smithson was well aware of the transcendental implications of enantiomorphism; in fact it is likely that he first encountered the concept of asymmetrical mirroring within the context of hyperspace philosophy. He snipped out a diagram of a pair of tartaric acid crystals from his copy of Martin Gardner's famous book *The Ambidextrous Universe*, which has an entire chapter on the fourth dimension as a "transcendent world" where asymmetries might be resolved. The transcendental implications of enantiomorphs were also evident in Bunn's *Crystals*. In one slightly tongue-in-cheek diagram, "Crystal Characters," Bunn plays on the associations inspired by each form of crystal; the enantiomorphs at lower right are labeled "The Mystics" (fig. 26). (Smithson was very familiar with this particular illustration, as he cut out the image of the "Romantic" crystal to use in another collage.) Linda Dalrymple Henderson, in her magisterial reconstruction of the fortunes of hyperspace in twentieth-century art, has identified the artists, writers, and scientists who did the most to perpetuate the philosophy of higher space during the nineteenth and twentieth centuries. Many, such as H. G. Wells, Lewis Carroll, Buckminster Fuller, Arthur C. Clarke, and the popular science writers Martin Gardner, J. W. Dunne, and Max Jammer, were key figures in Smithson's own intellectual development. And as Henderson argues in her forthcoming edition of *The Fourth Dimension and Non-Euclidean Geometry in Modern Art*, Smithson was himself exposed to active debate about the consciousness-expanding possibilities of hyperspace through his association in the mid-sixties with the artists of the Park Place Group.[27]

Indeed, if we reconsider Smithson's work of this period in terms of the discourse of hyperspace, we find that it is full of formal, temporal, and optical motifs long associated with hyperspatial puzzles. These include an appeal to simultaneity and stillness, a rejection of perspectival representation, the use of mirrors or shadows as indicators, and the construction of ill- or a-logical structures. All of these strategies have direct analogs in Smithson's work of this period (considering the appeal to the a-logical, for example, it is interesting to note that Smithson did an entire series of installations called *Alogons* in 1967). Smithson was also interested in alternating perspective figures or "Necker Reversals," which are commonly illustrated in books on the fourth dimension as tools to help the reader approximate a kind of hyperspatial perception. We might also note Smithson's interest in this period with negative/positive relations in photography. He commonly reproduced his photographs and collages as negative photostats, thus producing a kind of tonal enantiomorphism (see figs. 29, 35).[28]

Smithson's embrace of what Martin Gardner called "4-space" is also evident in his essay "Towards the Development of an Air Terminal Site." The article

appeared in *Artforum*'s special issue on American sculpture in June of 1967. This issue was a seminal compendium of texts and has since become legendary for the impact and diversity of the essays between its covers (other articles in the issue include part three of Robert Morris's "Notes on Sculpture," Michael Fried's "Art and Objecthood," and Sol LeWitt's "Paragraphs on Conceptual Art"). Smithson's "Air Terminal" article is among the most cryptic of his writings, but a close analysis reveals it to be a meditation on four-dimensional space and its temporal implications. Smithson wrote the essay after serving as an artist-consultant for the architecture firm Tibbets-Abbett-McCarthy-Stratton, which was in the process of entering a design competition for the terminal at the new Dallas-Fort Worth airport. While working on schemes for art installations designed to be seen from the air by passengers on arriving and departing airplanes, Smithson had become intrigued by the relationship between motion (change over time) and form.[29]

In the article, Smithson performs an extended meditation on the nature of time by developing a contrast between two ways of thinking about motion. He illustrates his distinction through a rather humorous discussion of the two modes of aircraft design that prove most appropriate for each time-motion paradigm. He begins by describing the traditional system of naming aircraft: "As it is now, many [aircraft] are still named after animals, such as DHC 2 Beavers; Vampire T.; Chipmunk T. Mk. 20; Dove 8s; Hawker Furies; Turkey; etc." These names, Smithson argues, reveal certain assumptions and biases: "The meaning of airflight has for the most part been conditioned by a rationalism that supposes truths—such as nature, progress, and speed." Airplanes named after wild animals were designed to express "the old rational idea of visible speed." What he means by this "old" idea is the commonsense notion that when we observe a speeding object we are seeing what is, in fact, a speeding object—a discrete unit of matter moving or being moved *through* space as time passes. Airplanes in this universe are named after animals because they are understood to move as if alive, as if they had volition (L. *volare*, to fly; L. *volo*, present indicative of *velle*, to will). These animal aircraft, in other words, occupy an *animistic* universe: elastic, kinetic, changing over time as objects shift about from place to place.[30]

Smithson then asks the reader to imagine a different kind of aircraft: one that is not designed (or named) to express speed but rather, as Smithson puts it, one that "discloses itself" on a "network."[31] *Disclosure* is the key notion here: when Smithson claims that an aircraft "discloses itself" rather than moves, he implies that what we perceive as the airplane's motion is really only the gradual coming-to-appearance of some greater form. Here Smithson adapts to his own needs a key concept of hyperspace philosophy: its prohibition of classical dynamism and its interpretation of motion as an illusory side effect of four-dimensional spatial forms. This rather thorny concept was first popularized by the British mathematician, physicist, and patent-office worker C. H. Hinton, to whom Smithson was likely introduced through his reading of J. W. Dunne's *Experiment with Time*. Dunne described the essential stasis of Hinton's four-dimensional universe at length: "A being who could see Time's extension as well as that of Space would regard the particles of our three-dimensional world as merely sectional views of fixed material threads extending in a fourth dimension, and would consider that the only thing in the entire cosmos that really moved was that three-dimensional field of observation which we call the 'present moment.'"[32]

Another eloquent proponent of this idea was the early twentieth-century Russian mathematician P. D. Ouspensky. His highly influential geometrical-mystical tract on the fourth dimension explained time as follows: "The contact with a certain space of which we are not clearly conscious calls forth in us the sensation of motion upon that space; and all this taken together, i.e., the unclear consciousness of a certain space and the sensation of motion upon that space, we call time. This last confirms the conception that the idea of time has not arisen from the observation of motion existing in nature, but that the very sensation and idea of motion has arisen from a "time-sense" existing in ourselves, which is an *imperfect sense of space*: the fringe, or limit of our space-sense." Thus, for Ouspensky, time and change are illusions: "We are receiving as sensations, and projecting into the outside world as phenomena, *the immobile angles and curves of the fourth dimension*." "In other words, every being feels as space that which is grasped by his space-sense: the rest he refers to time; i.e., *the imperfectly felt* is referred to time."[33]

When Smithson writes in his "Air Terminal" article that "the rationalist sees only the details and never the whole," when he says that the rationalist "cannot see the aircraft through the 'speed,'" he is echoing Ouspensky and Hinton by saying that motion is merely a "detail," a microscopic cross-section of a larger spatiotemporal form that is, in actuality, static.[34] As he wrote in an early draft of his essay "Quasi-Infinities and the Waning of Space," "Time's direction becomes a progression, within a terminal shape that is immobile." Although there is no evidence that Smithson read Ouspensky's original text, he would have been indirectly familiar with his ideas through his other readings on the subject. He was certainly reading Kazimir Malevich (who had been heavily influenced by Ouspensky), going so far as to quote him in a draft of his 1967 "Monuments of Passaic" essay: "The *changing* element of our consciousness and feeling, in the last analysis, is illusion."[35]

Thus Smithson appeals to the fourth dimension to offer a broader perspective on motion that will reveal it to be, in actuality, inert. Time does not "pass" (or, to return to the aviation metaphor, time does not "fly"); what we experience as temporality is, rather, the process of a three-dimensional consciousness passing through an eternal four-dimensional form. As Hinton described this four-dimensional universe: "We should have to imagine some stupendous whole, wherein all that has ever come into being or will come co-exists, which, passing slowly on, leaves in this flickering consciousness of ours, limited to a narrow space and a single moment, a tumultuous record of changes and vicissitudes that are but to us." Hinton describes here what would later be widely referred to, in 4-D rhetoric, as the "block universe" of eternal form.[36]

In the "Air Terminal" article, Smithson asserts that this motionless perspective on motion is beginning to become more evident through the latest developments in air and space technology. He claims that "as the aircraft ascends into higher and higher altitudes and flies at faster speeds, its meaning as an object changes—one could even say reverses." In other words, the higher and faster an airplane is flying, the slower it appears to be moving from a ground observer's standpoint. Smithson's ultimate example of this tendency is the satellite in geosynchronous orbit that, though moving very quickly in the classical sense, appears to us to be still. Smithson suggests that we should learn to perceive all objects in the same way we perceive satellites: "This immobilization of space becomes more apparent if we consider the high altitude satellite. The farther out an object goes in space, the less it represents the old rational idea of visible speed." Not only do the new satellites provide concrete demonstrations of four-dimensional inertia as they fly, they also embody hyperspace philosophy in their formal design. As if to emphasize this point, Smithson is careful to include in his article an illustration of the boxy, seemingly inert Secor surveying satellite (manufactured, he notes gleefully, by the Cubic Corporation) (fig. 27). We are a long way from the misguided animism of the DHC 2 Beaver here; the Secor satellite, with its gridlike articulation, is nothing so much as a metonym and microcosm of the eternally static "block universe" of hyperspace.[37]

Smithson's Secor illustration also bears a strong resemblance to the diagrams of crystal lattices found throughout his crystallography books (see fig. 30). Indeed, throughout the essay Smithson associates four-dimensional space with crystal structure: "The streamlines of *space* are replaced by a crystalline structure of *time*."[38] Future aircraft, Smithson claims, must reflect this. Smithson proposes that as the four-dimensional universe becomes more apparent, *all* aircraft design will cast off its outmoded vitalism and adopt the Cubic Corporation's more enlightened design principles: "It is most probable that we will someday see upon these runways, aircraft that will be more crystalline in shape. . . . Perhaps aircraft will someday be named after crystals. . . . At any rate, here are some names for possible crystalline aircraft: Rhombohedral T.2; Orthorhombic 60, Tetragonal Terror; Hexagonal Star Dust 49; etc."[39] Art, of course, must do the same; it must attain the radical stillness of the transcendent crystal and leave behind its frantic naturalisms.

During these years Smithson produced several collages that address this gradual replacement of the animistic worldview with the crystalline. In *Proposal for a Monument on the Red Sea* (fig. 28), a scientific diagram of a cube appears massive and alien in its juxtaposition with the coastal landscape. In *Proposal for a Monument at Antarctica* (fig. 29), a negative photostat of a collage produced in 1966, a gridded crystalline form sits ominously on a hill, as if threatening to spread

throughout the image and asphyxiate all the busy ship workers in the foreground. Smithson borrowed this geometric form (which actually looks very much like the Secor satellite) from his copy of Bunn's *Crystals*, from which he neatly cut out the form with a razor blade along each of its jagged faces (fig. 30).[40] If this image seems disquieting or dystopian, it is largely because Smithson's collage practice introduces jarring shifts into the viewer's visual experience of the space. The crystalline form perching on the hill appears conspicuous and "alien" (this image was long referred to as "Science Fiction Landscape") because it refuses to fit into the representational structure of the image itself. Whereas the landscape photograph of the harbor shows the familiar and reassuring signs of recessional space (objects diminishing in size as they approach the horizon, for example), the crystal form does not obey this sense of perspective. The gridded rhombohedral units obey an axonometric, rather than a linear, projection. By repelling the viewer's customary experience of viewpoint, the collage is a remarkably economical visual embodiment of the implications of Smithson's crystalline "spacetime," where limited three-dimensional perspectives do not operate. The image articulates the essential incommensurability of four-dimensional form and perspectival representation, and demonstrates, prophetically for Smithson's later career, that the "crystalline structure of time" is utterly alien to the prevailing traditions of naturalistic representation of landscape. The eerie stillness and opacity of the form contradicts the idea of space (or landscape) as a stage for action, movement, and historical drama.

Smithson's four-dimensional crystallographic airspace of the mid-sixties was very much linked to his earlier mystical leanings. As Henderson has documented, the idea of the fourth dimension has long been closely associated with mysticism. This connection can be easily reconstructed for Smithson, whose turn to crystallography constituted a secularized extension, rather than a refutation, of the concerns of his religious period. His earlier interest in William Blake's "eternal proportions," for example, finds a ready corollary in the four-dimensional block universe with its "immobile angles and curves." Indeed Blake can be understood as a progenitor of hyperspace philosophy. A corner-folded page in Smithson's copy of Evelyn Underhill's *Mysticism* makes this suggestion: "Often

Secor surveying satellite, as published in
"Towards the Development of an Air Terminal Site," 1967.
Courtesy Cubic Corporation, San Diego, California.

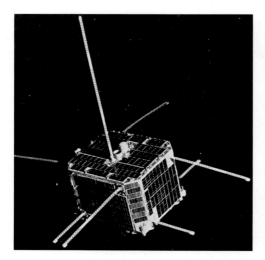

when we blame our artists for painting ugly things, they are but striving to show us a beauty to which we are blind. They have gone on ahead of us, and attained that state of 'fourfold vision' to which Blake laid claim; in which the visionary sees the whole visible universe transfigured." And the quietude of Smithson's crystalline block universe, its ability to contain all times at once in an eternal equilibrium, offered the same refuge of eternity, silence, and unified essence that St. Augustine had held out as the very image of God: "Try as they may to savour the taste of eternity, their thoughts still twist and turn upon the ebb and flow of things in past and future time. But if only their minds could be seized and held steady, they would be still for a while and, for that short moment, they would glimpse the splendour of eternity which is for ever still."[41]

What the mystical-spatial fourth dimension was also able to do for Smithson was to suggest a cool, hard space beyond limited anthropomorphic perception, a space wherein the seemingly fatal contradictions and paradoxes that he explored in his religious paintings might be resolved. The tragic enantiomorphic fragmentation of the divine body in the two-dimensional world of his icons (see figs. 23–25) is permitted an ultimate, if etiolated, resolution in the four-dimensional world of his time crystal. In terms of its temporal modeling, then, Smithson's crystallography must finally be understood not as a deconstructive but rather as a synthesizing paradigm. Smithson deployed crystallography to intimate a new form of trans- or extratemporal perception, a four-dimensional crystalline "space-time" that could offer what he called a "total crystalline consciousness of structure." This leap out of three-dimensional systems recalls Tony Smith's spiritualizing use of the infinite crystal grid and Malevich's Suprematist use of the fourth dimension as a scaffold for a transcendental realm free of all social and political specificities. Indeed, Smithson's "time-crystal" can be seen as an attempt to pursue a dialectical sublation of temporal flow itself. It provides a unified, or aggregate, perspective that includes all other perspectives, with their associated illusions of temporal passage, and resolves their apparent contradictions into a single, static system.[42]

The specific cultural implications of Smithson's crystalline view of history would begin to become

28

Robert Smithson, *Proposal for a Monument on the Red Sea*, 1966. Cut-and-pasted paper, pen and ink, and pencil on photograph, 8 1/4 x 6 1/2 in. (21 x 16.7 cm). The Museum of Modern Art, New York. Elmer A. Johnson, Jr., Bequest.

Robert Smithson, *Proposal for a Monument at Antarctica*, 1966.
Negative photostat, 8 x 12 in. (20.3 x 30.5 cm).
Estate of Robert Smithson.

30

From Charles William Bunn,
Crystals: Their Role in Nature and Science, 1964.

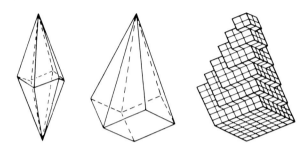

Left: a "dog-tooth" crystal of calcite. *Center:* a piece with cleavage surfaces at the bottom. *Right:* Haüy's idea of the relation of the natural faces to the stack of tiny rhombohedral units.

abundantly apparent as he moved into landscape in the late sixties (his crystalline treatment of Passaic, New Jersey, will be addressed in the following chapter). First, however, he began to see the crystallization of time as the governing logic of the minimal art that was beginning to fill the galleries of New York. In his famous article "Entropy and the New Monuments," Smithson explicitly discussed the new sculpture being produced by Donald Judd, Robert Morris, Dan Flavin, LeWitt, and others in terms of crystal accretion. Smithson knew that in the process of crystal deposition, each new molecule added represents a decrease in the energy potential of the system and thus an increase in entropy. The entire system is in equilibrium —"cooled" and stabilized. Smithson suggested that the new sculpture was "monumental" in the same way that a crystal can be seen as monumental—for Smithson, the sculpture registered the petrifaction of time and the calcification of space and pointed to the finality and obduracy of the universe's entropic future. He spoke of the artists' "fascination with inert properties," argued that their work "conveys a mood of vast immobility," and referred to their pieces as "obstructions." For Smithson the new sculpture, in which "lethargy is elevated to the most glorious magnitude," could be seen as a crystallization of space and time. A series of minimal forms represented a nullification or occupation of time and space, so that it was no longer available for further use: "The action is frozen into an array of plastic and neon."[43]

A remarkable passage in Smithson's critical essay on Judd reveals that Smithson was making an explicit connection between the biblical and crystallographical meanings of "Deposition": "Instead of bringing Christ down from the cross, the way the painters of the Renaissance, Baroque, and Mannerist periods did in their many versions of The Deposition, Judd has brought space down into an abstract world of mineral forms."[44]

Smithson then cited the minimalist format of "the slurbs, urban sprawl, and the infinite number of housing developments of the postwar boom" as evidence that this new Deposition was, like Pontormo's, beginning to reveal the exhaustion of history and the eternal infinity beyond it. It is to these "slurbs" that I now turn.

FORGETTING PASSAIC

On Saturday, September 30, 1967, Smithson took a bus ride from the Port Authority terminal in Manhattan to the city of Passaic, New Jersey. With Instamatic camera and notepad in hand, he spent the better part of the day exploring the downtown district of the city and rambling along the banks of the Passaic River, which were in the process of being excavated for the construction of a new highway. Smithson converted his field notes and six of his photographs into a travelogue that he published in the December 1967 issue of *Artforum* as "The Monuments of Passaic." A mock advertisement that he later drafted indicates his sardonic attitude toward the entire enterprise: "What can you find in Passaic that you cannot find in Paris, London, or Rome? Find out for yourself. Discover (if you dare) the breathtaking Passaic River and the eternal monuments on its enchanted banks. Ride in Rent-a-Car comfort to the land that time forgot. Only minutes from N.Y.C. Robert Smithson will guide you through this fabled series of sites . . . and don't forget your camera."[1]

Smithson's tour of Passaic was part of a series of New Jersey excursions that he took between 1966 and 1968. These short day trips across the Hudson had such seemingly unmemorable destinations as Bayonne, North Bergen, Secaucus, Loveladies Island, and the Pine Barrens. Smithson visited quarries in Montclair, Sandy Hook, and Franklin, and explored abandoned airstrips, industrial wastelands, and the debris-filled swamps of the Meadowlands. (He also, occasionally, visited his parents in Clifton.) Often taken with friends and fellow artists, these trips established the expedition as one of Smithson's fundamental artistic methods. Many of them, like the Passaic tour, eventually resulted in published magazine travelogues. Others served as specimen-gathering excursions for the new series of "Nonsite" gallery installations that Smithson developed during this period (fig. 31). Smithson's implicit appeals to the grand expeditionary tradition help

Robert Smithson, *A Nonsite (Franklin, New Jersey)*, 1968.
Painted wooden bins, limestone,
photographs, and typescript on paper with graphite and
transfer letters, mounted on mat board.
Bins: 16 $\frac{1}{2}$ x 82 $\frac{1}{4}$ x 103 in. (41.9 x 208.9 x 261.6 cm).
Collection Museum of Contemporary Art, Chicago.
Gift of Susan and Lewis Manilow.

account for the deflationary humor of these and other travel works; within rhetorical structures designed to convey epiphantic discoveries, Smithson presented disaffected narratives, anticlimactic bins of mineral samples, and lackluster black-and-white snapshots.[2]

Smithson's Passaic tour has long been esteemed for its peripatetic opposition to the centralization of the New York art establishment, and his aggressively drab Passaic photographs have been widely praised for their implicit critique of documentary transparency. "The Monuments of Passaic" has also become something of a cult classic in architecture, urban planning, and landscape architecture, where it serves as a benchmark for its exploration of what would later come to be called *terrain vague*: the liminal or interstitial landscape.[3] Another distinguishing feature of the project is its fundamental irreverence toward the idealistic bombast of traditional monuments. The photographs

that Smithson published in his article, each carefully labeled, feature such monuments as a rotating bridge *(The Bridge Monument)* (see fig. 39), an assembly of drainage equipment *(Monument with Pontoons: The Pumping Derrick)*, a group of wastewater pipes *(The Great Pipes Monument; The Fountain Monument)*, and a playground sandbox *(The Sand-Box Monument)*. Although Smithson published only six photographs in his *Artforum* article, he exposed seven rolls of film that day in Passaic. The other snapshots from these rolls, unpublished in Smithson's lifetime and unexamined as yet in the scholarship on Smithson, constitute the more comprehensive visual artifact of the Passaic tour. I will focus on them here.[4]

These unpublished snapshots go on to depict other, variously unexceptional "monuments"—puddles, vacant storefronts, concrete escarpments, parking lots. Many of them feature toppled, blemished, or down-

market equivalents of traditional monumental forms. The concrete cube in figure 32, for example, suggests the discarded base of some dismantled equestrian statue (or, perhaps, the imminent drowning of a unit of minimal sculpture). The leaky drinking fountain in figure 33 (another *Fountain Monument*) likewise disappoints. By categorizing these decidedly uninteresting objects as monuments and by composing them so anticlimactically in the frame (looking down upon the fountain and setting the cube indifferently in the middle distance), Smithson emphasizes their failure to produce the kind of metaphorical, didactic, or otherwise invigorating connection to the past that monuments are supposed to elicit. These monuments have all the mass, all the inertia of traditional monuments, but they have been drained of their capacity for inspiration or transportation. Resting blandly in the flat midday sun, they are lethargic monuments, and thus they have also been drained of their capacity for commemoration—the word *lethargy*, after all, derives from the Greek *Lethe*, the mythical river in Hades whose waters cause drinkers to forget their past. These are the waters that Smithson's leaking fountain monument offers up. And the Passaic River, bathing its ponderous cube in a dull mercuric gleam, becomes, at least for the duration of Smithson's tour, the river of oblivion.

Smithson claimed in 1969 that "oblivion to me is a state when you're not conscious of the time or space you are in." It could be found, he said, in "places without meaning." This is precisely the state that Smithson presents to us in his tour of Passaic, which is why it is so successful as an inversion of a traditional historical tour. Indeed, after combing through "The Monuments of Passaic," one is hard-pressed to shake the feeling of suffocating oblivion that it imparts. The *Artforum* article is masterfully elliptical, indeed it is difficult to call it a "site specific" work in the ordinary sense because it conveys so little specific information about the place it engages. In one of the better-known passages from the article, Smithson explicitly addresses this evacuation of meaning in Passaic, describing the city as a place without a predicate: "Passaic center loomed like a dull adjective. Each 'store' in it was an adjective unto the next, a chain of adjectives disguised as stores. I began to run out of film, and I was getting hungry. Actually, Passaic center

33
Robert Smithson, untitled snapshot from *Monuments of Passaic* project (small fountain monument), 1967.
Black-and-white commercially developed print,
3 ¹/₂ x 3 ¹/₂ in. (8.9 x 8.9 cm).
Robert Smithson and Nancy Holt papers,
1905–87, Archives of American Art, Smithsonian Institution.

was no center—it was instead a typical abyss or an ordinary void."[5]

Smithson's Passaic travelogue leaves some of the most basic questions about this area unanswered. Where is Passaic, exactly? How far away from Manhattan? Who lives and works there? Is it an industrial city or a bedroom community? What is its history? Smithson mentions that a railroad track once passed through the center of town (I shall return to this later) but doesn't tell us where it headed or when it was operational. There's a brief hint of a nineteenth-century past: "A rusty sign glared in the sharp atmosphere, making it hard to read. A date flashed in the sunshine . . . 1899 . . . No . . . 1896 . . . maybe," but its indecisive syntax suggests the refraction of historical narrative into a scattered series of illegible clues.[6]

In some ways Passaic in 1967 did indeed present itself as an "ordinary void" without history, but we do little justice to the sophistication of "The Monuments of Passaic" if we see it simply as a documentary reflection of the state of affairs in the city. It is ultimately more productive to examine Smithson's project in terms of its active conversion of Passaic's historical past (as well as its impending future) into a "place without meaning." The crystalline tropes running throughout the article provide an immediate clue to the nature of Smithson's interventions: many of the temporal strategies discussed in the previous chapter, including Smithson's use of enantiomorphic reversal or mirroring to neutralize temporal direction and movement, his appeal to history as a material deposit, and his evocation of an all-embracing, terminal utopian stillness, are also at work in "The Monuments of Passaic." By tracing these motifs in the urban arena of their development, as Smithson worked them through a real place and its histories, I will begin to examine Smithson's time-crystal model in terms of its intersection with the politics of public memory in the late sixties. Along the way, I will carefully reconstruct some of the other histories that had a claim on Passaic in 1967 (especially its history of race relations).

The reader may well argue at this point that any such attempt at historical reconstruction goes against both the spirit and the letter of Smithson's innovative project. This is precisely my point, although I hasten to add that this should not be construed as an attack on Smithson. It is instead an attempt, by looking awry at "The Monuments of Passaic," to bring Smithson's project into dialectical relief. My aim is not to propose a more objective or meaningful history of the city, but to restore some of the historiographical complexity out of which Smithson's own version emerged. This has the advantage, to my mind, of complicating the aura of objectivity that can tend to accrue around Smithson's gritty and uninspiring photographs. It is indeed tempting to grant Smithson a uniquely clear-eyed view of the bathetic "realities" of the American suburb. I will argue instead that the soporific blandness of Smithson's Passaic was itself a historical act, one that attempted to resolve a number of conflicts. A strategic reconstruction of some of those conflicts — whose fragmentary outlines remain buried throughout Smithson's texts and images — will help us better to restore the historical irresolution that Smithson confronted in Passaic, as well as the historical implications of his responses to it.

Other Histories of Passaic

By examining Smithson's field notes and the full sequence of his snapshots along with his published narrative, it is possible to provide a partial reconstruction of his route through Passaic on that September Saturday. His travels covered a narrow strip of land, skirting along the west bank of the Passaic River. Beginning at the Union Avenue bridge connecting Rutherford and Passaic (see fig. 39), Smithson ambled northward along the riverfront highway construction, then turned west away from the river and along Main Avenue toward the city center, where he photographed buildings, parking lots, and other "monuments," and had lunch at the Golden Coach Diner at 11 Central Avenue. He then returned southward, completing his narrative with the *Sand-Box Monument* (see fig. 48) at a playground adjacent to Passaic Stadium, near his starting point. Figure 34 shows the locations of several of the stops on Smithson's tour.

If Smithson had been interested in leading a traditional historic tour of this area, he might have mentioned that the Passaic River had once powered a thriving manufacturing economy. As early as 1792, Alexander Hamilton and his investment group, the Society of Useful Manufactures, had used the Great Falls area of what is now Paterson (just upriver from Passaic) as the centerpiece of a blueprint for the first

34

Area of Smithson's tour through Passaic, with locations of selected monuments numbered in order of their appearance in the "Monuments of Passaic" narrative, 1967. Map compiled by the author from two United States Geological Survey maps (at left, Orange Quadrangle 1955, photorevised 1970; at right: Weehawken Quadrangle, 1967). (1) *The Bridge Monument* (Union Avenue Bridge; see figs. 37, 39). (2) General vicinity of all highway and river monuments (see figs. 32, 38, 43). (3) Former railroad station in central Passaic, site of Smithson's lunch stop (11 Central Avenue) and the "parking lot monument" (see fig. 46). (4) Taras Shevchenko Park, location of the playground monuments including *The Sand-Box Monument* (see figs. 33, 48).
(Below) area of detail.

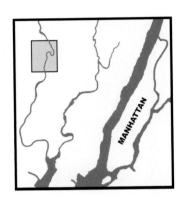

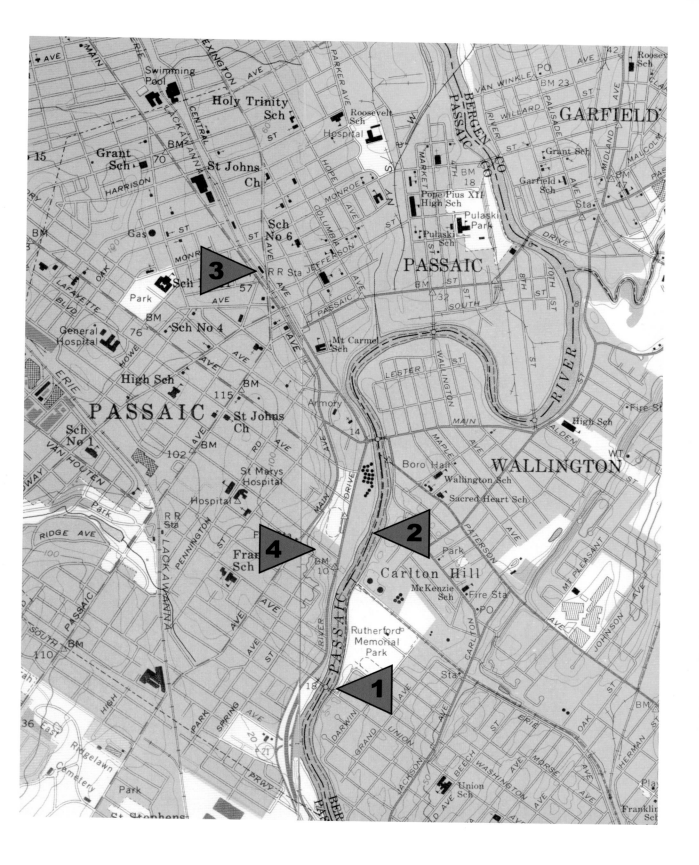

planned manufacturing center in the United States. Passaic, like Paterson, boomed in the nineteenth century, becoming one of the world's largest centers of worsteds and woolens manufacture. Its industrial success supported and encouraged an exponential growth in population, fueled primarily by skilled Slavic and Austro-Hungarian immigrant workers. In the early years of the twentieth century the city was predominantly white but was by no means a typical white-bread suburb: by 1910 its percentage of foreign-born population was the highest in the country. The labor unrest that gripped the entire region in the mid-twenties, including the Passaic Textile Strike of 1926, has become legendary in American history because it led directly to momentous Progressive-Era changes in labor law.[7]

Unfortunately, the strikes also accompanied the ruinous decline of the industrial base of the Paterson/Passaic area, which by mid-century was experiencing widespread blight and dilapidation. By 1967, the dangerously polluted Passaic River flowed past abandoned factories. Passaic's downtown retail district (through which Smithson traveled on his tour) was being rapidly abandoned, suffering from competition from new exurban shopping centers like the Garden State Plaza and the Bergen Mall. Between 1948 and 1966 the city had lost 36 percent of its retail establishments; this rate of decline was the highest in New Jersey. Moreover, as I examine more closely at the end of this chapter, the entire city was beginning to suffer from the effects of intensifying racial conflict stemming from the resistance of established ethnic groups to a major influx of African-American and Puerto Rican residents in the years following World War II.[8]

Significantly, another history that Smithson chose not to mention in "The Monuments of Passaic" was his own. Born in Passaic, Smithson had spent his entire childhood in two adjacent towns. Soon after his birth his parents moved the family across the Passaic River (across, that is, the Bridge Monument, fig. 39) to Rutherford, where they lived during the war years. In 1948 (when Smithson was ten years old), the family moved back across Passaic to the town of Clifton, which surrounds Passaic to the north and west (traveling north on Main Avenue in Passaic, where Smithson encountered the adjectival storefronts, brings one quickly to Clifton).[9]

Passaic, "Ultramoderne," and the Landmarks Preservation Debate

Smithson's decision to suppress these historical narratives in his article was all the more significant for the fact that the question of history and its relationship to urbanism was the subject of conspicuous and contentious debate at the time. The Passaic tour coincided exactly with the rise of the historic preservation movement in the New York metropolitan area. Smithson's sequence of Passaic snapshots investigates the decay of Passaic's urban infrastructure and the disruption caused by new large-scale construction projects, all within a larger project of redefining the historical monument. Simply by attending to these themes and their conflation, Smithson placed his Passaic project squarely—if polemically—within the context of preservationist discourse. In New York City, the landmarks preservation movement developed in response to the postwar construction boom that had begun to bring about the widespread and largely unchecked demolition of older buildings and neighborhoods. The debate reached a critical point in the mid-sixties, after Penn Station was demolished over widespread community objections to make way for Madison Square Garden. The Landmarks Preservation Act was signed into law on April 19, 1965, creating a legislative body with the power to designate and enforce landmark status on structures and districts within the city. (Federal efforts on this score were also underway; the National Historic Preservation Act was passed in 1966.)[10]

Smithson could not have remained unaware of the debates surrounding historic preservation during these years. By 1966 and 1967, the Landmarks Preservation Commission was conferring landmark status at a furious pace; the New York Times regularly covered these landmark designations as well as the debates over property rights that inevitably followed. One of the most contentious questions in the early history of the Landmarks Commission involved the designation of the entire area of Greenwich Village—Smithson's own neighborhood—as a historic district. This blanket designation, first proposed in 1965, was intended to protect some two thousand structures occupying a sixty-five-block area (a space larger than all the other New York historic districts combined). A bitter battle between Village preservationists and real estate interests ensued. After multiple public hearings and widespread controversy, the official designation was declared (pending final legal approval) in March 1967. Thus, on the morning of Smithson's September trip to Passaic, he got out of bed in a sector of urban space that was all but certain to be frozen in time as New York's largest historic district.[11]

The historic preservation movement intersected at multiple points with Smithson's own historical preoccupations. Smithson's time-crystal model dealt broadly with preservation inasmuch as it posited history as the material persistence of all time. Yet it differed markedly from the kind of preservation advocated by the landmarks panel, whose protectionist approach was inspired by the form of historical value famously described by the early twentieth-century art historian Alois Riegl: "The cult of historical value must aim above all at the most complete conservation of the monument [or building] in its present state, and this requires that the natural course of decay be stayed as much as is humanly possible."[12] The problem with this approach, from Smithson's perspective, was, of course, that it attempted to circumvent entropy and therefore could not possibly succeed in its aims.

Much of Smithson's work of 1965–68 responds, with varying degrees of obliquity, to the rise of preservationism and its anti-entropic gambits. Indeed, it seems likely that the historic preservation movement provided one of the key conceptual pressures that galvanized Smithson to develop and deploy his own critique of traditional history. Consider his "Ultramoderne" project from 1967, for which he photographed Art Deco buildings around New York City, particularly in the Central Park West area. His photographs emphasize repetitive brickwork, setback-inspired pyramidal massing, cross-mirrored surfaces, and multifaceted motifs (fig. 35). Smithson published several of these photographs in the September–October 1967 issue of *Arts Magazine*, along with his own idiosyncratic text celebrating the style. The text made clear that Smithson's understanding of the crystalline nature of time was entangled in his observations about these buildings: "There are two types of time—organic (Modernist) and crystalline (Ultraist)." The text is also linked to his "Air Terminal Site" article and its appeal to a higher, four-dimensional version of eternity: Ultramoderne buildings, according to Smithson, produce a "vertigi-

35

Supplemental photograph taken in connection with *Ultramoderne* project, 1967.
Negative photostat print, 8 1/2 x 8 1/2 in. (21.6 x 21.6 cm).
Estate of Robert Smithson.

nous immobility" and trap temporal movement in a larger "trans-historical consciousness." To enter an Ultramoderne architectural space is to be transported out of familiar linear or progressive temporalities and to glimpse, if only through disorientation, the radical simultaneity of the eternal time-crystal: "Within the boundaries of the 'thirties, that multi-faceted segment of time, we discover premonitions, labyrinths, cycles, and repetitions that lead us to a concrete area of the infinite." To occupy the crystalline time field of Ultramoderne architecture is to be at one with time and with all times, to be in synchrony with the universe at large. Distance and difference are captured in a jewel-like network. "The Ultramoderne exists *ab aeterno!*"[13]

Although it does not explicitly announce itself as such, Smithson's "Ultramoderne" article amounts to a full-fledged rhetorical intervention in the landmarks preservation debate; indeed much of its persuasive energy derives from the ironic friction that it generates when examined in this context. The article reads as an absurdist or parodic version of a preservationist architectural paean; this is due, first, to Smithson's choice

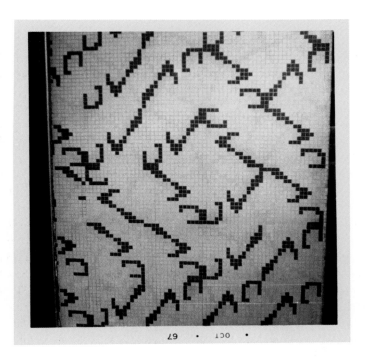

36
Robert Smithson, untitled snapshot from
Monuments of Passaic project (square spirals), 1967.
Black-and-white commercially developed print,
3 $^{1}/_{2}$ x 3 $^{1}/_{2}$ in. (8.9 x 8.9 cm).
Robert Smithson and Nancy Holt papers,
1905–1987, Archives of American Art, Smithsonian Institution.

of thirties Art Deco modernism as his subject matter. Buildings constructed in this style, most of them just over thirty years old, were a low priority for preservation at the time. The Landmarks Preservation Commission was certainly not paying much attention to them.[14] Second, because Smithson interprets Ultramoderne buildings as crystalline and historically static, they not only evade but also inherently repudiate the construction of historical narratives. Ultramoderne buildings, for Smithson, operate as machines for scrambling the directional arrow of history upon which historicism and preservationism depend. As Smithson claimed, Ultramoderne architecture compressed "the many types of monumental art from every major period" into a tangle of "primitive inertia," thus confusing specific historical references and expressing the "basic disease of the historical function."

Note that "Ultramoderne" attacks Landmarks Preservation not by disavowing preservation entirely but rather by attempting to redefine it. Ultramoderne buildings produce their own, superior form of "historic preservation" because the past, by intermingling kaleidoscopically with the present and future in an eternal stasis, is always at hand. "Ultramoderne," then, proposes an upgrade to the preservation idea, a form of hypertrophic preservationism in which everything— everything—is saved. By containing "all the arduous efforts of all the monumental ages," Ultramoderne architecture results in the "absolute inertia or the perfect instant, when time oscillates in a circumscribed place." For Smithson, a single Ultramoderne building was better qualified to preserve history than are all the crumbling fragments of nineteenth-century neoclassicism that the Landmarks Commission was so keen on preserving. However, even as they preserve history in an infinite archive, these buildings render that archive useless by making it impossible to retrieve specific historical narratives from it. In their ability to crystallize all histories, these buildings oscillate between memory and oblivion, preservation and loss.

It is important to take "Ultramoderne" into consideration when analyzing the Passaic tour because the two projects are closely related, both chronologically and thematically. They were published nearly simultaneously, and both explored zones and spaces where Smithson felt that the ultimate crystallization of historical time was beginning to reveal itself. In fact, Smithson's Passaic negatives reveal that when he set out for his tour, his camera was still loaded with an unfinished roll of film from the Ultramoderne project. Moreover, as he walked through Passaic he continued to seek out architectural details of the Ultramoderne ilk. For example, somewhere in downtown Passaic, between a TV store and a small municipal "Pocket Park," he stopped to photograph an ever-receding square spiral that would have been right at home on Central Park West (fig. 36).

Gridlock

Although the spiraling pattern of the tile work in figure 36 provided Smithson with a prefabricated crystalline motif that he could collect as if it were a kind of natural specimen, other Passaic snapshots show Smithson using his camera more actively, to construct intricate crystalline artifacts out of the available visual materials. Consider the compositional precision of the photographs in figures 37 and 38, one showing the open steel roadbed of the *Bridge Monument* and the other featuring shadows underneath an unfinished overpass for the new highway. In figure 38, the broad diagonal bands of the traffic barrier meet a near-perfect reversal in the striped shadows beneath the bridge, which are then reversed again, at a lesser angle, by the vertical supports of the steel bridge at the top of the photograph. These dynamic reversals are fixed in turn by the horizontal stratification of the image, in which a visual pattern of stacked slabs (steel bridge, concrete abutment, wooden planks) packs the image into a tight geometrical interlock. Figure 37, too, features a visual interlock. Here, the recessional pull of the image (defined by the V shape made by the seam running through the roadbed from lower right to upper left as it meets the curb in the background) is echoed in infinite miniature in the cross-hatching of the roadbed, and then snapped back to the picture plane by its reiteration in the bold zigzags of the truss in the foreground. Note that this "gridlock" strategy operates at the level of subject matter as well: each photograph features a roadway whose connotations of progression have been invalidated by the vectoral indecision of Smithson's composition (the "Road Closed" sign in figure 38 thus becomes a particularly appropriate internal caption).

The refutation of progress encoded in these photographs reminds us that in order to imagine Passaic as a historical terminus, a place where time itself would cease its motion, Smithson needed to be able to imagine the arrest not only of the past but also, equivalently, of the future. His understanding of the neutralizing power of enantiomorphic reversal was especially useful in this regard. As discussed in Chapter 2, Smithson was drawn to the crystallographic concept of enantiomorphic symmetry because it allowed him to articulate an infinite stillness formed from the cross-cancellation of the vectors of the past and the future. The Passaic tour makes liberal use of such enantiomorphic strategies; indeed, perhaps the most compelling idea that it has bequeathed to contemporary urbanism derives from this concept. It is tempting to assume that Smithson's monumentalization of everyday structures was his most innovative strategy in the Passaic article, but I would argue that this is not what is most radical or even "postmodern" about the project. In fact, this kind of conflation has a long modernist heritage—Le Corbusier, for example, identified American grain elevators as monuments in the 1930s. The idea of a tour of industrial ruins was also well established; "industrial tourism" had been common since at least the nineteenth century. Not even the deflationary quality of the sights on Smithson's tour was unprecedented. According to tourism theorist Dean MacCannell, there was a new interest in "negative sightseeing" —tours of sites of social and environmental wreckage—during the late sixties. In 1967 one could take a guided tour of Harlem with the Penny Sightseeing Company, and in 1970, during Earth Week, one could take bus tours of the "ten top polluters in action."[15]

What *was* unusual about Smithson's tour was his assertion that the *new* construction projects around him were also monuments, monuments which he called "ruins in reverse": "This is the opposite of the 'romantic ruin' because the buildings don't *fall* into ruin *after* they are built but rather *rise* into ruin before they are built." This paradoxical equation of progression and regression produces an enantiomorphic stoppage of historical motion. In Passaic, where progress is perpetually mirrored by decay, the very movement of time has been cancelled. Indeed, by suggesting that we see Passaic's backward-looking ruins and forward-looking construction projects as equivalent, Smithson

69

Robert Smithson, untitled snapshot from *Monuments of Passaic* project (crystalline grate on *The Bridge Monument*), 1967. Black-and-white commercially developed print, 3 ¹/₂ x 3 ¹/₂ in. (8.9 x 8.9 cm). Robert Smithson and Nancy Holt papers, 1905–87, Archives of American Art, Smithsonian Institution.

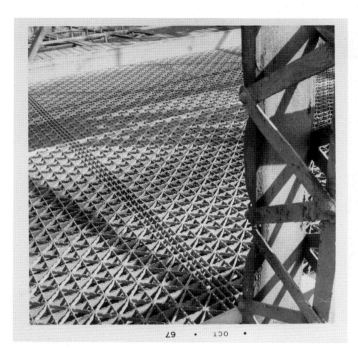

invites us to adopt the position of a fourth-dimensional observer in an eternal block universe in which the contingencies of direction, change, and motion are irrelevant. Smithson sprinkles clues to this crystalline suspension of direction throughout the article. On the way to Passaic, for example, he is careful to note that the bus turns onto "Orient Way," but once it crosses the river into Passaic there is only disorientation. Upon arriving in Passaic, he watches the *Bridge Monument* rotate to allow a barge to pass: "The Passaic (West) end of the bridge rotated south, while the Rutherford (East) end of the bridge rotated north; such rotations suggested the limited movements of an outmoded world. 'North' and 'South' hung over the static river in a bipolar manner. One could refer to this bridge as the 'Monument of Dislocated Directions.'"[16]

I do not mean to imply that Smithson's Passaic project amounted to a purely fantastical exercise in applied crystallography. The landscape of the Passaic valley in the sixties did lend itself, in many ways, to Smithson's "ruins-in-reverse" idea. Indeed, few landscapes were better suited to inspire a connection between decay and construction. By 1967 the widespread urban decay was being brought into stark apposition with massive civil engineering projects that were often designed specifically to remedy (or at least to bypass) the stagnation of the area. The adjacency of the half-ruined and the half-finished was everywhere apparent. Smithson witnessed this landscape often in his frequent travels back and forth between New York City and the northern New Jersey suburbs during this time, and it would have perhaps been more surprising had he not made a visual and conceptual connection between the two processes. In his field notes for the Passaic trip, Smithson noted "the eternally ramshackled construction" that he passed on the way to his destination: he was probably referring to the gargantuan project of draining and developing the Meadowlands, which was getting under way at the time. He would also have witnessed the construction of the New Jersey Turnpike.[17] Indeed, this was a particularly busy historical moment for the New Jersey Department of Transportation; massive highway projects were tearing up landscapes throughout the state, including Route 21, the new north–south highway being built along the Passaic River, that Smithson documented in his tour. But although Smithson was clearly attend-

ing to these "improvements," by identifying them as a form of reversed ruin and therefore claiming their construction as an enantiomorphic equivalent of decay, Smithson precludes the very possibility of urban renewal. In Smithson's Passaic, highway projects do not bypass stagnation but rather, inevitably, contribute to it.

Smithson was not alone in this fatalistic interpretation of the prospects for change in Passaic. One Passaic housewife, interviewed for a 1968 *New York Times* article about the decline of the city, unwittingly echoed Smithson's "ruins in reverse" motif: "Passaic is decaying and all we get from the politicians are promises. . . . Promises to make the streets safer. Promises to build new housing. I don't have any faith left. If they started a new building here Saturday it would fall down Wednesday." Thus it is not entirely accurate to say that Smithson simply imposed a prefabricated notion of enantiomorphic cross-cancellation onto an unwitting landscape; more likely the landscape —in all its historical and political dimensions— inspired and reinforced the model. Smithson's time-crystal, with all its pretensions to historical transcendence, is inextricable from the specific conditions of the exurban New Jersey landscape of the late sixties.[18]

Like "Ultramoderne" and Smithson's other urban projects of the late sixties, "The Monuments of Passaic" served as a kind of modern-day geological survey (or, better, crystallographical survey) report. The tour was an expedition to a place where Smithson felt that eternal equilibrium could be found in its natural state. It was thus also an inverted or backwards historical tour, in this sense a distinct example of "Mirror-Travel." To travel from Greenwich Village to Passaic was to reverse the traditional direction of historical tourism by leaving an official historic district in order to visit a fringe zone of "infinite disintegration and forgetfulness." To do so, however, was nevertheless to arrive at a higher plane of historic preservation. Preservation activists surely felt that they had managed to stop time in Greenwich Village (Smithson's low opinion of this emerges throughout the Passaic article in his frequent references to the futility of attempting to evade entropy). But for Smithson, the city of Passaic had managed to evoke an even more stable and inclusive brand of eternal stasis without even trying. In yielding passively to progress (unlike the Village, Passaic had no wealthy, influential, or cohesive neighborhood groups that could stop the highway from cutting through the historic fabric of the city), Passaic was allowing itself to crystallize. It was "stopping time" far more finally and effectively than was Greenwich Village. As Smithson asked, only half-jokingly, "Has Passaic replaced Rome as the Eternal City?"[19]

A Crystallography of Perspective

Smithson conceived of his own work in Passaic as contributing to, rather than simply recording, the crystallization of Passaic. Consider Smithson's snapshot of the concrete cube sitting in the Passaic River (see fig. 32), which bears a close resemblance to the photocollage, titled *Proposal for a Monument on the Red Sea*, that he produced a year earlier in 1966 (see fig. 28). Clearly Smithson saw some connection between the collage and the snapshot; notice that as he photographed the cube in the river, he took care to preserve the basic topographical outlines of the earlier collage. In Chapter 2 I discussed *Proposal for a Monument on the Red Sea* as one of a group of experimental images that Smithson produced in an attempt to imagine the crystalline "block universe" of four-dimensional space as it began to intrude upon the everyday three-dimensional world. The cube looms disconcertingly in the seascape because its shading is inconsistent with that of the nearby rocks and, more importantly, because the axonometric perspective of its delineation is misaligned with the recessional space of the rest of the landscape. The photographic seascape, with its necessary ties to linear perspective, embodies the kind of limited, contingent, singular viewpoint that the transcendent cube-crystal (in Smithson's universe) was set to overtake. Yet the cube snapshot from the Passaic project suggests a different understanding of the relationship between photography and crystallization. Whereas previously the crystalline associations of the cube were established differentially, through opposition to the photographic vision of the seascape, now the cube is integrated seamlessly into the photographic space itself.

Smithson's Passaic snapshots suggest that throughout his tour he was experimenting with new methods of using photography itself as a crystallizing tool. One strategy that he tested, as we have already seen in figures 37 and 38, was to use the camera to lock the subject matter into crystalline patterns. But most of Smithson's Passaic photographs are not as obviously "crystalline" in their pictorial logic as these. His published image of the *Bridge Monument* (fig. 39), for example, frees the triangular facets of the bridge from the tight organization around the picture plane that they exhibit in figure 37, permitting the perspectival recession of the image to rush backward unimpeded. In fact, a close analysis of Smithson's Passaic snapshots demonstrates that many feature exaggeratedly recessional compositions marked by the convergence of orthogonal lines and the diminution of forms as they stretch into the distance (see fig. 43). The railings, curbs, roadways, concrete barriers, and other recessional subject matter in these snapshots (most of which have not been illustrated here) seem to have been chosen not for their topical interest but rather because they serve so well to indicate the perspectival distortions forced upon them by the act of photography itself. Smithson's emerging interest in this exaggerated recessional technique is suggested by the fact that he further explored and refined it in subsequent projects. In an expedition to Bergen a few months after the Passaic trip, for example, he took a series of snapshots labeled "Points on the Edge of a New Jersey Swamp." In this photographic tour (which generated five rolls of exposed film) Smithson concentrated his efforts even more directly on the production of photographic perspectives (figs. 40, 41). In Passaic and Bergen, Smithson attempted to explore the spatial structure inherent in all photographic images. In these recessional views, he emphasized what has often been described as the very essence of photographic representation: its mechanization of linear perspective.[20]

What makes these perspectives embody a crystalline vision (rather than foil or frustrate it, as in Smithson's previous collages) is the broader depositional strategy underlying their production. If we think of each of these photographs as the material deposition of a single shard of vision (a "solid diminution," as he later put it), we can see them in series as a crystalline aggregate. In fact we can better understand Smithson's photographic process in Passaic if we consider it as part of his sculptural production. Smithson himself tended to deploy a sculptural vocabulary to convey the process of vision (photographic and otherwise). He spoke often, for example, of "casting glances." As art

39

Robert Smithson, *The Bridge Monument Showing Wooden Sidewalks*, from "The Monuments of Passaic," 1967. Collection Museet for Samtidkunst, Norway.

40

Robert Smithson, untitled snapshot from *Points on the Edge of a New Jersey Swamp* project (fence), 1968. Black-and-white commercially developed print, 3 ¹/₂ x 3 ¹/₂ in. (8.9 x 8.9 cm). Robert Smithson and Nancy Holt papers, 1905–87, Archives of American Art, Smithsonian Institution.

41

Robert Smithson, untitled snapshot from *Points on the Edge of a New Jersey Swamp* project (railroad), 1968. Black-and-white commercially developed print, 3 ¹/₂ x 3 ¹/₂ in. (8.9 x 8.9 cm). Robert Smithson and Nancy Holt papers, 1905–87, Archives of American Art, Smithsonian Institution.

42

Robert Smithson, untitled snapshot from *Monuments of Passaic* project (traditional monument), 1967.
Black-and-white commercially developed print,
3 ¹/₂ x 3 ¹/₂ in. (8.9 x 8.9 cm).
Robert Smithson and Nancy Holt papers,
1905–87, Archives of American Art, Smithsonian Institution.

critic John Perreault recalled from a trip that he took with the artist in 1968, "Out on the ice-cold Palisades . . . Smithson had repeatedly spoken of 'casting a glance': 'I'm not interested in casting material, but in art that's made out of casting a glance.'" And in his essay "A Sedimentation of the Mind: Earth Projects," Smithson made it clear that the artist's vision should be considered as a solid: "A great artist can make art by simply casting a glance. A set of glances could be as solid as any thing or place."[21]

Thus the solid artifacts among the monuments of Passaic include not only bridges, buildings, and water fountains but also Smithson's snapshots themselves. Indeed, as the contact sheets from the Bergen and Passaic photo tours demonstrate, Smithson frequently alternated between recessional photographic views of empty space and views of traditional monumental forms. Throughout, he equivocated between his camera-crafted pyramids and the pyramidal obelisks that he photographed along with them (fig. 42). It is as if Smithson was attempting to use the perspectival apparatus of the camera to mold (or cast) empty space into pointed monuments. Thus Smithson's photographs not only explore photography's mechanization of perspective, but also theorize the unerringly medusan quality of the medium. His gorgonization of perspective space connects the Passaic photographs with much of his other sculptural work of the mid-sixties, which often conflates perspective and matter (notably in the perspectival arrangements of specimens in his Nonsites; see fig. 31). It also relates to the work of other artists interested in the solidification of space; indeed, Smithson's unassuming photographs of roadsides and railroad tracks are just as closely related to Bruce Nauman's castings of negative space as they are to the tradition of tourist and documentary photography.[22]

By thinking of photography as a kind of injection molding process, Smithson reverses the Cartesian understanding of linear perspective as a tool for the sublimation of the material world. Material objects, when represented in perspective, cede their particularity, their heft, and their conceptual opacity to a rational infrastructure. Smithson takes that infrastructural matrix and gives it a heft of its own. This intervention in the history of perspective was fully intentional; Smithson went out of his way to study the historical development

43
Robert Smithson, untitled snapshot from
Monuments of Passaic project (concrete form), 1967.
Black-and-white commercially developed print,
3 ¹/₂ x 3 ¹/₂ in. (8.9 x 8.9 cm).
Robert Smithson and Nancy Holt papers, 1905–87,
Archives of American Art, Smithsonian Institution.

of perspective and deserves to be counted among its most brilliant and compelling theorists. As his fossilization of perspective space in the Passaic photographs suggests, he shared none of the Cartesian ambitions of "Golden Age" Renaissance linear perspective. Rather, as his notes and papers demonstrate, he preferred the eccentric and Manneristic "perspective exercises" of sixteenth- and seventeenth-century German and Flemish artists. A good example of these is the perspective diagram of 1604 by Jan Vredeman de Vries; the skewed objects strewn about the page, which, coincidentally, bear a striking resemblance to Smithson's own concrete perspectival artifacts in one of his *Monuments of Passaic* snapshots, suggest the "perspective pyramids" of a dozen glances cast in place (figs. 43, 44). The oblique forms appear as fallen, wasted views and offer more of an obstruction to the viewer than an abstraction of the viewer's visual penetration of the space.[23]

These Mannerist explorations of perspective were attractive to Smithson because they proclaim and embrace the artificiality of perspective systems rather than treat such systems as neutral expressions of visuality. Smithson felt that, since the Mannerist era, the inherent artificiality of perspective had been obscured by painterly atmospherics. As he wrote in his 1967 essay "Pointless Vanishing Points": "With the rise of 'naturalism' and 'realism' in the arts the artificial factors of perspective were lost in thick brown stews of chiaroscuro." Smithson's use of photography in the Passaic project aims to objectify and therefore denaturalize perspectival representation.[24]

Smithson's solidification of visual perspective, produced as it was in the context of a monumental tour, also served to denaturalize the perspectival metaphors underlying the traditions of memory and history. If his library is any indication, Smithson frequently would have encountered the analogy between historical and visual perspective constructions in his reading. In Husserl's *Phenomenology of Internal Time-Consciousness* we find that "an articulated part of the process 'draws together' as it sinks into the past —a kind of temporal perspective . . . analogous to spatial perspective. As the temporal object moves into the past, it is drawn together on itself and thereby also becomes obscure." In another of Smithson's books, philosopher George Santayana claims that "memory . . . sets up a temporal perspective, believing firmly in its

Jan Vredeman de Vries, plate 3 from *Perspective*, 1604.
By permission of the Houghton Library, Harvard University.

45

Lorenz Stoer, plate 7 from *Geometria et Perspectiva*, 1567.
Typ520.67.810F, Department of Printing and Graphic Arts,
Houghton Library, Harvard College Library.

recessional character. . . . Memory and prophecy do in time what perception does in space."[25]

By calcifying memorial and photographic space simultaneously, Smithson's snapshots ultimately prevent the spectator from enjoying a transparently perspectival relationship to the past. Art historian James Elkins has noted that sixteenth-century perspective exercises often convey a sense of desertion or ruination. We might well ask why this is the case. Why would an artist such as Lorenz Stoer feel compelled to render his 1567 woodcut, also known as a "perspective garden" (fig. 45), as a ruin, complete with broken arches, blasted trees, and weeds growing between the forms? Perhaps Stoer was elaborating upon the desolate sense already suggested by the refractory quality of the forms themselves—each form crystallizes a perspectival system which is coherent in itself but otherwise multiply misaligned, not only with the viewer but also with the other forms on the page. Woodcuts like Stoer's elaborated upon techniques often used in the backgrounds of Mannerist paintings, which featured unsettling architectural scenes formed by the displacement of linear perspective (so that the viewer felt "off-line" with the image, as if seated too far to the side at a play with perspective scenery). Smithson, not surprisingly, was especially interested in Stoer's work. In one of his notebooks, he drafted a paragraph of commentary on Stoer's "geometrical landscapes" and also mentioned the work of Wenzel Jamnitzer, an artist who produced similar perspective constructions. Smithson was fascinated by these hardened, inaccessible perspective objects, objects that (like the past) can offer nothing to the viewer but a sense of misalignment and belatedness.[26]

What is truly ruinous about Smithson's mortification of perspective is its suggestion that, once a view has been deposited, it cannot be reoccupied. The die has been cast by the eye. In this sense Smithson's monuments of Passaic, like Stoer's geometrical landscapes, are more radically, irretrievably "past" than all the perspectively orthodox ruins depicted in picturesque landscape paintings. This is why Smithson's monumental photography—every glance preserved intact and piled upon the previous in an infinite photosculptural rubble—lends his view of Passaic its bleak and brittle sense of history. It is worth noting that Smithson's visual anachronism in Passaic was linked

not only to the current dialogues about history and monuments, but also to prevailing art-world discussions about the relationship between vision and memory. Clement Greenberg and Michael Fried had recently developed an aesthetics of visual renewability into modernist gospel. As I discussed in Chapter 1, the success of a work of art for Greenberg depended on its "at-onceness." This at-onceness, in turn, depended upon the complete and unfailing repeatability of the experience of seeing it: "The 'at-onceness' which a picture or a piece of sculpture enforces on you is not, however, single or isolated. It can be repeated in a succession of instants, in each one remaining an 'at-onceness,' an instant all by itself. For the cultivated eye, the picture repeats its instantaneous unity like a mouth repeating a single word."[27]

For Greenberg, the view of a monument (in this sense the modern artwork) is a fully renewable resource; its occurrence produces no mnemonic byproducts that might block or inflect the return view of the work of art. The metaphysical sleight of hand that underlies Greenberg's assertions is that if each view is to be equal to the first, the phenomenal field must be constantly "reset" so that the memory of previous views will not get in the way of the perfect apprehension of the succeeding. The "cultivated eye" must be able to return to the object and have the same experience over and over again; it must not encounter the residue of its own previous view, for this would block the purity of the repetition. Of course it is precisely this residue or visual waste product that Smithson embodies in his entropic "cast glances." His Mannerist and materialist understanding of perspective insists upon the mundane memorability of vision, defies any notion of renewable experience, and maintains a Siberian indifference to the repeated advances of the cultivated eye.

"Stigmatic Vistas" and the Problem of Nostalgic Affect

Smithson's monumental snapshots, then, preclude memory even as they preserve it. Just as each moment is preserved by Smithson's Instamatic, it is simultaneously rendered opaque to mnemonic revisitation. Smithson's monumental photographs do not remember Passaic so much as they bury Passaic under an infinite deposition of mnemonic artifacts. The exaggerated, unchecked "historic preservation" that results renders history infinite and thus impossible. Smithson was not alone in exploring this conceptual inversion, at infinity, between history and oblivion. We find a vivid parallel in one of his favorite Jorge Luis Borges stories, "Funes the Memorious." Funes is a character who, because he can forget nothing, can remember nothing. He exists in "a multiform, instantaneous and almost intolerably precise world," where memory becomes isomorphic with time itself and thus cannot function selectively: "Two or three times he had reconstructed a whole day; he never hesitated, but each reconstruction had required a whole day." Borges's story, like Smithson's hypermonumentality, contends with the specter raised by Proust at the beginning of the century, in which "it is quite possible that [the philosophy] according to which everything is doomed to oblivion, is less true than a contrary philosophy which would predict the conservation of everything." Smithson's camera, in its infinite memorializing of Passaic, functions paradoxically as *oubliette*. Smithson is, we might say, looking to forget.[28]

Smithson would train his amnesiac camera on many other cities and landscapes after 1967. But here, in "The Monuments of Passaic," his photo-monumental strategies take on an especially acute significance. After all, we must not lose sight of the most provocative aspect of the project: Smithson has chosen the city of his own birth as the site for his experiments in forgetting. "The Monuments of Passaic" takes what might easily have been a mawkish exercise in nostalgia and memory and transforms it into a high-concept oblivion rendered with flawless ironic detachment. The strategy is brilliant: for an artist hoping to attain a "total crystalline consciousness," free of the limitations of specific histories and situated perspectives, what better way to test one's mettle than to subject one's own most personal, specific, and situated memories to the eternalizing treatment?

Smithson's neutralization of both memory and sentiment in the Passaic project is so successful that it is sometimes easy to lose sight of the difficulty of the task to which he set himself. His use of perspective is a case in point. After studying Smithson's photographs in their disaffected aggregate, we need to stop and remind ourselves that an image like figure 39, showing the *Bridge Monument* rushing back into the distance, would need little or no alteration to be printed on a

greeting card (a romantic figure holding baguettes or a fishing pole, walking away into the distance, would seem right at home on the walkway). As suggested above, visual and historical perspective have long been connected in the West; an image like this activates an entire battery of cultural metaphors linking spatial recession and memory. Recessional photographs threaten to raise any number of sentimental specters by setting into play what Jeff Wall calls the "adventure of loss" of perspective. The stigmatic action of the camera can turn even the most quotidian landscape into a playground of affect.[29]

Smithson was abundantly conscious of the affective tendencies of perspective. In fact, I've borrowed the term *stigmatic* from Smithson himself, who explicitly referred to photographs as "stigmatic vistas." His choice of this term, of course, immediately connects his photographs back to his religious paintings, where stigmatization figured prominently as a mark of suffering and broken unity (see figs. 23–25). He once also described perspective recession as a form of wounding: "Through the windshield the road stabbed the horizon, causing it to bleed a sunny incandescence." All this suggests that for Smithson the "viewpoint" of the photographic memory had some connection to the nails of the crucifixion (indeed, as art historian Jill Bennett has argued, the image of the nail entering Christ's bloody wounds was enlarged and lovingly detailed in some medieval devotional images in order to fix through bodily sympathy the viewer's memory of the scene). Perhaps we might even consider Smithson to be the first medieval photographer. At any rate, Smithson's annotations in his library reveal his association of perspectival diminution with all sorts of feeling, not only pain but also desire. For example, he underlined a passage in a text by Saint John of the Cross claiming that "the instant desire seizes upon anything, it is narrowed." The dramatic attenuation of the receding objects in Smithson's photographs embody, at some level, the very structure of desire, which in the temporal arena is synonymous with nostalgia and memory.[30]

Because Smithson so well understood the emotional baggage of his "stigmatic vistas," his preservation, mortification, and infinite crystallization of perspective in the Passaic project served, at least in part, as a renunciation of historical nostalgia. By "casting" his views he plastered the mnemonic wounds; by multiplying them to infinity he reduced their individual power to pierce. His crystallizing treatment of Passaic blunts, confounds, and ultimately transcends the affect of history. His infinite deposition of temporal fragments into a crystalline simultaneity attempts to allow the perception of time above and beyond its perspectival association with desire and nostalgia. "The Monuments of Passaic" is just as much an exercise in mystical detachment as it is a documentary treatment of highway construction. Its rhetoric of dullness and passivity is a hard-fought liberation from the wounds of memory and the habits of desire for the past. As Smithson underlined in his copy of T. S. Eliot's "Four Quartets":

> This is the use of memory:
> For liberation — not less of love but expanding
>   of love beyond desire, and so liberation
> From the future as well as the past.[31]

Race in the Parking Lot

The personal drama of "The Monuments of Passaic" is also political, however, for other residents of Passaic were also swept up in its crystallization of history.

Smithson's tour of Passaic began drawing to a close after he finished his lunch at the Golden Coach Diner (see fig. 34). Starting back southward toward the Union Avenue bus stop where he began, he encountered the penultimate monument of his journey: "I walked down a parking lot that covered the old railroad tracks which at one time ran through the middle of Passaic. That monumental parking lot divided the city in half, turning it into a mirror and a reflection — but the mirror kept changing places with the reflection. One never knew what side of the mirror one was on. There was nothing *interesting* or even strange about that flat monument, yet it echoed a kind of cliché idea of infinity; perhaps the 'secrets of the universe' are just as pedestrian — not to say dreary. Everything about the site remained wrapped in blandness and littered with shiny cars — one after the other they extended into a sunny nebulosity. The indifferent backs of the cars flashed and reflected the stale afternoon sun. I took a few listless, entropic snapshots of that lustrous monument."[32]

Notwithstanding Smithson's insistence that there was nothing interesting about it, his parking lot

monument (fig. 46) is quite interesting, both in its perfect encapsulation of Smithson's conception of crystalline time (in its condensation of tropes of stoppage and stillness) and also in the way it can be made to reveal the more comprehensive political and historical implications of Smithson's Passaic project. It serves, first, as a remarkable compendium of long-standing anxieties animating Smithson's career. Most importantly, the parking lot raises — and attempts to resolve — the problem of the automobile with which Smithson had so conspicuously struggled in his religious paintings (see figs. 5, 11). There, the speeding "infernal" machines had served as anxious symbols of temporal passage and fallen history. Here, however, in the "sunny nebulosity" of the Passaic afternoon, the automobile is redeemed by the regular repetition and enforced stasis of the parking lot. The gleaming glass and metal surfaces of the cars suggest a species of transcendental facetry. The parking lot as an index of stasis is further suggested by its relationship to the railroad tracks it has literally superseded. As Smithson notes, the parking lot has its origin in the paving over of a railroad track. This paving action links the monument to Smithson's ongoing interest in asphalt (see *Asphalt Rundown*, fig. 47) as an agent of hardening and congealment; a material that automatically "runs down," performing its own entropic immobilization.

The power of the asphalt to defeat the kinetic potential of the tracks underneath is paralleled by Smithson's curious treatment of the history of the railroad in his written narrative. Smithson's discussion, with its vague reference to the railroad tracks that ran through Passaic "at one time," gives the railroad's history an indistinct, muffled, and faraway quality. It is true that the railroad tracks were old — they had been part of the Erie-Lackawanna line that had run along Main Avenue since 1831. Surprisingly, however, they had been removed only four years before Smithson's tour, in 1963. They had been torn up in order to open the moribund downtown shopping area to much-needed parking and to help facilitate the construction of Highway 21.[33]

It had also been hoped that the new parking lot would contribute to the urban renewal of Passaic by remedying the profound racial and economic segregation that had historically divided the city. The idea that these tracks so recently had a "wrong side" raises the

46
Robert Smithson, untitled snapshot from *Monuments of Passaic* project (parking lot), 1967.
Black-and-white commercially developed print,
3 1/2 x 3 1/2 in. (8.9 x 8.9 cm).
Robert Smithson and Nancy Holt papers, 1905–1987,
Archives of American Art, Smithsonian Institution.

possibility that Smithson's parking lot might be about the crystallization not only of speed but also of race. Indeed, this parking lot opens a new perspective on Smithson's project by demonstrating that his operations upon history are part of a much larger adumbration of difference and conflict in Passaic.

In Smithson's text, the disused railroad tracks serve as an enantiomorphic fold across which the entropic sameness of Passaic reveals itself. Acknowledging the urban cliché of the city split by railroad tracks into a right and wrong side, Smithson claims that the tracks "divided the city in half." But by refiguring this division as a mirror relation, he envisions that scission as caught up in a process of equivocation, as a difference in the process of dedifferentiation, locked in a larger cross-referential wholeness ("One never knew what side of the mirror one was on"). Like the mirrors in Smithson's gallery installations that both sever and heal the material they transect, the ruined railroad tracks project a kind of still, "listless" harmony upon the town.

Others, however, took a different view of the situation. Dr. Wallace Haddon, an African American dentist interviewed in 1968 for a *New York Times* article about Passaic, claimed that "there's a color line right down the middle of town, where the railroad tracks used to run." It turns out that this unassuming parking lot still served as a highly charged index of a form of difference that was, in reality, unlikely to heal itself anytime soon. Already destabilized by the decimation of its textile economic base, Passaic was, during the sixties, undergoing rapid demographic changes that led to increased racial tension. Between 1960 and 1970 the percentage of whites decreased from 91.2 percent to 64.2 percent of the total population. The African American population increased 10 percent, to 17.9 percent of the total population, while the percentage of Hispanic, primarily Puerto Rican, residents leaped from 3 percent to 18 percent of the total population. Racial tensions were high and virtually defined the complex politics of Passaic at the time. As Dr. Haddon testified, segregation remained as absolute as ever: "A Negro catches hell" if he tries to move into the predominately white section of town.[34]

When Smithson's Passaic article is considered in this light, other aspects of an oblique racial subtext emerge as well: not only in his reference to the railroad

47

Robert Smithson, *Asphalt Rundown (Rome)*, 1969.
Estate of Robert Smithson.

48

Robert Smithson, untitled snapshot from
Monuments of Passaic project (alternate view of
The Sand-Box Monument), 1967.
Black-and-white commercially developed print,
3 ¹/₂ x 3 ¹/₂ in. (8.9 x 8.9 cm).
Robert Smithson and Nancy Holt papers,
1905–87, Archives of American Art,
Smithsonian Institution.

tracks, but also in an experiment he includes for the demonstration of the action of entropy. Toward the end of the article, while contemplating the *Sand-Box Monument* (fig. 48), Smithson writes: "I should now like to prove the irreversibility of eternity by using a *jejune* experiment for proving entropy. Picture in your mind's eye the sand box divided in half with black sand on one side and white sand on the other. We take a child and have him run hundreds of times clockwise in the box until the sand gets mixed and begins to turn grey; after that we have him run anti-clockwise, but the result will not be a restoration of the original division but a greater degree of greyness and an increase of entropy."[35]

To be sure, the language of color in this demonstration—black, white, and grey—is perfectly explicable in terms of the broader discourse of black-and-white photography running throughout the article, and can easily be read as being so abstract an image of dialectical entropy as to be emptied out of all social or political content. But it should be noted that Smithson made a conscious choice to design his sandbox experiment in black and white. He borrowed the experiment almost verbatim from a book called *Turning Points in Physics*. Here is the original text, which he carefully marked in his copy of the book: "The experiment is simple and convincing. Fill a jam jar half with white sand and half with red sand, and then stir the contents a hundred times in a clockwise direction. The result is pink sand. Stirring now a hundred times in anti-clockwise [*sic*] direction will not separate the sand again into white and red. In fact, the sand will be even pinker." The sand in the original text was red and white; Smithson changed it to black and white for the purposes of Passaic. Given the conspicuousness of the racial tensions at the time, as well as the frequency with which Smithson employs color rhetoric in the article (elsewhere, for example, he notes that "the houses mirrored themselves into colorlessness"), it is difficult not to see Smithson's sandbox as a place where race is very much in play, even as Smithson's forward entropic projection wants to claim that the game is already over.[36]

Smithson's sandbox, then, functions as a listless utopia of sorts. It serves as an abstract demonstration of entropic sameness, but it also addresses (even as it attempts, prematurely, to resolve) the rising crisis in race relations that was gripping the country at the time. Smithson rarely commented overtly on race issues, but he was knowledgeable and concerned about them. In fact, in April of 1967, just a few months before embarking on his Passaic tour, he had contributed a sculpture to the Annual Art Exhibition and Sale of the Scholarship, Education, and Defense Fund for Racial Equality. If we were to attempt to assign an ethical intentionality to the sandbox, we would do best to interpret it as an instrument for the production of racial equality through the dissolution of racial disharmony as well as all other distinctions. But the sandbox also displaces the exigency of difference by projecting—and naturalizing—its entropic endpoint. And at heart, with its rhetoric of dullness, sterility, and acedia, it projects a hope that racial conflicts might inevitably resolve themselves slowly, gradually, sleepily. Given the explosive race rioting that, by September of 1967, was already beginning to alarm the nation, Smithson's entropic black-and-white sandbox seems both poignant and willful. Just two months before Smithson arrived for his tour, the city of Passaic itself had experienced its first race riots—two nights of looting and firebombing in July. In the two years ahead the city would experience not Smithson's sleepy grey-scale unity but rather continued and intensifying violence.[37]

Smithson's sandbox, then, serves not only to stifle the memory of the city's segregated past and present. It also serves to forget, before it has even happened, Passaic's violent future. In doing so it encapsulates in microcosm all of the essential hopes of the Passaic project as a whole. Throughout "The Monuments of Passaic," Smithson works to neutralize Passaic's history: his "ruins-in-reverse" trope equates progress and regress, thus obviating all historical trajectories; his photographic "cast glances" transform the affect of historical retrospection into an indifferent accumulation of perspectives; and his entropic monuments attempt to override the violent struggles of difference that so often mark historical change. But, as I hope to have suggested here, history can still occupy the scene of its entropic exclusion; there is still some digging to do in Smithson's sandbox.

SMITHSON AND STEPHENS IN YUCATÁN

I actually value indifference. I think it's something that has aesthetic possibilities.

—Robert Smithson, 1967

Robert Smithson and John Lloyd Stephens were both New Jersey–born residents of Manhattan, wherefrom each embarked on a well-publicized excursion to the Yucatán Peninsula. One departed from New York on Monday, October 9, 1841, aboard the cargo ship *Tennessee*; the other left on Tuesday, April 15, 1969, aboard Pan Am flight 67. Both published narratives of their travels: Stephens's *Incidents of Travel in Yucatán* was a two-volume book published by Harper & Brothers in 1843, while Smithson's "Incidents of Mirror-Travel in the Yucatan" appeared as an article in the September 1969 issue of *Artforum*. Both narratives included abundant illustrations. [1]

The immediate similarities end there. Stephens's antebellum adventure, steeped in nineteenth-century imperialist and positivist rhetoric, bears so little direct resemblance to Smithson's meandering, skeptical treatment that the two barely seem worth discussing in the same breath. Indeed, Smithson himself downplayed his connection to Stephens; although he knew Stephens's writings and suggested in his title a desire to reflect upon them, he avoided any direct reference to Stephens in the body of his article. When he did speak explicitly of Stephens, it was only to negate him—in one interview he referred to his Yucatán trip as the "anti-expedition" to Stephens's. [2]

Yet despite Smithson's apparent ambivalence about Stephens and his nineteenth-century baggage, his Yucatán project can be fruitfully examined in terms of the dialogue it invites with the American expeditionary tradition. Both travelers, for example, applied the rhetoric of historical indifference to the landscape and to the inhabitants of the Yucatán Peninsula. Stephens's narrative puts "indifference" into

play as a pejorative; by constructing the people of Yucatán as indifferent to their own history, Stephens authorizes his extraction of archaeological artifacts from the region. Smithson subjects such imperialist operations to a blistering and sophisticated critical inversion. Nevertheless, in some of the most sophisticated aspects of Smithson's narrative, particularly in his attempts to imagine a form of "dedifferentiated" vision and history, Stephens's notion of indigenous indifference is necessarily retained. My goal is to help initiate critical debate about the historical implications of Smithson's expeditionary methodology and to suggest, despite Smithson's frequent renunciations of "anthropomorphism" and politics, that his expedition to the Yucatán Peninsula constituted both an anthropology and a politics of peripheral encounter.

Stephens and Catherwood

During the 1830s and early 1840s, John Lloyd Stephens embarked on several major expeditions to regions beyond the fringes of Anglo-American influence. The exoticism of his destinations (such as Turkey, Russia, Egypt, Arabia, Jerusalem, and Central America), combined with what one twentieth-century critic approvingly described as his "delightful style overflowing with anecdote and salacious adventure," made Stephens one of the most successful and influential American travel writers of the nineteenth century. His best-selling books not only found favor with the general public, but also influenced a generation of American writers, among them Poe and Melville. Stephens's Central American travel narratives have remained important references; still in print, they are considered classic texts in Mesoamerican archaeology. [3]

Between 1839 and 1842, Stephens took two trips to the Yucatán Peninsula, each of which resulted in a two-volume illustrated expedition narrative published by Harper and Brothers in New York. Stephens was accompanied on both occasions by the British architect Frederick Catherwood, whose drawings illustrated the published narratives and gave U.S. audiences their first glimpses of ancient Mesoamerica. In the late 1830s, most of the ruins of what are now known to be ancient Maya cities had been abandoned for centuries. Although European accounts (mostly unreliable) had been published for a few of the sites in the late eighteenth and early nineteenth centuries, Stephens and Catherwood were the first explorers to undertake a systematic survey of the ruins, proving that an extensive ancient civilization had once flourished on the American continent. Within the United States, their discoveries inflamed vigorous debate about the origin of the mysterious ancient builders; about their connection, if any, with the region's current inhabitants; and about the position of the United States within the suddenly expanded scope of the New World's course of empire.[4]

Stephens and Catherwood first encountered Maya ruins at Copán (then, as now, in Honduras), where the ancient structures and stelae stood tangled in a centuries-old jungle chokehold. The discovery came near the beginning of the expedition; having landed in Belize, the travelers began their explorations in the dense, mountainous rainforests of Central America, then gradually made their way to the drier, more thinly forested landscapes of the northern part of the Yucatán Peninsula. The effect of this itinerary upon the published narrative is to suggest a correlation between the progress of the expedition and the unfolding of the landscape, and for the inaugural chapters of the travelogue this means that the opening of vision, the founding of historical perception, and the clearing of the landscape all participate in the same dramatic narrative. Stephens's descriptions of the obstacles faced in Copán emphasize the most basic challenges of visual and historical differentiation, dramatizing the landscape's resistance to narrative and representation. At first, according to Stephens, Catherwood found it difficult to produce even a coherent drawing from the tangled scene around him. Inscribed with illegible hieroglyphs which seemed to mimic the overgrown vegetation that covered them, the ruins proved challenging to discern, much less to comprehend: "The designs were very complicated, and so different from anything Mr. Catherwood had ever seen before as to be per-

fectly unintelligible. The cutting was in very high relief, and required a strong body of light to bring up the figures; and the foliage was so thick, and the shade so deep, that drawing was impossible."[5]

Only after indigenous laborers had been employed to cut down the trees around each stela to "lay it open"—and only after several failed attempts at drawing—was Catherwood finally able to separate the monuments from the foliage and, as Stephens had phrased it, to "bring up the figures" before him. The resultant engravings, the first to be encountered in Stephens's book, reproduce for the (presumably Anglo-American) viewer the difficulty of this first struggle for representation. In this image of a stela at Copán (fig. 49), the stylized turbulence of the vegetation filling the background makes the design on the stone and the design of the forest seem mutually derived; even the scale of the clumps of leaves matches that of the monument's carved patterns. Only the deeper contrast of the figure differentiates it from the vegetation and tenuously relegates the forest to a safe atmospheric distance. The engraving recalls the stela's original immersion even as it proclaims Catherwood's ultimate conquest of the scene; the residue of camouflage encodes within the representation its own primordial resistance. This residue of camouflage, this reminder of the stela's previously undifferentiated status, accords an ontological force to the act of perception itself.[6]

In 1844 Catherwood republished many of these illustrations in a folio volume of colored lithographs; the dramatic chiaroscuro in figure 50 conveys the same romance of perception, with an eerie illumination emphasizing the precariousness of monumental form in the context of the overgrown forest. With illustrations such as this, Stephens and Catherwood announce Western expeditionary vision to be something more than simply passive perception. It is a concentrated, focused, *generative* perspective; one that the modern travelers have had to import. Like contemporary "Magic Eye" stereographs, which reveal their three-dimensional images only to the practiced eye, Catherwood's images proclaim that only with straining and training can difference—the difference between figure and ground, monument and forest, past and present—be forged from the indiscriminate jungle.

Throughout Stephens's narratives, this struggle between discernment and camouflage is also arti-

49

Frederick Catherwood, *Stela at Copán*, 1841.
Engraving by A. L. Dick. From John Lloyd Stephens,
Incidents of Travel in Central America, Chiapas, and Yucatán.
By permission of the Houghton Library,
Harvard University.

culated as a historiographical theme. Stephens frequently used light as a metaphor for historical knowledge, discussing a "ray" or "beam" picking a picture from the surrounding historical obscurity. As in many of Catherwood's 1844 lithographs, in which the light seems to have searched out the historical monuments from beyond or before the picture plane (see fig. 50), Stephens implies that historiographical perspicacity is not available locally. It is efficient, deictic, and discriminating, and must be manufactured by the historicizing eye of the modern traveler.[7]

Industry and Idleness

Stephens and Catherwood develop the theme of visual/ historical manufacture as an explicit counterpoint not only to the indifference of the jungle, but also to what they construct as the indifference of the Yucatecans themselves. According to Stephens, the historical obscurity of the ruins was compounded by the fact that the indigenous inhabitants of the area, although they seemed certain to be blood descendants of the ancient builders, had retained virtually no knowledge of their own history. Nor did they seem interested in attaining that knowledge; in his narrative Stephens often seems less amazed at the monuments themselves than at what he calls "the ignorance, carelessness, and indifference" of the inhabitants toward the monuments. As Catherwood wrote in 1844, "Unfortunately for the antiquarian [the Indians] are totally without historic traditions, nor is their curiosity excited by the presence of the monuments amongst which they live."[8]

Catherwood's visual representations of the "Indians" only reinforced this impression of indigenous indifference. Even when the ruins he depicts stand outside the thick jungles of Copán or Palenque, the framing function of historical obscurity remains active in the image, borne by the indigenous figures themselves. In his illustration of the partially cleared exterior of the Casa de las Monjas at Uxmal (fig. 51), for example, the Indians demonstrate their historical incapacity by ignoring the newly cleared monument behind them. Pinned to the proscenium, they and their glances are indifferent to the background, as they seem uninterested in the historical axis of their environment. Thus, even as they serve the role of archaeological staffage, they remain detached conceptually from the archaeology they frame. Catherwood associ-

ates them with only the space (and, it is implied, the
order) of the vegetation which provides a foil to the
historical buildings. The woman at the left seems to
have sprung intact from the maguey plant at her feet,
while the akimbo limbs of the reclining man at right
mimic the fleshy sprawl of the adjacent cactus. As
autochthonous figures, acting almost as after-images of
erstwhile underbrush, they are identified less with
the historic architecture than with the tenseless vegetation that had, until recently, obscured it.[9]

In the course of his narratives Stephens associates indigenous historical indifference with a more
generalized lack of industriousness — a lack which then
functions throughout the narrative as a foil to Stephens
and Catherwood's vigorous habits of modern historical inquiry. In the following outburst of managerial
exasperation, Stephens bemoans the indigenous

laborers' reluctance to clear vegetation from the monuments at Copán: "The Indians, as in the days when
the Spaniards discovered them, applied to work without ardour, carried it on with little activity, and, like
children, were easily diverted from it. One hacked into
a tree, and, when tired, which happened very soon,
sat down to rest, and another relieved him. While one
worked there were always several looking on. I remem-
bered the ring of the woodman's axe in the forests
at home, and wished for a few long-sided Green
Mountain boys."[10]

This lack of "ardour" signals for Stephens the
historical failure of Mesoamerican civilization; it is a
spent civilization, one so lethargic that it cannot muster
the energy to overcome its terminal state of slothful
equilibrium. In the United States the sin of sloth had
lost most of its theological connotations by the late

eighteenth and early nineteenth centuries and had come instead to be classified as a sin against the national economy and against the linear, uniform, unidirectional kind of time upon which that economy relied. Stephens's various descriptions of indigenous acedia do indeed suggest that the people of Central America and Yucatán inhabit a different sort of time: lazy, circular, and stagnant. Throughout the narrative, many of the scenes and "incidents" Stephens chooses to relate are thinly disguised allegories for this unproductive inertia; he clearly believes that the Yucatecans' siesta-bound culture precludes any possibility of their further participation in the "onward impulse"[11] of history: "Moving on to the high stone structure forming the platform of the well, I saw a little boy, dressed in a straw hat, dozing on an old horse, which was creeping round with the well-beam, drawing in broken buckets a slow stream of water, for which no one came. At sight of me he rose from the neck of his horse, and tried to stop him, but the old animal seemed so used to going round that he could not stop, and the little fellow looked as if he expected to be going till some one came to take him off."[12] That "some one" is of course Stephens, the Yankee whose attempt to reconstruct a historical narrative from the ruins will provide the only linear motion to counter the ramshackle inefficiency of the circular local currents.

This temporal disjunction between Stephens's productive historical time and the Indians' timelessness has been shown to be typical of anthropological narrative. Anthropologist Johannes Fabian, who calls this strategy the "denial of coevalness," has discussed it at length in his indispensable critique of the uses of time in anthropological discourse. Although I am focusing here on Stephens's representation of indigenous culture, it should be noted that Stephens also "denies coevalness" to the Americans of Spanish extraction whom he finds in the Yucatán. He represents even the highest social castes as stunted dead ends of modern European progress, as if they were preserved specimens of Old Europe, trapped in the amber of Central American ahistory: "The countries in America subject to the Spanish dominion have felt less sensibly, perhaps, than any others in the world, the onward impulse of the last two centuries, and in them many usages and customs derived from Europe, there long since fallen into oblivion, are still in full force."[13]

For Stephens and Catherwood, then, both vision and historical awareness require a commitment to progress and industry. Stephens's narrative and Catherwood's illustrations dramatize a difficult genesis, a rending open of the claustrophilic, primordial jungle into a Western space where figure and ground, fore and aft, present and past, can be rationally plotted within a spatial and temporal continuum. The viewer's line of sight in these drawings follows a channel of visual and historical power, recalling in many respects Michel Foucault's "sovereign gaze." But it differs from Foucault's model in one crucial aspect: whereas one characteristic of the "Eye of Power," especially as it has been discussed in relation to American art of this period, is that it operates inconspicuously, smoothing over the power relations inherent in representation by naturalizing the representational apparatus itself, Stephens and Catherwood seem preoccupied with emphasizing the frictional energy of this intersection. Art historian Kenneth John Myers has argued that, by 1840, the picturesque mode of seeing in the United States (which had begun as a set of exclusively upperclass British conventions) had been thoroughly naturalized, and that American viewers in general were able to "forget the labor of admiring" a landscape. But in Yucatán and Central America, it seems, there is a lag—the labor of admiring is not forgotten but rather obsessively revisited, as if, in the contact zone, the picturesque had to be reinvented. Stephens and Catherwood emphasize, rather than mask, the labors of installing modern vision and modern history in an obscuring, indifferent environment.[14]

Other Operations

During a portion of their expeditions, Stephens and Catherwood were accompanied by a third traveler— Dr. Samuel Cabot, a Boston surgeon and ornithologist. Cabot had come along primarily to collect zoological specimens, but while the group was waiting in Mérida for supplies he offered to bestow his surgical services on the people of the town. He particularly wanted to try out a new surgical procedure that he had recently learned for the ocular affliction strabismus. In strabismus, also known as "lazy eye," defects in the muscles surrounding one or both eyeballs cause the eye to roll off center, preventing the proper functioning of binocular vision. People with this condition experience an unresolved visual field, making it difficult to focus and to perceive depth.

The surgery required that Stephens and Catherwood assist by pinning the squirming patients' heads to the operating table and spreading their eyelids apart while Cabot made precise incisions in the offending muscles (Stephens never mentions any form of anaesthetic) (fig. 52). Recounting the surgeries, Stephens can hardly contain himself over the intrinsic violence of this ostensibly charitable enterprise. He describes the operations in lurid detail over several pages and finally proclaims that his head was "swimming with visions of bleeding and mutilated eyes."[15]

Although strabismus was also common in the United States, Stephens's narrative has the effect of associating the disorder with the Yucatecans. This is partially because Stephens notes what seemed to be a higher than usual incidence among them: in Mérida "there seemed to be more squinting eyes, or biscos, as they are called, than are usually seen in any one town." More importantly, however, the etiology of strabismus as discussed in contemporaneous medical treatises featured traits and behaviors that Stephens had already pejoratively attached to the Yucatecans. For example, strabismus was strongly associated with mental incapacity because of the "dulness of look" it produced and the fact that it was often a symptom of neurological diseases and other "cerebral irritations." It also suggested infantilism (its onset is nearly always in childhood) and lassitude (it was believed that the wandering eye could often be controlled by a well-disciplined patient willing to make the effort toward "proper practice and education").[16]

It may seem curious that the inability to orchestrate one's eyeballs into position for binocular vision could have been interpreted as immaturity or laziness, but it was during precisely this period that binocular vision was first fully understood as the brain's active resolution of the images it receives from the two separate eyes. This had important implications for the prevailing model of vision, which would now be understood not as the passive reception of a preconstituted image, but instead as the ability to actively construct a coherent scene from a raw field of divergent visual data. Art historian Jonathan Crary has shown that this new model of vision was part of a broader "mapping of the eye as a productive territory" in the early nine-

52

Nathaniel Currier, *Untitled* (illustration of surgery for strabismus), 1841. Tinted lithograph. From Alfred C. Post, *Observations on the Cure of Strabismus*. Courtesy of the Library of Congress.

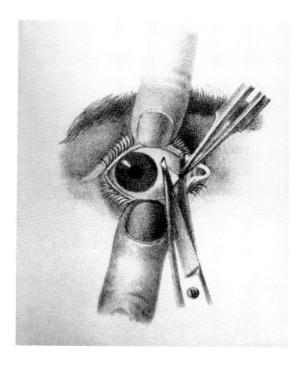

teenth century, and he argues that as vision (along with other physiological processes) was absorbed within metaphors governed by the emergent paradigm of factory production, binocularity itself became equated with a kind of industriousness. As he notes in his discussion of the stereoscope: "The apparently passive observer . . . by virtue of specific physiological capacities, was in fact made into a producer of forms of verisimilitude. . . . The content of the [stereoscopic] images is far less important than the inexhaustible routine of moving from one card to the next and producing the same effect, repeatedly, mechanically." Although Crary's hints of drudgery here give binocularity the taint of factory labor, one should also consider the managerial connotations of the process—after all, binocular vision involves the coordination and control of two potentially "lazy" eyes.[17]

Consequently, when associated with an indigenous population and implicitly opposed to civilized, industrious vision, strabismus could be made to signify not merely a visual disorder but also a cultural one — a culture unable to break out of an indolent parallax and perform the perspective functions of modern industrial civilization. And given the pervasive equation of vision with historical knowledge throughout Stephens's narrative, strabismus also signals a historical disorder — a culture unable to manufacture the necessary perspective to differentiate its foreground from its background, its present from its past. Within Stephens's narrative, strabismus neatly reinforces, at the level of the body itself, the Yucatecans' indifference. Into his lengthy, sanguinary account of the strabismus operations Stephens seems to have displaced all of the latent violence of the archaeological operation ahead, with its aims to overcome the local historical myopia by slicing through all obstacles to visual and historical perspective.

Historical Prospecting

Most of the meager literature on Stephens takes a brighter view of his attitudes toward indigenous culture in Yucatán and Central America. This is because Stephens was the first to argue that the Mesoamerican ruins had been erected by Native Americans, ancestors of those he found when he arrived. The nearly universal assumption at the time was that structures of such caliber could only have been conceived extrahemispherically, by a lost tribe from the Old World (favorite candidates included Egyptians and Israelites) or from a lost continent such as Atlantis. But Stephens's magnanimous attribution must be qualified by the lengths to which, as I have shown, he and Catherwood went to demonstrate that the nineteenth-century Maya did not inherit the historical mantle of their ancestors. According to these travelers, the antiquarian ineptitude of the Maya effectively disqualifies them from any claim to their own history — an abdication which then renders it conveniently available to the United States, whose modern, disciplined intellects become the worthy heirs of this American heritage and the rightful directors of any project designed to illuminate it.[18]

Stephens has also been praised for his enlightened views on race. According to critic and historian Van Wyck Brooks, Stephens saw the deplorable condition of the contemporary Maya as "wholly the result of circumstances, for he did not believe in the existence of inferior races." Stephens did frequently interpret the indigenous conditions in historical, rather than essentialist, terms, largely because he could rightly attribute the Mesoamerican denouement to the atrocities and "monkish fanaticism" of the Spanish. As he put it, "With the arrival of the Spaniards the sceptre of the Indians departed." He did not, then, imagine the historical indifference that he found in Yucatán as a state of primordial savagery, nor did he see it as an innocent Arcadia. Rather, to choose a canvas from Thomas Cole's series *Course of Empire* (with which Stephens would certainly have been familiar; it was exhibited in New York three years before he left for Central America), the Indians inhabit a state of Desolation (fig. 53), their course of empire exhausted, their history, indeed, their very awareness of history, extinguished.[19]

By placing the nineteenth-century Maya within the historical frame of the Desolate, Stephens was able to recognize the operations of a certain historical causality without going so far as to imagine that history, which had once disenfranchised the Maya, might be equally capable of reempowering them. In this regard he drew upon the historical philosophy of American exceptionalism — an attitude shared by many of his contemporaries in the United States. The view held that, while all other prosperous empires had suffered declines and falls, subject to the law of the circular "Course of Empire," the United States would enjoy a forever progressive course. Art historian Angela Miller has concisely described this belief as a "historical double standard," since it allowed the United States to benefit from the fall of other empires while reserving for itself a historical immunity. In this case, the double standard leads Stephens to see the decline of the Maya as inevitable and inarguable, their heritage useful only inasmuch as it will bolster the progress of its permanent new curator. Stephens's assessment of the Maya renders them eligible for the "salvage paradigm" of archaeological science, by which historically successful nations aim to rescue golden age artifacts from cultures that have degenerated beyond the capacity to care for them.[20] Thus, even as Stephens constructs himself as the agent of history's return to the area, he need not accept any responsibility for its permanent reinstallation. At no point are the Maya to regain

53
Thomas Cole, *The Course of Empire: Desolation*, c. 1836.
Oil on canvas, 39 $^1/_4$ x 63 $^1/_4$ in. (99.7 x 160.7 cm).
Collection of the New-York Historical Society.

command over their heritage; Stephens's aim is the extraction of historical artifacts and their relocation to the United States, the new Pan-American historical epicenter. Consider his gleeful description (under the subheading "An Operation in Prospect") of his plans "to buy Copán! remove the monuments of a by-gone people from the desolate region in which they were buried, set them up in the 'great commercial emporium,' and found an institution to be the nucleus of a great national museum of American Antiquities!"[21] Although Stephens takes great pains to distinguish his archaeological explorations from the earlier pillagings of the Spanish, through his antiquarian's eye the Maya are conquered again.

One might wonder why, given what he believed to be the essential enervation of the Maya, Stephens felt it necessary to take the trouble to reconquer the Maya at all. Why the emphasis on the heroic exertion of vision and historiography? Why the hurry to establish a managerial mandate over the ruins? Why the rush to appropriate artifacts? Stephens's emphatic attitude here reveals a specific condition determining the United States' assimilation of Mesoamerican history in the early 1840s. The United States' claim to that history needed to be established not so much over the Maya (too indifferent to be of concern), nor even the Spanish Americans (whom Stephens represents throughout the narrative as emasculated, bumbling, imperial has-beens), but rather over other European nations that might attempt to arrogate this newly discovered history to their own pedigrees and collections. Given this threat, and given that their expedition occurs in the wake of the Monroe Doctrine, Stephens and Catherwood's Herculean labors of vision/history function almost like homesteading claims. Simply to have viewed this landscape, to have organized this indifferent field along Western lines of visual and scientific perspective, to have "laid it open" to "rays of historical light," is to have cultivated it. In recording one of his bedtime ruminations Stephens narrates: "Other ruins might be discovered even more interesting and more accessible. Very soon their existence would become known and their value appreciated, and the friends of science and the arts in Europe would get possession of them. They belonged of right to us, and, though we did not know how soon we might be kicked out ourselves, I resolved that ours they should be; with

visions of glory and indistinct fancies of receiving the thanks of the corporation flitting before my eyes, I drew my blanket around me, and fell asleep."[22]

1969: A Series of Standstills

Stephens extracted hundreds of artifacts from the Maya sites, returning to New York with sculptural and architectural remnants that were to form the core collection of his Museum of American Antiquities. But his museum was never built; tragically, he installed the artifacts in Catherwood's new panorama building downtown, only to see the structure and all of its contents destroyed by fire a few weeks later. The only comfort in this incalculable misfortune was the fact that a few large stone pieces had yet to arrive by steamer and thus escaped the conflagration. Stephens gave these to his friend John Church Cruger, who proceeded to install them on his private island in the Hudson River among faux-gothic ruins that he had constructed in emulation of a Thomas Cole painting. Here the artifacts remained for some eighty years, until 1919, when the American Museum of Natural History in New York learned of their existence and acquired them from one of Cruger's octogenarian daughters. The museum prominently displayed them in the collections of Mexican and Central American antiquities (fig. 54), and it was there in the 1940s that the young Smithson would first have seen them on one of his many boyhood visits to what was (and would continue to be) his favorite museum.[23]

Smithson, accompanied by his wife, Nancy Holt, and his friend (and dealer) Virginia Dwan, embarked on his own Yucatán expedition in April of 1969. As the title of his own expedition narrative suggests, Smithson knew of Stephens's work. He had a Dover paperback edition of the *Incidents* in his small collection of books on Mexico and the Maya, and he also had a copy of Catherwood's frontispiece to the 1843 edition. It is unclear exactly how closely Smithson read Stephens's narrative, but just as the title of his essay announces that his expedition will involve "mirror-travel" to Stephens's "travel," Smithson's work on the peninsula constitutes an extended reflection on Stephens's brand of nineteenth-century archaeological exploration.[24]

In nearly every respect, Smithson's work in Yucatán can be interpreted as an inversion or undoing of Stephens's operations. In language reminiscent

Installation of "Stephens Stones," American Museum
of Natural History, c. 1965.

of his crystalline neutralization of motion in Passaic,
Smithson begins his travelogue by challenging the
paradigms of narrative and progress that had defined
Stephens's entire enterprise. While driving south from
Mérida in his rental car, Smithson muses that "one
is always crossing the horizon, yet it always remains
distant. . . . The distance seem[s] to put restrictions
on all forward movement, thus bringing the car to a
countless series of standstills." Whereas for Stephens
the hard-fought view into depth had anchored the
coherent perspectival organization of space and time,
assuring its visual, physical, and historical travers-
ability, here it ensnares the traveler in an impassable
network of infinite distances.[25]

   During the expedition, these "standstills" took
the form of temporary sculptural installations that
Smithson arranged at various sites, photographed,
and then dismantled. The best known of these are the
"mirror displacements," which both illustrate and

55
Robert Smithson setting up
Yucatan Mirror Displacement #1, 1969.
Photo by Nancy Holt.

56
Robert Smithson, *Yucatan Mirror Displacement #1*, 1969.
Chromogenic-development slide.
Solomon R. Guggenheim Museum, New York.

structure his written article (each mirror displacement becomes a subheading within the text). For the
displacements, Smithson installed the same group
of twelve-inch-square mirrors at nine different sites
throughout the region, arranging the mirrors in
roughly parallel arrays, either balanced among tree
limbs or cantilevered into the soil (figs. 55, 56). Although
my focus is primarily on the displacements, Smithson's work in the area also included an *Upside-Down
Tree* at Yaxchilan, a series of *Overturned Rocks* at
Palenque and Uxmal, a group of root and rock constructions near Palenque, the *Hypothetical Continent of
Gondwanaland* at Uxmal, and a set of slides shot at the
Hotel Palenque, which Smithson would present in
1972 as model of "anti-architecture" in a lecture at the
University of Utah (see fig. 62).[26]

Perhaps Smithson's most conspicuous inversion of Stephens's precedent is that none of the famous
Maya ruins appears in any of his photographs, even
though several of the installations were assembled
within eyeshot of the major archaeological sites. Dis-
persed and half-covered by sediment or branches,
the blocky mirrors do *suggest* the ruins, but their empty
reference to the desired historical spectacle proposes
a systematic erasure of Stephens's visionary enterprise
(fig. 57). This refusal to *see* the Maya ruins amounts
in many ways to their re-covering, to their removal
from the conditions of archaeology which, over the past
century and a half, had endorsed their use as imperialist trophies or their recontextualization as art objects.[27]

The Collapse of Vision

But Smithson's anti-archaeological tactics in this project
go beyond his simply *not picturing* the ruins. His use
of mirrors as a medium, especially when considered
in the context of the enantiomorphic rhetoric of his earlier work, signals a more systematic attempt to oppose
Stephens's visual imperialism. In his 1964 piece

Robert Smithson, *Yucatan Mirror Displacement #2*, 1969.
Chromogenic-development slide.
Solomon R. Guggenheim Museum, New York.

Enantiomorphic Chambers (see Chapter 2), Smithson developed a model of binocular vision that would structure his entire Yucatán project (see fig. 22). His 1967 essay "Pointless Vanishing Points" had described the piece as a sculptural deconstruction of binocular vision, as a stereoscope that thwarts, rather than facilitates, three-dimensional perception. The two steel chambers were meant to evoke eyes, and the "vanishing" of the viewer standing between them intended to suggest the evacuation of a centralized consciousness that might gather and coordinate the images in each of the chambers. The piece thus used mirroring, with its connotations of alignment failure, to call into question binocular vision, which relies upon precise stereo-optical coordination. The *Enantiomorphic Chambers* essentially synthesize crystallography with physiological optics, locating the enantiomorphic slippage or "vacancy" right between the eyes of the viewing subject. As Smithson explained, the sculpture would produce an experience of "infinite myopia" rather than vision in depth. "The two separate pictures that are usually placed in a stereoscope have been replaced by two separate mirrors in my *Enantiomorphic Chambers*—thus excluding any fused image." Smithson appealed here to the essential binarism of human vision to propose that there can be no such thing as an eidetic perception: "The binocular focus of our eyes converges on a single object and gives the illusion of oneness, so that we tend to forget the actual stereoscopic structure of our two eyes or what I will call 'enantiomorphic vision'—that is seeing double."[28]

Is this "seeing double" not an uncanny return to strabismus, a correction of Dr. Cabot's corrections, an anti-surgery that might restore what Stephens had described as the "crisscross expression" of the indigenous perspective? As Smithson asks in his Yucatán essay, "Why not reconstruct one's inability to see?"[29]

Indeed, at many points in the essay Smithson recounts this "inability to see," evoking the physiology of strabismus and other binocular disorders: "The eyes, being infected by all kinds of nameless tropisms, couldn't see straight. Vision sagged, caved in, and broke apart. . . . Squinting helped somewhat, yet that didn't keep views from tumbling over each other. . . . How could that section of visibility be put together again? Perhaps the eyes should have been screwed up into a sharper focus. But no, the focus was at times

cock-eyed, at times myopic, overexposed, or cracked." Smithson describes himself as a blinded traveler; inhabiting the overlapping, kaleidoscopic visual field of "lazy" eye, he cancels out Stephens's efforts to impose any kind of perspective upon the Yucatán Peninsula. He offers "a type of 'anti-vision' or 'negative seeing'" against Stephens's penetrating vision. Thus the Yucatán project shares many of the same antiperspectival aims of the Passaic project; but whereas in Passaic Smithson had critiqued perspective by fossilizing and multiplying it until both its clarity and its directionality were neutralized, here he destroys it from within.[30]

Art historians generally agree that Smithson's deconstruction of binocularity is one of his most influential and praiseworthy artistic innovations. Ann Reynolds has detailed Smithson's learned and withering critique of Clement Greenberg's then-hegemonic aesthetics, based as they were on an ideal of disembodied, pure "opticality" which Smithson exposed as a logical and corporeal impossibility. Gary Shapiro and Rosalind Krauss have demonstrated the deeper philosophical implications of this refutation of modernist opticality, equating Smithson's critique of the *video* (the seeing subject) with the philosophical project of interrogating the Cartesian *cogito* (the thinking subject). Krauss puts it concisely: with Smithson's deconstruction of binocular vision comes "the disappearance of the first person." This is certainly borne out in the above excerpt, in which Smithson positions him-"self" not as a unitary subject but rather as irretrievably bicameral; the subject of his sentences is not "I" but "the eyes."[31]

But Smithson's "negative seeing" requires that additional attention be paid to its inspirations and implications. Although the subversive intentions and the intellectual sophistication of Smithson's models of blindness cannot be dismissed, it is nonetheless important to recognize the primitivist underpinnings of his reversion to "lazy eyes," to scrutinize the image (I use the word *image* advisedly) of the Maya and of Mexico that this reversion encourages, and to explore the ways in which this image, deployed as it was in the late sixties, constitutes a specific political position.

Double Vision as Low-Level Perception

The Yucatán mirror displacements present two pictorial fields simultaneously: a view of the landscape at which the camera points, partially obscured *by* the mirrors, and another view (usually skyward), partially caught *on* the mirrors. Neither view is complete, nor can the two be consolidated into a unified spatial whole. The mirrors' reference to ruination (in their scattered, half-buried arrangement) thus extends to their effect upon the space around them—they act literally to decompose or to ruin the illusion of continuous space. Moreover, note that this decomposition is produced bilaterally. The mirrors do not aim randomly into haphazard corners of space—such a chaotic arrangement would actually act to draw the surrounding space into the installation, and, through that, implosion would paradoxically serve to affirm the centrality of the mirrors, their function as anchors. Rather what is striking about the mirrors is the care with which Smithson has installed them so that each face parallels the others. Thus the mirror displacements, rather than scattering the view into an infinite tangle, produce their decomposition by means of a binary overlap. As in double vision, the unitary visual field of perspective space splits apart, crosses over, and shallows out. It is as if space has been *infolded*, as if the two visual planes were collapsing around a single hinge.

Smithson's double vision suggests the eternal misalignment of the travelers' perceptions. He muses on this misalignment at length in the Yucatán essay, using it to call the entire travel narrative tradition—traveling, seeing, representing—into question: "Some 'enantiomorphic' travel through Villahermosa, Frontera, Ciudad del Carmen, past the Laguna de Terminos. Two asymmetrical trails that mirror each other could be called enantiomorphic after those two common enantiomorphs—the right and left hands. Eyes are enantiomorphs. Writing the reflection is supposed to match the physical reality, yet somehow the enantiomorphs don't quite fit together. The right hand is always at variance with the left." In the context of the expeditionary tradition, this amounts to a humble (and humbling) statement, one that approaches contemporary postcolonialism in its recognition of the recalcitrance of the colonized Other. Yet in another, deeply paradoxical sense, Smithson uses this misalignment as a tool of access, a way of allowing, rather than precluding, an understanding of (and immersion in) the primitive.[32]

To begin with, although his "enantiomorphic travel" seems to recognize the impossibility of

any fusion with the Other, Smithson describes that travel through the sculptural and verbal vocabularies of indolence and regression, thus reproducing for himself the same "indifferent" status that Stephens had originally predicated upon the Yucatecans. Smithson joins the Yucatecans in their primordial, indifferent, strabismic condition—that is, their perceptual insouciance. We might say that as Smithson travels his eyes fall out of alignment with each other and into alignment with nature. The eyes are relaxed, the ardor of binocular vision forsworn. Primordial visual perception, unburdened by binocular exertion, simply *mirrors* the environment around it: "Small bits of sediment dropped away from the sand flats into the river. Small bits of perception dropped away from the edges of eyesight. . . . Particles of matter slowly crumbled down the slope that held the mirrors. Tinges, stains, tints, and tones crumbled into the eyes."[33]

This rhetoric of visual passivity was part of Smithson's broader fascination with the theme of lethargy. In his writings Smithson speaks (with a thesaurus's compass) of listlessness, laziness, acedia, tedium, torpor, ennui, dissipation, fatigue, boredom, and stagnation. Although this interest in disinterest is perhaps most easily explained by his fascination with entropy and its accompanying cosmic exhaustion, Smithson also drew upon a broad spectrum of literary sources. These included the writings of T. E. Hulme, T. S. Eliot, and Wyndham Lewis, whose conservative disdain for modern busy-ness was an early influence on Smithson; Flaubert's novels, those "Epics of Immobility" which, through various means, produce the impression of narrative petrifaction; Borges's geometric narratives, which trap narrative progression in structural labyrinths; and the lyrical novels of André Gide and others whose passive protagonists, according to literary critic Ralph Freedman, resemble mirrors in that they substitute perception for action. Also especially important to Smithson were art theorist Anton Ehrenzweig's theories of low-level perception, Claude Lévi-Strauss's concept of the "cold society" (both of which will be discussed below), and, of course, the prevailing "aesthetic of indifference" of minimalism, pop, and conceptual art.[34]

Smithson often used the phrase "low-level scanning" to describe the perceptual insouciance here; in one interview, for example, he described his method of apprehending a site as "a kind of low-level scanning, almost unconscious." He borrowed the term "low-level scanning" from Ehrenzweig's 1967 book *The Hidden Order of Art*. Ehrenzweig, whose influence on Smithson's working method would be difficult to overstate, developed a psychology of artistic creativity that advocated the value of unconscious modes of vision and attention. Ehrenzweig describes low-level vision as syncretic, a form of vision that can ignore the distinctions between figure and ground by "hold[ing] them in a single unfocused glance" and that can apprehend a mass of concrete detail without consciously identifying it. He valorizes "the artist's vacant unfocused stare" (recalling as he does the strabismic "dulness of look"). Low-level vision operates beneath the conscious systems that differentiate incoherent aspects of vision: "Unconscious scanning—in contrast to conscious thought which needs closed gestalt patterns—can handle 'open' structures with blurred frontiers" (Smithson, for his part, referred to the various peripheries he visited as the "unfocused fringes").[35]

Ehrenzweig included this low-level syncretism within his broader concept of "dedifferentiation," which was another keyword that Smithson often deployed and which was perhaps the closest synonym to "indifference" in the sense that Smithson intended it. For Ehrenzweig, low-level vision uses low levels of energy; it is a simple "gathering," a purely receptive faculty, indifferently absorbing undifferentiated visual refuse. Smithson's enantiomorphic model of vision produces the same effect—without the viewer expending stereographic effort, the eyes remain disconnected receptacles: "The eyes became two wastebaskets filled with diverse colors, variegations, ashy hues, blotches and sunburned chromatics."[36]

Leaving Difference Alone

Smithson's mirror displacements recognize the essential difference at the heart of all cognition, all vision, all memory, but they leave that difference alone, in what we might call its primordial state, without attempting (as Stephens did) to refine, resolve, or process it into an illusion of perspectival space and linear historical time. Smithson's "Incidents of Mirror-Travel" attempt simply to perceive, to the extent that it is even possible, the collapse occasioned by what Jacques Derrida

called "incidences of primordial nonpresence."[37] The displacements are *relaxations* of vision and, thus, of landscape—they permit the landscape, still propped open, perhaps, by the work of modern vision, to fold back in upon itself, back to the indifferent overlap that Stephens had originally troped in his dramatization of indigenous strabismus. The enlightenment space that Stephens had cleared and held open with his stereoscopic exertions (fig. 58) is systematically collapsed by the strabismic interfolding of Smithson's mirror displacements (fig. 59).

Smithson's cultivation of low-level perception, along with his rhetorical breakdown of the boundaries between subject and nature, verges on nostalgia for a mythic state of noble savagery. But Smithson goes further than that, taking his regression back to a proto-human, not just a proto-civilized, condition. Two months before his Yucatán trip, he had said that an artist thinks "somewhat like a dog scanning over a site. You are sort of immersed in the site you are scanning." And, in an earlier draft of the Yucatán essay, "One must see the world through the eyes of small foraminifera, corals, brachiopods, molluscs, and crinoids." In the published version of the essay he evokes the compound eyes of insects, of which the fractured visual arrays of the mirror displacements seem a particularly appropriate illustration. Indeed, there is a section in the essay where Smithson recommends his work in the region as being especially suitable for the local fly population. Discussing his "upside-down tree" installations, he notes that "flies would come and go from all over . . . and peer at them with their compound eyes." *"Why should flies be without art?"* he asks.[38]

This attempt to reinhabit the visual apparatus of primordial creatures is an attempt to get as close as possible to a nature which, slouching as it is toward entropic heat death, is itself collapsing. Enantiomorphic vision, according to Smithson, mimics the essence of nature itself, and he was interested not in any "idealistic notion of perception" but rather in "zeroing in on those aspects of mental experience that somehow coincide with the physical world." For example, Smithson repeatedly describes the light in Yucatán as if it were itself indifferent, unwilling to gather itself into purposeful rays, overtaken by the forces of gravity: "The rays are shattered, broken bits of energy, no stronger than moonbeams." He speaks of the "load . . .

of perception" and notes that "in the jungle all light is paralyzed." In regard to this heavy or groggy light, the word "Incidents" in his title is significant. The English word *incident* derives from the Latin *incidere,* meaning to fall upon. The terms *incident light* and *incident ray* refer to light as it falls upon a surface, as opposed to light that emanates from or passes through it. Smithson was well aware of this etymology—he pointed out in an interview soon after his Yucatán trip that "incident itself means falling." Smithson's incident light is *fallen* light: "Reflections fall onto the mirrors without logic." And it is fallen in all its postlapsarian connotations—"If colors can be pure and innocent, can they not also be impure and guilty?"[39]

This concern with "impure" colors is part of an extended discourse on color in the essay and further emphasizes the exhaustion of the natural environment. Smithson describes the region as suffering under an excess of color, which, as he says, "is the diminution of light." Color for Smithson is light at a lower energy level, spent light, light wrecked into its prismatic elements and destined, like Humpty Dumpty (one of Smithson's favorite illustrations of entropy), to remain dismembered. Once fallen, once broken into color, it contributes to the general gravity of the area: "an excess of green sunk any upward movement" (fig. 60). "Refracting sparks of sunshine seemed smothered under the weight of clouded mixtures—yellow, green, blue, indigo and violet."[40]

Finally, a persistent trope throughout his discussion of color and light is infection: "light is suffering from a color-sickness"; "particles of color infected the molten reflections"; and "certain shades of green are carriers of chromatic fever." Indeed, the notion of contagion articulates Smithson's sense of perception quite nicely, suggesting the discomfiture which modern vision suffers upon exposure to the entropic environment. To see in Yucatán is to have one's modern perspective infected—"the eyes, being infected by all kinds of nameless tropisms, couldn't see straight." The mirror displacements themselves combine mirroring and minimalist seriality in such a way as to suggest infection or some other insidious form of reproduction —their clusters suggest patterns of viral or bacterial replication, and their splitting of the landscape view performs an ongoing perceptual mitosis. The traveler's perceptual apparatus, thus infected, is sapped of energy

and rendered incapable of operation. Here again we find Smithson both doing and undoing Stephens's work. He invokes the landscape's malarial reputation as if to restore the bouts of fever that had slowed, and eventually stopped, Stephens's progress through Central America, but in so doing perpetuates the image of the area as essentially dissolute.[41]

The collapse of the visual field in Yucatán is attended in Smithson's narrative by the collapse of the historical field. In a 1966 essay he had explained his preferred sense of time: "Its balance is fragile and precarious, and drained of all notions of energy, yet it has a primordial grandeur. It takes one's mind to the very origins of time—to the fundamental memory." This passage, with its fascination with "origins" and its evocation of a phenomenon "drained of all notions of energy," shares the same vocabulary that Smithson used to invoke an indifferent, primordial mode of vision.[42]

In accordance with this temporal energy drain, Smithson's mirror displacements function as models of passive memory. In a draft of the Yucatán essay, he wrote that "the color of past time is forever passing through the sky," and that "the sky reflected down its 'involuntary memory' in 12" squares of blue" (fig. 61). Smithson referred here to Marcel Proust, or rather to Samuel Beckett's book *Proust*, which he owned and annotated heavily. Beckett, in this early piece of criticism, discussed at length Proust's interest in "involuntary" memories (e.g., the madeleine episode of *Swann's Way*) as a gateway not to a past composed of rationally, actively constructed historical narratives but to the field of inattention, of everyday routines and situations, precisely those normally considered boring or unmemorable: the field, as Beckett wrote, of "dullness" and "habit." In acting as receptors for a Proustian species of involuntary memory, Smithson's mirror displacements equate memory not with history but with habit, not with energy but with ennui. They suggest a being-reminded-of instead of a compositional remembering (this is a distinction dating back to Aristotle). Smithson's mirrors catch light in an incidental fashion— because they are untrained and unfocused, light merely befalls them—and thus bring Stephens's light beam of history (still ricocheting, perhaps, through the air) down again to earthy tangles, dispersing it, displacing it, and draining it of both its directional force and its illuminating power.[43]

Frederick Catherwood, *Idol and Altar at Copán*, 1844.
Colored lithograph by W. Parrot, Plate V of *Views of Ancient
Monuments in Central America, Chiapas and Yucatán*.
Typ. 805.44.2624PF, Department of Printing and Graphic
Arts, Houghton Library, Harvard College Library.

Robert Smithson, *Yucatan Mirror Displacement #5*, 1969.
Chromogenic-development slide.
Solomon R. Guggenheim Museum, New York.

Robert Smithson, *Yucatan Mirror Displacement #4*, 1969.
Chromogenic-development slide.
Solomon R. Guggenheim Museum, New York.

The Crystallization of Difference:
Smithson and Lévi-Strauss

Unsupported by historical effort, the edifice of time in
Yucatán collapses, like the edifice of vision, into an
indifferent field of binocular overlap. The repeated "fold-
ings" allowed by each displacement produce a progressive invagination of the entire landscape or region.
Taken as a whole, the project creates a progression of
refractions (literally: *incidents*), a series of cleavages,
that structure the contraction of the landscape. With
the obliquity of primordial difference left to itself, the
landscape is not so much "viewed" or "pictured" but
rather is allowed to crystallize in its natural form.

What kind of history might exist in this landscape? Although resulting from what might be called
a natural process of primordial historicity and relying
upon distance, belation, and separation, it nevertheless recuperates, as a whole, a sense of eternity, immersion, and even presence. A similar concept of mirrored, crystalline time crops up in one of Smithson's
favorite novels: J. G. Ballard's *The Crystal World* (1966).
In a story that is particularly interesting for its parallels with Smithson's Yucatán project, Ballard imagines
a tropical forest in Africa that freezes into an inter-
locking, impassable tangle of delicate crystal forms. The
forms result from an apocalyptic process in which
time abandons its linear flow and locks itself into space,
"deliquescing" into mirrored spatial reverberations.
As one character marvels: "It's as if a sequence of displaced but identical images of the same object were
being produced by refraction through a prism, but with
the element of time replacing the role of light." Ballard's crystalline forest recalls Smithson's own Yucatán
vitrifications, not only in its intimations of doubling,
inertia, and collapse, but also in the suggestion that the
end state of time amounts to a return to a primordial
beginning: "This illuminated forest in some way reflects
an earlier period of our lives, perhaps an archaic
memory we are born with of some ancestral paradise
where the unity of time and space is the signature
of every leaf and flower."[44]

Smithson's most important source for his
conception of crystalline "archaic memory," however,
was anthropologist Claude Lévi-Strauss. Lévi-Strauss had
explained the ahistorical character of "savage" thought
by evoking an infolded structure. In one passage, the
last part of which Smithson carefully underlined in his

copy of the 1967 *Yale French Studies* special issue on structuralism, Lévi-Strauss compares primordial myth to music and shows how both are able to convert their inherent diachrony into an essentially synchronic structure. He may as well be describing Smithson's mirror displacements: "This relationship to time is of a very special nature: everything takes place as though music and mythology needed time only in order to deny its place. Both, in effect, are mechanisms designed to do away with time. . . . *The act of listening to the musical work has immobilized the passage of time because of the work's internal organization; like a cloth billowing in the wind, it has caught up and infolded it.*"[45]

Elsewhere Lévi-Strauss compares primitive logic to a kaleidoscope and writes that within the mind of the primitive "a multitude of images forms simultaneously, none exactly like any other, so that no single one furnishes more than a partial knowledge."[46] Smithson's Yucatán project clearly betrays Lévi-Strauss's influence; he makes the connection abundantly clear by using a long quote from *The Savage Mind* as one of the two epigraphs of "Incidents of Mirror-Travel in the Yucatan": "The characteristic feature of the savage mind is its timelessness; its object is to grasp the world as both a synchronic and a diachronic totality and the knowledge which it draws therefrom is like that afforded of a room by mirrors fixed on opposite walls, which reflect each other (as well as objects in the intervening space) although without being strictly parallel." Primitive temporality becomes a paragon of structuralist synchrony, trapping the flow of time within a crystalline play of mirrors in order to neutralize it and make it static.[47]

Lévi-Strauss's model of primitive timelessness also related to Smithson's interest in lethargy and indifference. According to Lévi-Strauss, modern, or "hot," societies, in order to maintain their progressive goals and their highly differentiated functions, expend energy quickly, whereas "cold," or primitive, societies attempt to maintain their social and economic structures in a state of equilibrium. Lévi-Strauss bases this binary model on a thermodynamic interpretation of society and culture:

In short, societies are rather like machines, and it is a well known fact that there are two main types of machine: mechanical machines and thermodynamic machines. The former are those which use the energy with which they were supplied at the outset and which, in theory, could go on operating indefinitely with this energy, provided they were very well constructed and were not subject to friction and heating. Thermodynamic machines, on the other hand, such as the steam-engine, operate on the basis of a difference in temperature between their component parts, between the boiler and the condenser; they can do a tremendous amount of work, far more than the others, but in the process they use up and destroy their energy.[48]

Smithson was greatly affected by this idea that different kinds of societies have fundamentally different relationships to energy, not least because of his career-long fascination with entropy. In a casual interview a few months after his trip to the peninsula, he was specific not only in his praise of *The Savage Mind* as a thermodynamic model of culture, but also in his preference for the "cold" approach.[49]

Lévi-Strauss argues, moreover, that the thermodynamic status of a given culture not only determines its economic and cultural life, but also predicts its attitudes toward history. History is a high-entropy endeavor: whereas cold societies attempt, "by the institutions they give themselves, to annul the possible effects of historical factors on their equilibrium and continuity in a quasi-automatic fashion," hot societies operate by "resolutely internalizing the historical process and making it the moving power of their development." In these passages (which Smithson underlined in his copy of *The Savage Mind*) is an echo of the distinction I have been making between Stephens's historiographic industry and Smithson's historiographic idleness. Historical indifference is passive, natural, "quasi-automatic," while historicism is literally a form of industriousness.[50]

Thus, in thermodynamic terms, history is a form of work which draws its energy from a differential established between past and present. And just as Smithson had theorized the differential operation of binocular vision as an anthropomorphic production disconnected from nature, Lévi-Strauss sees the differentiating exertions of modern historicism as a departure from the crystalline temporal unity with nature that primitives enjoy: "Primitives distrust history because they see in it the beginning of the separation, the beginning of the exile of man adrift in the cosmos."

Primitive societies, then, have never warmed up to historical difference: they remain static, "crystalline"; they "function at a temperature of absolute zero—not zero as understood by the physicist, but in the 'historical' sense." Smithson's attachment to the "cold society," exercised as it is in the Maya region, inspired as it is by Lévi-Strauss, shows how comfortably minimalism's "cool" sensibility and conceptual art's "aesthetic of indifference" could be aligned with structural anthropology's version of primitivism.[51]

Of course, Lévi-Strauss harbors no illusions of a truly present "Presence" of primitive timelessness. He recognizes that the savage mind is caught up in temporality. But he imagines that mind folding temporal difference in against itself, crystallizing difference into an armorial structure that remains inviolable to historical narrative. History is "annulled" in a "quasi-automatic" fashion. This is why, in his essay "Structure, Sign, and Play in the Discourse of the Human Sciences," Derrida argues that Lévi-Strauss's method "compels a neutralization of time and history" that amounts to the projection of a sort of secondhand eternity onto the culture under study. This is also the reason why Derrida suggests that, despite Lévi-Strauss's profound awareness of difference, "one no less perceives in his work a sort of ethic of presence, an ethic of nostalgia for origins, an ethic of archaic and natural innocence."[52]

One perceives something of the same ethic in Smithson's work. Smithson's Yucatán mirror displacements provide a certain low-level inoculation of difference, one which will crystallize and prevent the penetration of politics, historical narrative, and other contentious forms of modern differential behavior. He wrote in his "Ultramoderne" essay about the "invincible idleness" of primitive time: "The 'shape of time,' when it comes to the Ultramoderne, is circular and unending—a circle of circles that is made of 'linear incalculables' and 'interior distances.' All the arduous efforts of all the monumental ages are contained in the ultra-instants, the atemporal moments, or the cosmic seconds. This is a return to a primitive inertia or invincible idleness."[53]

Dehistoricizing the Maya: The Broader Context

It remains to be shown how Smithson's embrace of "primitive inertia" relied not just on a generalized 1960s primitivism but also on specific contemporary attitudes toward Mexico, Central America, and pre-Columbian civilization. In the United States in the late sixties, the prevailing view of Maya society was that it had been essentially prehistoric. On the first page of Victor W. Von Hagen's *World of the Maya* (which Smithson carried with him as he traveled through the area), we learn that the ancient Maya, despite their "glyph-writ system," were a "preliterate people." Mexican poet and essayist Octavio Paz stated in 1970 that "from the Mexican high plateau to the tropical lands of Central America, for more than two thousand years, various cultures and empires succeeded one another and none of them had historical consciousness. Meso-America did not have history but myths and, above all, rites."[54]

The ancient Maya were imagined as a prehistoric, mysterious, ritualistic cult, ineluctably estranged from European historical and philosophical systems. On one level, this estrangement of the Mesoamerican Other can be applauded—after all, it resists absorbing the ancient Maya (as Stephens did) into the analytical order of the Western historical lineage. But on another level, this very resistance had its own cultural, anthropological, and political functions, many of which served to fulfill various Western fantasies. During the sixties, the ignorance of Maya history allowed Maya culture to be used as a vessel for the Western cosmic, colonial, and eschatological imagination, especially for the futuristic projections of what writer Adam Gopnik has called "sci-fi primitivism." Spurred primarily by developments in structural anthropology, the late sixties saw a preoccupation with the alignment of the pre- and the posthistoric. Communications theorist Marshall McLuhan, who demonstrated a loose affiliation with Lévi-Strauss in his definition of primitive cultural media as "cool," predicted an impending "electronic retribalization" as technology returned society to a condition of spontaneity and wholeness: "The man of the tribal world led a complex, kaleidoscopic life. . . . The modes of life of nonliterate people were implicit, simultaneous, and discontinuous." The prehistoric was seen as a template for the posthistoric—the future was the obsolete in reverse. Smithson, of course, subscribed to a version of this pan-historic equation. The inevitable increase in entropy, after all, would lead to a universal sameness, a dedifferentiation, that would provide a mirror image of the original primordial unity. He equated primordial time with end time: "I am convinced that the future is lost somewhere in the dumps of the non-historical past."[55]

The prevailing conception of Maya temporality as tangled with time but impervious to historical narrative accorded well with Smithson's crystalline field of temporal indifference/dedifferentiation. In other ways as well, Smithson's Yucatán narrative was fully commensurate with the broader cultural project of dehistoricizing the Maya, for it repressed both the historical experience of the ancient Maya and the political existence of the contemporary Maya. Smithson evokes the Maya exclusively through mythology—perpetuating what philosopher of religion Mircea Eliade called "the corrosive action of mythicization" upon history. The ancient Maya appear in Smithson's text not as historical cultures but as muses; they arise only as gods, eternally haunting the peninsula, appearing unexpectedly in Smithson's rearview mirror or addressing him through the air conditioner of the rented Dodge Dart. This is not to say that Smithson uses the myths simplistically—on the contrary, as art historian Rebecca Butterfield has shown—but merely to point out that his project takes no interest in the Maya as historical actors.[56]

One might argue that at least Smithson respects the mythological integrity of the site. Unfortunately even that is compromised by the fact that most of the gods with speaking parts in the text are Aztec, not Maya. They dispense commentary and advice which often have nothing to do with Maya mythology—for example, Texcatlipoca (*Aztec* god of the smoking mirror) implores Smithson to "travel at random, like the first Mayans"—advice which derives not from any Maya codex but from the 1961 Michel Butor novel *Degrees*. Among the mirror displacements and other illustrations in Smithson's article, there is one photograph of a Mesoamerican artifact—but it is Olmec. Smithson's notion of Maya culture tends toward a hodgepodge of Mesoamerican primitivism.[57]

The "Invincible Idleness" of Mexico

In 1972 Smithson gave a slide lecture at the University of Utah about the Hotel Palenque (he had taken the slides during the 1969 expedition but did not include them in his "Incidents of Mirror-Travel" article). He equated the ramshackle contemporary hotel with the ancient ruins nearby (fig. 62):

My feeling is that this hotel is built with the same spirit that the Mayans built their temples. Many of the temples changed their facades continually: there are sort of facades overlapping facades, facades on facades. You know this window is actually looking out over the things that we went there to see but you won't see any of those temples in this lecture; that's something that you have to go there to see for yourself, and I hope that you go to the Hotel Palenque so that you learn something about how the Mayans are still building. The structure has all of the convolution and terror, in a sense, that you would find in a typical Mayan temple—especially of the Uxmal variety which is . . . called Mayan Baroque and made out of serpentine facades loaded with spirals and rocks carved in the shape of woven twigs and things; it's quite nice. So that to me this window, this seemingly useless window called forth all sorts of truths about the Mexican temperament.[58]

Advocating a processual architecture of ruin and renewal, of dysfunction and "de-architecturisation," Smithson's Palenque talk deserves a place among the seminal texts of early deconstruction. But what are the "truths about the Mexican temperament" that have inspired this radical revision of modern architectural theory? The truths are certainly not historical—Smithson's image of "facades overlapping facades, facades on facades" proposes, as do his mirror displacements, a jewellike ensnarement of history.

What is troublesome about these "truths," in fact, is that Smithson has rendered them eternal—exhibiting a textbook primitivism, Smithson folds all of Yucatecan history and politics into this homogeneous "convolution." Smithson makes no distinction between "the Mexican temperament" and the Mayan; the people of Mexico in 1969, despite centuries of conquest, revolution, and creolization, remain changeless icons of the mythological Maya. According to Smithson, the Hotel Palenque's (and the entire region's) "complete wreckage situation" derives from eternal natural laws, not from specific social or historical conditions: "One can't figure out why they put that door there but it seems to belong, it seems to have some incredible sort of Mayan necessity. It just grew up sort of like a tropical growth, a sort of Mexican geologic, man-made wonder."[59]

Since the cancellation of historical time is perhaps Smithson's primary concern in the Yucatán project, such eternalizing strategies are hardly surprising.

Yet given the political crises consuming the area in 1969, it is important to recognize the obstinacy of Smithson's evasion of history here. He could not have been unaware, for example, of the alarming rise in guerrilla and terrorist violence in Guatemala (more than a thousand murders between the summer of 1967 and the summer of 1968), or of the growing concerns in the American media about the failure of the U.S.-sponsored Alliance for Progress. Even the primordial junglescapes of the mirror displacements must have seemed synonymous with guerrilla warfare to a Vietnam-era artist.[60]

Violence does occasionally erupt into Smithson's essay, but only inasmuch as it is displaced, like the design logic of the Hotel Palenque, into a mythologized, primordial principle: "Through the windshield the road stabbed the horizon, causing it to bleed a sunny incandescence. One couldn't help feeling that this was a ride on a knife covered with solar blood. . . . Just sitting there brought one into the wound of a terrestrial victim. This peaceful war of the elements is ever present in Mexico—an echo, perhaps, of the Aztec and Mayan human sacrifices." Thus eternalized and mythologized, the political violence adopts the cloak of inevitability. Smithson's Yucatán becomes host to an enduring, primordial "war of the elements." Notions of political causality, historical change, or progressive activism become both futile and irrelevant in such territory. Smithson's treatment of the horizon theme is telling in this regard: the horizon functions as a symbol not of hope or anticipation but rather of apathy: "Driving away from Mérida down Highway 261 one becomes aware of the indifferent horizon. Quite apathetically it rests on the ground devouring everything that looks like something." There is no point in attempting progress. The Yucatán landscape will indifferently disperse every effort at visual, historical, and political resolution.[61]

Although Smithson's Yucatán project tends to express this political fatalism indirectly, particularly in the way it de-emphasizes the agency of the artist/traveler, it is not difficult to locate a similar tone in more manifestly political analyses of Central and Latin America at the time. A survey of discussions on the subject in Smithson's library, all of which stress the enormity of the social and political problems facing the region, reveals a palpable undercurrent of hopelessness.

62

Robert Smithson, *Hotel Palenque #7*, 1969. Chromogenic-development slide. Solomon R. Guggenheim Museum, New York.

Alternating between sympathy and condescension for the populations of the area, much of this literature views the violence, anarchy, and corruption in Central America as endemic and insurmountable. For example, just as Smithson had used the trope of infection to express the area's incurable toxicity, so too does political scientist Peter Nehemkis see its problems in epidemic terms: "For the truth of the matter is that Latin America is a sick society. It is sick politically. It is sick economically. It is sick spiritually. Each sickness feeds upon the others and the malaise is total." Where Smithson's mirror displacements scramble attempts at perspective vision, journalist Richard Gott writes that "nobody ever realistically opens much of a perspective for Latin America." Smithson essentially did not have to look far in Latin American political theory to find echoes of his own sense of entropic indifference: Latin American military regimes, according to Gott, "have a certain blandness," and even the currently peaceful regions can attain only "a depressing air of aimless stability." Nancy Holt has attested that Smithson considered the Latin American nations to be models of "entropic" government. And Smithson claims that this futility is naturally embodied in the attitude of the "natives," who acquiesce calmly to "the grand nullity of their own past attainments." Smithson constructs their soporific resignation as a model for his own attitudes—they are, after all, already prepared for the world's entropic endpoint.[62]

Smithson's fatalism here not only echoes contemporaneous political discussions about Latin America, it also accords with Smithson's own broader political philosophy. Informed by entropic theory and having found apparent confirmation in the global political crises of the late sixties, Smithson was, during this period, interpreting political events as part of the inevitably entropic tendency of all world systems. Thus, to the perpetual frustration of his more politically active colleagues, he eschewed political activism as counterproductive: "I think that if you strive towards some kind of ideal you'll inevitably end up in a terrible mess. And other messes will be developing right along. What I say is that all one can do, unfortunately, is perceive these messes as they take place."[63]

The pervasive passivism of Smithson's Yucatán project can, in fact, be read as a specific rebuttal to the political activism of many of his colleagues. The Art Workers' Coalition (AWC) held its first open hearing at the School of Visual Arts (three hundred New York artists attended) on April 10, 1969, just five days before Smithson left for Yucatán. According to art critic Lucy Lippard, Smithson was no friend of the coalition; she identified Smithson, Richard Serra, and Philip Leider as "notorious sightseers" of the AWC: "As long as they play with themselves in the bar, telling everyone how absurd or mismanaged the AWC is . . . they will be the bane and to some extent the downfall of the Coalition."[64]

Smithson's trip to Yucatán, then, occurred just as his carefully constructed philosophies of indifference were coming to loggerheads with the activist awakening of the New York art community. His dismissal of his colleagues' activism can be explained (if not excused) by noting that his stance was not exactly apathetic— passivity was a reasoned choice for him, the only response to contemporary politics which was consistent with his intellectual background. From Smithson's entropic perspective, struggles against political injustice would only waste energy and aggravate the situation. As he said in 1970, "One keeps dropping into a kind of political centrifugal force that throws the blood of atrocities onto those working for peace." It is interesting that he uses the image of the centrifuge here; it recalls his earlier illustration, in his "Monuments of Passaic" article, of the futility of attempting to overcome the forces of entropy (see Chapter 3): "Picture in your mind's eye [a] sand box divided in half with black sand on one side and white sand on the other. We take a child and have him run hundreds of times clockwise in the box until the sand gets mixed and begins to turn grey; after that we have him run anti-clockwise, but the result will not be a restoration of the original division but a greater degree of greyness and an increase of entropy." Political action amounts to little more than running around in circles; regardless of the direction, disorder can only be increased.[65]

Faced with this situation, Smithson felt that the task of the artist was to cultivate a thoroughgoing acedia: "The artist should be an actor who refuses to act." "Immobility and inertia are what many of the most gifted artists prefer." When asked in 1970 about his position regarding political action that should be taken by artists, Smithson answered, "My 'position' is one of sinking into an awareness of global squalor and futility." The quotes Smithson places around the word "position" are typical of his broader suspicion of linear perspective, of single "points of view." When pressed on his political positions, Smithson's usual tactic, at least in his published interviews, was to attack the notion of positionality itself. His position was, he said, "basically a pointless position. . . . I think the more points the better, you know, just an endless amount of points of view."[66]

Smithson's expedition to Yucatán can be understood as an exploration and performance of precisely this position. Seeking to sink into a form of perception that might coincide methodologically with the fatigue and dissolution (disillusion) of entropic futility, Smithson found a model in the landscape of Yucatán. "Incidents of Mirror-Travel in the Yucatan" functions as a primer of indifferent perception and of political passivity. The landscape and the population of Yucatán as Smithson and his contemporaries constructed them—inscrutable, irresolute, impassive—exemplify the "invincible idleness" that Smithson considered to be the only viable political strategy. Thus, for all his inversions of Stephens's narrative, Smithson perpetuates, even amplifies, Stephens's belief in Yucatecan amnesia, indifference, and myopia. Both Smithson and Stephens picture the Yucatán Peninsula as desolate in order to extract from it a heritage. For Stephens, the contemporary desolation of the Maya authorizes his appropriation of the region's archaeological artifacts. For Smithson, the desolation, now seen as eternal, is *itself* the artifact. It provides a primordial endorsement for passivity and a heritage, a "fundamental memory," of indifference.

SPIRAL JETTY / GOLDEN SPIKE

There were many photographs taken of the driving of the Golden Spike in 1869, but Andrew J. Russell's iconic *East & West Shaking Hands at Laying of Last Rail* (see fig. 3) is unquestionably the most famous. Among the reasons for this, I would suggest, is that the photograph's visual structure replicates precisely what is so satisfying about the form of historical thought that the spike-driving ceremony embodies. Compositionally, the image is strikingly simple: starting from the lower left corner of the photograph, one can trace a straight diagonal line along the shoes of the men standing in front of the engines, through the center of the chief construction engineers' handshake, and along toward the upper right corner of the image. The same line can be extended from lower right to upper left, resulting in a chiastic structure that has the effect of summoning all the hardscrabble particulars of the scene into a central point of juncture (an X, in other words, literally marks the spot). The crisp, triangular wedge of space that is thus created along the ground in the scene, with its equilateral sides recessing obediently toward the center of the image, appeals to the conventions of linear perspective. Indeed, the composition builds a perspectival redundancy into the image. The single-point perspective matrix of the photograph, already assured by the monocular technology of the camera, is reiterated by the figures, whose arrangement substantiates the enabling conditions of the image itself.

In 1869, the optical armature of Russell's photograph served to reinforce the message of the spike-driving ceremony at virtually every level. By gathering the visual space of the photograph into a single point, it helped to make the geopolitical operations at work in the Golden Spike ceremony—centering and consummating the American nation—seem as "natural" as vision itself. The driving of the last spike was a ceremony uniquely positioned to symbolize this kind of gathering. Coming after decades of rapid expansion and sec-

63
William T. Garrett Foundry, San Francisco,
after a description by David Hewes (1822–1915).
The Last Spike, 1869.
17 ^{6}/$_{10}$ carat gold, alloyed with copper,
5 ^{9}/$_{16}$ x ^{7}/$_{16}$ x ^{1}/$_{2}$ in. (14.1 x 1.1 x 1.3 cm).
Iris & B. Gerald Cantor Center for Visual Arts at
Stanford University, 1998.115. Gift of David Hewes.

tional conflict that had recently culminated in the Civil War, the wedding of the rails helped to provide a much-needed guarantee of the divinely sanctioned union of an unsettlingly centrifugal society. To quote the May 29, 1869, issue of *Harper's Weekly*, "This railway counteracts [any] natural tendency to disunion, [it] has prevented a separation and binds the States of the Atlantic and Pacific into one nation." The new railroad promised to bring these disparate regions, which could not easily be comprehended as a union, into an immediate relation. It served—literally, in Russell's case—to put Reconstruction-era America into perspective.[1]

The Golden Spike ceremony effected this "binding" not only visually but also temporally. The completion of the railroad soon led to the standardization of clock time across the country, as the need for consistent railroad schedules forced the elimination of discontinuous local time zones. More immediately, however, the ceremony promised—with the clang of a hammer—to gather the nation into a single point at a single moment. The rhetorical power of the ceremony depended largely upon its punctuality—upon the sense that the arduous, dangerous, and contentious process of building a transcontinental railroad (and, by extension, a national identity) could be compressed into a single moment. The ceremony purported to offer its spectators a moment in which the entire history of the nation could be effectively nailed down. Moreover, in this way the ceremony encouraged and prefigured its own historicization. For just as Russell's photograph helps to place its viewer, who "looks back" at the event, in a determinate and intelligible relationship to history (a perspectival relationship, with a predictable sense of scale, diminution, and hierarchy), so, too, did the driving of the Golden Spike stake out a precise point in the field of time around which historical perspectives might later be anchored. By transforming the transcontinental railroad from an exten-

sion to a point, from a process to a moment, both the photograph and the ceremony enacted what Heidegger called "the specific making present that makes measurement possible."[2]

The Golden Spike itself (fig. 63) serves as a marvelously overdetermined artifact of this operation, because it neatly hypostatizes this punctual model of presence and consummation in both its design and its function. Even its goldness is significant, for at root the temporal punctuation I have been discussing evokes a kind of historical alchemy. What is the Golden Spike if not a miraculous transmutation? In it, the raw time and matter that went into the construction of the transcontinental railroad, the grueling years of rail-hauling, spike-driving, and tunnel-blasting, are distilled into a gleaming immediacy.

No wonder that Smithson, who had spent his entire career interrogating "stigmatic vistas" like Russell's, built the *Spiral Jetty* next door to the Golden Spike National Historic Site. The introduction to this book established that the *Spiral Jetty* and the Golden Spike are geographically and experientially inseparable; as I've begun to suggest here, the two monuments are connected in many other ways as well. By the time he arrived in the Salt Lake area in 1970, Smithson had already spent years attempting to dismantle the visual-historical models that seem to be so perfectly embodied in the Golden Spike legend and its relics. In project after project he had discredited the punctual-perspectival production of history, whether by neutralizing perspective representation by subjecting it to infinite reification and accumulation, as in "The Monuments of Passaic," or by appealing to binocularity and enantiomorphism in order to dislocate its apparent unity, as in his Yucatán tour. When Smithson came to Utah he was well prepared to engage this landscape and the historical meanings that occupied it.

The Golden Spike Centennial, 1969

In the century following the completion of the railroad, most of the physical reminders of the Promontory area's frontier past had eroded or disappeared entirely. The entire 125-mile section of track that had stretched through Promontory around the north side of the Great Salt Lake was bypassed in 1904 by the Lucin Cutoff, a shorter, more level route stretching across the lake itself (see fig. 65). The site of the original rail junction was abandoned; not even a ghost town remained. The tracks that the Central and Union Pacific railroads had raced to build there in 1869 were ripped up and sold for scrap metal.[3]

Antiquarian interest in the site slowly began to increase in the mid-twentieth century, and the area was ultimately placed under the aegis of the National Park Service as a National Historic Site in 1965. A visitors' center was constructed and the road to the site was paved. In May of 1969, soon after Smithson returned from Yucatán and just ten months before he arrived in Utah to begin work on the *Spiral Jetty*, nearly thirty thousand people converged on the area to celebrate the centennial of the spike-driving ceremony. The highlight of the celebration was a scripted and costumed reenactment of the original ceremony, the authenticity of which the Centennial Celebration Commission took great pains to ensure. Exact replicas of the two original locomotives were displayed on a few hundred feet of track that was re-laid at the location of the original juncture. The original Golden Spike (see fig. 63), which had long resided at the Stanford University Museum, was shipped back to the site. Actors (many of them descendants of the original participants) dressed up in period costume and re-drove

the Last Spike at the precise time of day of the 1869 event (fig. 64). The Western Union telegraph message that had been sent in 1869 to President Ulysses Grant—"The transcontinental railroad is completed"—was repeated, also in telegraph form, now for the benefit of Richard Nixon, who was vacationing in Florida at the time. The reenactment was surrounded by months of symposia, banquets, dedications, exhibitions, and other fanfare. Dignitaries and celebrities, including Johnny Cash and John Wayne, attended the events (Wayne was on hand for the Golden Spike International Preview of his film *True Grit* in Salt Lake City).[4]

Also attending the ceremony, but in a considerably less celebratory mood, were small but vocal bands of protesters. Many were there to try to draw more attention to the immense contributions that Chinese laborers had made toward the Central Pacific's side of the railroad line. Others objected to the celebration of a railroad that had served as a genocidal vehicle for nineteenth-century Native American populations. The protesters seem to have had good reason for concern about the way that these other aspects of the transcontinental railroad had been erased from the historical narrative. The archives of the centennial celebration (still housed at the Golden Spike National Historic Site) reveal the extent to which the centennial reenacted not only the original spike-driving but also the entire ideology of nineteenth-century Anglo-American nationalism that originally produced it. Just as Russell's 1869 photograph had been carefully posed to exclude the hundreds of Chinese workers standing just outside its frame, so too did the 1969 celebrations tend to set the Chinese outside of the historical picture. At the reenactment ceremony, Secretary of Transportation John Volpe gave a speech that notoriously slighted the contribution of the Chinese laborers. Widely reported in the national press—for both its content and the protests it sparked—the speech asked, "Who else but Americans could drill ten tunnels in mountains 30 feet deep in snow? Who else but Americans could chisel through miles of solid granite? Who else but Americans could have laid ten miles of track in 12 hours?"[5]

Perhaps even more problematic than Volpe's outright omission of the Chinese workers was the discussion in the official centennial publication of

64

Centennial reenactment of the driving
of the Golden Spike, May 10, 1969.
Utah State Historical Society, Gift of the Utah Travel Council.

the local newspaper, which spoke of "little yellow men" who "trooped in from Sacramento in their blue blouses, and basket hats, pantaloons flapping in the breeze, carrying small outfits, and chattering like so many monkeys." This publication (of which Smithson had a copy) also discussed the frequent clashes of the Chinese with their "red-faced, blustering Irish bosses." Native Americans fared no better in the centennial rhetoric; an advertisement for the Golden Spike commemorative Winchester rifle, under the banner "The Railroad, the Sioux, and the Repeating Rifle," proposed that "two things kept the railroad moving: the Indians did not know how to rip up track—and the Winchester arrived. 15 shots per man."[6]

The ethnic mainstreaming of the reenactment celebrations was perhaps not surprising, given that the Spike's ritual act of punctual unification was enlisted to serve much the same purpose in 1969 as it did in 1869. Occurring as it did in the midst of widespread cultural upheaval and political instability, the centennial's patriotism and nostalgia for a unified, mainstream culture was all the more intense. The reenactment seemed to offer a chance to reexperience a mythical national unity, but what it truly reflected, in the collection of protests disrupting the celebration, was a deeply divided American society about to enter the summer of 1969. The standard questions that we would now ask of the original Golden Spike ceremony— including who and what were left out of it—were first being publicly raised at the 1969 centennial. This means that Smithson's *Spiral Jetty* took form in a doubly complicated historiographical space: it revisited a distant historical precedent at precisely the moment that its historiographical recuperation was becoming the subject of intense public debate. By inserting itself into a historiographical climate that was already destabilized and politicized, the *Jetty* could not help but join an active debate about history and its constitution. As Smithson knew, the *Jetty* would come to occupy not some mythic Western "wide open space" but rather a space that had already been shaped by a conspicuous historical event, the peculiar mechanics of its commemoration, and the politics of its continued historical construction.

The ambivalent imprint of those historiographical politics remains inscribed upon the *Jetty* itself. Smithson was very well aware of the Golden Spike—

and the Golden Spike centennial—as he planned and constructed the *Spiral Jetty*.[7] As mentioned in the introduction, the site Smithson chose for the *Jetty* was a short drive over dirt roads from what was then the new Golden Spike visitors' center (fig. 65). At the visitors' center Smithson would have seen, probably many times (along with the typical postcard racks and interpretive displays), an abbreviated reenactment of the "wedding of the rails." In this regularly and noisily staged event, still performed hourly today, the two replica engines leave their positions at the opposite ends of the short run of track, approach each other, and, with great fanfare and exhalations of steam, nudge noses before backing up to take their positions for the next show (fig. 66). Smithson mentioned the Golden Spike and the first transcontinental railroad explicitly in the essay he wrote about the *Jetty*. He had a copy of *The Story of the Wedding of the Rails*, the special publication that had been produced for the centennial by the Box Elder *News-Journal*, a local newspaper. While building the earthwork, he stayed in Brigham City at the Golden Spike Motel (which, according to Virginia Dwan, held endless fascination for him) (fig. 67). Even a year after the *Jetty* had been completed, he was still contemplating the relationship of the two monuments, drawing up preliminary plans for a museum about the *Spiral Jetty* to be built near the Golden Spike site (fig. 68).[8]

Modern Sculpture and the Alchemy of History

Although Smithson left no written record of his direct responses to the Golden Spike spectacle, the *Jetty* itself is an articulate partner in the cross-monumental dialogue going on in northern Utah. This is due largely to the vocabulary of time and work that both monuments share. Smithson brought with him from New York a set of concerns about labor and process that were entirely pertinent to the historiographical questions at hand in Utah. The Golden Spike model of punctual consummation, for example, was not peculiar to the world of Western railroading; Smithson had already wrestled with it back home, where something very much like it formed the aesthetic foundation of Clement Greenberg's art criticism. Smithson, who had been closely monitoring Greenberg's writing during the sixties, would surely have noted that the entire spike-driving spectacle eerily reproduced, almost to

65

Northern Great Salt Lake area, showing location of
Golden Spike National Historic Site and Spiral Jetty
(indicated with arrow).
(Below) area of detail.

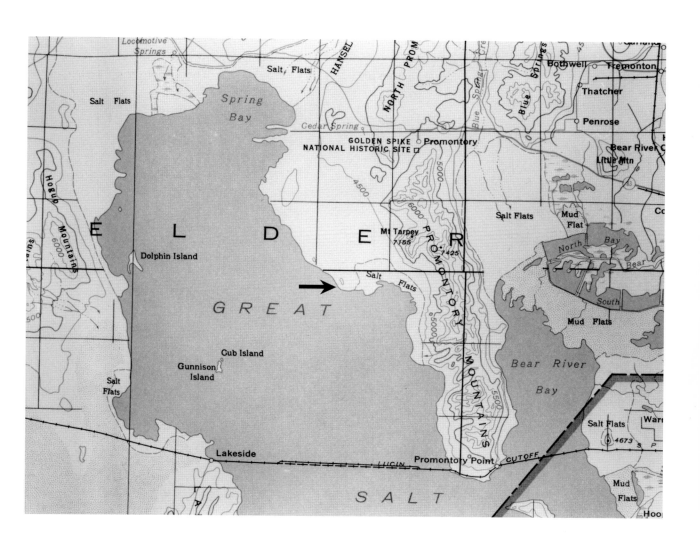

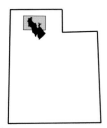

66

Replica engines used for hourly reenactments
of "The Wedding of the Rails," 1996.
Golden Spike National Historic Site, Promontory, Utah.
Photo by the author.

67

Advertisement for the Golden Spike Motel
from Smithson's copy of *The Story of the Wedding of the Rails*
(special Golden Spike Centennial issue of
the Box Elder *News-Journal*), 1969.
Robert Smithson and Nancy Holt papers, 1905–87,
Archives of American Art, Smithsonian Institution.

68

Robert Smithson, *Plan for Museum Concerning
Spiral Jetty near Golden Spike Monument*, 1971.
Pencil, 9 x 12 in. (22.9 x 30.5 cm).
Estate of Robert Smithson.

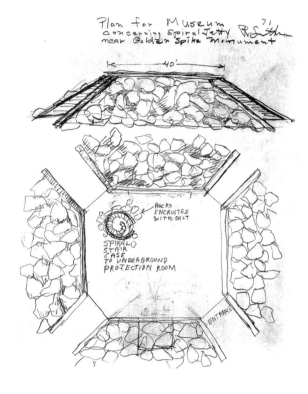

the letter, Greenberg's dictum that the viewer in front of a piece of modern art was to be "summoned and gathered into one point" by the work. The Golden Spike, by encapsulating Manifest Destiny in an instantaneous object, also paralleled Michael Fried's famous claim that modern art should be instantaneous and thus at every moment "wholly manifest." Indeed, the Golden Spike, if translated into the art-critical lexicon of Smithson's period, emerges as a passable prototype for a high-modern sculpture, a perfect embodiment of the kind of pseudo-instantaneous "portable abstraction" that Smithson was then working to defeat in his own work and writing.[9]

Similarly, although Smithson did not likely wish to express any specific opinions about nineteenth-century labor politics on the railroad, he did have opinions about twentieth-century labor practices in the art world that were entirely applicable to the situation in Utah. During the late sixties and early seventies, Smithson began to develop a critique of the operations of the art market based on its relationship to the artist's time. Smithson's understanding of time as a process of continuous material deposition meant that, for him, the work of art existed materially at every moment leading up to and following the point at which it would be traditionally seen as "completed." The art market, on the other hand, ignored all of the artist's time spent in the process of creation in order to fetishize the completed work of art, the "product."

In his 1968 essay "A Sedimentation of the Mind: Earth Projects," Smithson had argued that artists must resist the process of temporal commodification that results from this object-oriented view of art. Under the subheading "The Value of Time," Smithson argued for the equally positive value of *each moment* of the artistic process—a value that, if granted, would make it impossible to isolate the artistic process from the art object: "For too long the artist has been estranged from his own 'time.' Critics, by focusing on the 'art object,' deprive the artist of any existence in the world of both mind and matter. The mental process of the artist which takes place in time is disowned, so that a commodity value can be maintained by a system independent of the artist. Art, in this sense, is considered 'timeless' or a product of 'no time at all'; this becomes a convenient way to exploit the artist out of his rightful claim to his temporal processes. . . . Any critic who

devalues the *time* of the artist is the enemy of art and the artist. The stronger and clearer the artist's *view* of time the more he will resent any slander on this domain. . . . Artists with a weak view of time are easily deceived by this victimizing kind of criticism, and are seduced into some trivial history."[10]

The kind of absolute positivity of the temporality of production that Smithson endorsed would, he felt, thwart the commodification of art by denying special privileges to any moment falsely nominated as a completion or consummation. It would preclude the possibility of building an art history around isolated works of art, because it would make it impossible for critics to locate the significant points around which they would normally organize art-historical narratives. It would disallow the extraction of "finished" objects from the continuous raw history into which they are inalienably knitted. Smithson was essentially setting his theory of history as "spiral wreckage" against the standard art-historical trope of the "breakthrough," which carved artistic careers into long stretches of stagnant or unproductive time, punctuated by abrupt, spasmodic moments of creative consummation. Smithson encouraged artists to think of their work process as continuous and nonhierarchical—not, as Fried had described sculptor Anthony Caro's accomplishments, "a succession of climaxes."[11]

This positivity of process frustrates the operations of the art market because it does not permit the essentially alchemical procedure of allowing the history of a work to disappear in order to return, concentrated and transvalued, in an isolable material object. As a new temporal economy, Smithson's model resembles those developed in the twentieth century by many theorists of supplementarity, including Jean-François Lyotard's notion of the nonpropagative time of cinema, Georges Bataille's concept of expenditure, or Jacques Derrida's theory of time as a gift that permits of "no reciprocity, return, exchange, countergift, or debt."[12] The artist's time is not "spent" in the classical economic sense, not given up now in exchange for its transfigured restoration in the value-laden, climactic art object later. Rather it is simply "spent" in the sense of "exhausted," and it remains on the scene indefinitely. If what I have called the historical alchemy of the Golden Spike emerged from its fixation on the railroad's golden moment of completion rather than on the extended period of labor and process that preceded it, Smithson's entrance into Utah, his strong view of time in tow, was to offer an alternative.

For Smithson, the antidote to the kind of commodified "trivial history" set into play by the art object (or Golden Spike) is an insistence on the obduracy and persistence of each instant of the artist's (or railroad worker's) interaction with matter. Of course such an idea was not unique among New York artists of the seventies, who embraced process art and were becoming increasingly familiar with Marxist critiques of the art market. Smithson's arguments also recall conceptual art's emphasis on the value of the time spent thinking through the work prior to any physical production. But Smithson's "strong view of time" also had roots in his earlier engagement with the discourse of hyperspace (see Chapter 2). The work of art, when perceived according to the strong view, exists fully at each moment of its creation, stretching forward and backward in history as a four-dimensional object. A strong view of time reveals the full four-dimensional contour of the work of art, while a "weak view" sees only the three-dimensional object sold and exchanged among art collectors. These objects are merely fragments or cross-sections of the true "work," yet (and herein lies Smithson's main objection to Fried and Greenberg) they are treated by critics as if they were unified, transcendent wholes.[13]

The *Spiral Jetty* aims to occupy this strong view of time in several ways. It has often been noted that Smithson's earthwork resists formal closure because its size and physical imbrication in the site make it difficult to isolate as a bounded object (it is impossible to determine exactly where the Utah landscape ends and the *Jetty* begins). But the same can—and must—be said for its relationship to its historical margins. Smithson's treatment of history in the *Spiral Jetty* project ensures that the earthwork cannot be plucked out of its historical "continuance." The experience of visiting the *Jetty* makes this abundantly evident. As discussed in the introduction, travelers to the *Jetty* must first pass through the Golden Spike National Historic Site. Then, further along the way to the earthwork, visitors find the remains of a failed oil extraction operation from the 1930s (see fig. 4). These remains include the ruined foundation of a shack, a battered trailer, a holding tank, a truck, an amphibious vehicle, and a much larger

69
Abandoned oil tank and jetty near *Spiral Jetty*, 1996.
Photo by the author.

70
Abandoned truck near *Spiral Jetty*, 1996.
Photo by the author.

and more conventional straight jetty (figs. 69, 70). A high-altitude aerial survey photograph taken in 1993 clearly demonstrates the close relationship between the massive oil jetty (right) and the delicate *Spiral Jetty* (left) (fig. 71). Although these historical "distractions" are rarely discussed in the literature on the *Jetty*, they are, for visitors, as conspicuous as the *Spiral Jetty* itself (if not more so—especially during the periods when the *Jetty* is underwater). The oil operation's remains are inextricable from Smithson's *Jetty*, which arrogates the failed efforts of the oil field into its own four-dimensional contour, as Smithson notes: "Two dilapidated shacks looked over a tired group of oil rigs. A series of seeps of heavy black oil more like asphalt

71

Rozel Point showing *Spiral Jetty* (left)
and straight jetty from abandoned oil extraction
operation (center), June 26, 1993.
United States Geological Survey (USGS), National Aerial
Photography Program.

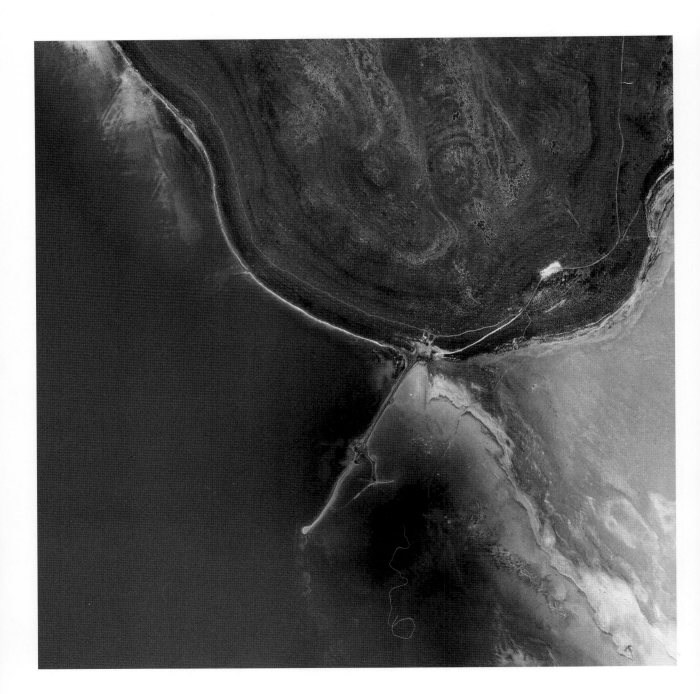

occur just south of Rozel Point. For forty or more years people have tried to get oil out of this natural tar pool. Pumps coated with black stickiness rusted in the corrosive salt air. . . . A great pleasure arose from seeing all those incoherent structures. This site gave evidence of a succession of man-made systems mired in abandoned hopes." All history, whether or not it ultimately contributed to something called "progress," becomes a part of the *Spiral Jetty*.[14]

Smithson's abundant documentation of the construction of the earthwork also provides a "strong view" of its history. The *Spiral Jetty* film documents (at sometimes tedious length) the process of construction, incorporating time spent scraping, loading, dumping, and moving rocks into position. These cinematic frames each correspond to an instant of the time spent in construction, and function as cellular deposits of the production time of the *Jetty*. In this sense they are analogous to the earthwork project itself; history dumps itself onto the film much as the rocks are dumped into the Great Salt Lake. Smithson's documentation also knits the construction of the *Spiral Jetty* into a kind of "continuance" with that of both the oil jetty and the transcontinental railroad. Many of Smithson's construction photographs, for example, allude to the "abandoned hopes" at the oil jetty by courting the possibility of failure. The truck in figure 72 leans precariously as it dumps its load of rocks, recalling Smithson's reference to the "tar pool" at the oil jetty and suggesting that Smithson's project, too, may end up "mired" (as Smithson knew, this was in fact a danger, for the salt flats forming the bottom of the lake at this point are fragile, and the weight of the trucks might easily have caused the lakebed to buckle). At the same time, the *Jetty*'s construction process—building a high embankment or bedding for a path to be traveled—refers directly to the process of railroad building (figs. 73, 74). In fact, the *Jetty* was built with the same machinery and techniques—and indeed, by some of the same men —as those used earlier in the twentieth century for the railroad causeways across the Great Salt Lake. Finally, Smithson projects the *Jetty* into its other temporal margin: the future. The *Spiral Jetty*'s history did not stop when Smithson sent the dump truck drivers home— rather, as Smithson knew it would, history continued to accumulate at the site in the form of the continuous deposition of salt crystals over the entire surface of

72

Robert Smithson, *Untitled* (Construction of *Spiral Jetty*), 1970. Contemporary print from Smithson's original negative. Robert Smithson and Nancy Holt papers, 1905–87, Archives of American Art, Smithsonian Institution.

the *Jetty*. Because the *Jetty* takes continual contributions from the lake itself, its work is never done.[15]

By appending Spiral to Spike, Smithson proposes an inclusionary brand of history, one based on extension rather than contraction, continuance rather than instantaneity. The *Spiral Jetty* promises to recuperate forgotten or marginalized histories and to fully incorporate all of the "mind and matter" that the Golden Spike can only attempt to summarize, in a distorted and fragmentary fashion, through its perspectival / historical representation. In the historiographical context of the Promontory area, Smithson's insistence on the accumulative positivity of the work that goes into constructing a work of art cannot help but take on a polemical role. We might say that the *Jetty* performs a centennial counter-reenactment here, reenacting not the timeless and universal product of labor, the Golden Spike, but rather that which the Golden Spike model of history must repress—the duration, extension, and materiality of that labor. The *Jetty* provides a form of rescue of the time that went into the railroad's construction, and thus poses a monumental rejoinder to the goings-

73

Spiral Jetty, 1970.
Photo by Gianfranco Gorgoni.
Estate of Robert Smithson.

Andrew J. Russell, *Granite Cañon, Black Hills*, 1869.
From Russell, *The Great West Illustrated*.
Yale Collection of Western Americana,
Beinecke Rare Book and Manuscript Library.

Spiral Jetty, 1970.
Photo by Gianfranco Gorgoni.
Estate of Robert Smithson.

on a few miles away at the Golden Spike National Historic Site. It functions as the Spike's supplement, as if the spiral, spreading out into the lake, were a plume made up of all the interstitial time that was being swept out of the way by the punctuated temporality at Promontory. The *Jetty*, with its relentless positivity of time, functions as a kind of waste of time — the Great Salt Lake becoming an enormous tailings pond for the historical effluent of official American frontier history.

An Ear to the Ground: The Resonance of History

By locking the *Jetty* so thoroughly into the past, present, and future of its site, Smithson knits all three monuments (Golden Spike, oil field, and the *Jetty* itself) together in a larger historical field. This, he hopes, will preclude the possibility of the excision and replacement of any one of them into some other "trivial history." Yet his precautionary measures go even further than this. For it is not only the outer margins of the *Jetty* that must be protected from the objectifications of the historian, it is also its inner margins. We can begin to address this inner form of historical resistance by examining Smithson's comparison of the *Spiral Jetty* to a "spiral ear": "[The *Jetty*] echoes and reflects Brancusi's sketch of Joyce as a "spiral ear" because it suggests both

a visual and an aural scale, in other words it indicates a sense of scale that resonates in the eye and the ear at the same time. Here is a reinforcement and prolongation of spirals that reverberates up and down space and time. So it is that one ceases to consider art in terms of an 'object.'" In this passage, Smithson mentions the *Jetty*'s evasion of object status and connects this to the operation of scale relationships and a thematics of aurality (the *Jetty* does indeed have a cochlear appearance, fig. 75). Smithson alludes to a portrait of James Joyce by sculptor Constantin Brancusi to epitomize this cathexis of themes (the portrait is a simple spiral-shaped drawing), but I would like to begin this discussion of scale, aurality, and history by invoking another art-historical ear that haunts Smithson's project.[16]

Giovanni Morelli was a late nineteenth-century Italian writer who became famous for the forensic method of connoisseurship that he invented. Against prevailing models of authentication and attribution, he argued that only by closely examining certain incidental details of paintings can the true identity of their artists be determined. According to Morelli, it is in painting unimportant details like the earlobes and fingernails of figures, when they are not burdened by careful consciousness of tradition or of the grander themes of a painting, that artists reveal their personal idiosyncrasies and thus "give themselves away." Morelli's books were illustrated with drawings of ears supposedly corresponding to the unique styles of particular artists (fig. 76). For Morelli, these ears are the locus of the painter's true work, the seat of un- or pre-reflective, nonalienated art labor. Just there, hiding in the folds of paint building up the earlobe — the spontaneous presence of the artist. This form of connoisseurship, like others, confers value through instantaneity, but it does so by burrowing into the seemingly incidental details of the work, down at the very verge of its microscopic presence as matter.[17]

Smithson had in his library a well-thumbed essay about Morelli and his ears: Edgar Wind's "Critique of Connoisseurship." Published in 1965 in Wind's book *Art and Anarchy*, the essay attacked Morelli for his equation of spontaneity with value and his consequent devaluation of the artist's durational "labours of execution." Wind identified Morelli as a key progenitor of the "romantic cult of the spasm" that had gone on to define modern art history; this was because Morelli equated the artist's true presence with the instanta-neous fullness of an unreflective moment. Wind's cri-tique of Morelli is interesting in this context because it so closely parallels Smithson's own critique of the alchemy of art history, which confers all its value on an isolated moment of consummation. Smithson, like Wind, deplored the tendency of modern critics to define the work of art around an instantaneous moment; this moment or "spasm" could be too conve-niently cleaved from its durational context and rein-serted into a historical narrative of the critic's choosing. No wonder, then, that Smithson decided to refer to Joyce rather than to Morelli when broaching the sub-ject of ears. Even so, it is useful to keep Morelli in mind, for Smithson's "spiral ear" presents us with so perfect a frustration of Morelli's model that it seems to have been designed specifically to thwart the Morel-lian art-historical approach.[18]

Morelli's model of criticism, although all ears, ultimately defeats the acoustic possibilities of art history. Smithson's *Spiral Jetty* project, on the other hand, attempts to define an aural historiography. Hearing is a form of sensual apprehension more complex and slippery than the Cartesian possession traditionally ascribed to vision. To listen for something, we might say, is never quite to find it. Its specific location cannot be pinpointed because it is perpetually complicated by resonances that pull it into other registers or scales. This sensual slippage makes hearing ill-suited for any forensic or evidentiary paradigm like Morelli's. Smith-son, however, defines the *Spiral Jetty* as an aural work, and by doing so helps to immunize it against connois-seurship. The "Spiral Jetty" essay, for example, sets names into resonance in order to retract the possibility of deriving from them a stable historical attribution. Smithson's essay is flagrantly "incidental," full of all sorts of seemingly unimportant historical details. Smithson devotes several pages to documenting his rambles around the lake while looking for a site, listing the local people he met and often mentioning various inci-dents in their tales of life growing up around the lake. But these nominalist details prove unstable; they have a fantastical or eerily coincidental aspect about them that suggests a historical echo. This is especially true of proper names: he cites a writer named "William Rudolph," who turns out to be the author of a quote about red salt lakes (*Rudolph*, of course, coming from

Lionardo.

the same root as "red"). John Silver, Smithson points out, lives on Silver Sands Beach. Another local character is, incredibly, named "Mark Crystal." These incidental proper names, which in the Morellian universe would constitute stable attributions, slip uneasily into other scales, registers, and histories. Smithson rejects the spontaneous presence of any historical detail, insisting that it remain connected through resonance to a larger historical structure.[19]

Smithson mentioned in his essay that the *Spiral Jetty* resonates in the eye and the ear at once. And indeed, in the process of visually representing the work, Smithson creates the same slippage or demateral-ization of the concrete detail. The most popular image of the *Spiral Jetty* is the aerial photograph taken by Gianfranco Gorgoni (under Smithson's direction) in 1970 (fig. 77). This image quickly became, and remains, iconic. Smithson reproduced this and eight other photographs in his "Spiral Jetty" essay, which was first published in 1972 in a volume of writings edited by Gyorgy Kepes.[20] When the essay was originally published, Smithson guided the reader through a set of nine photographs of the *Jetty* that proceeded in a telescopic progression, each successive image closing the distance to the *Jetty*, each a closer "detail," each representing a closer looking (or, perhaps, listening) in. Although the photographs were published out of order in posthumous reprintings of the essay, in the original publication Smithson carefully sequenced and captioned the photographs so that they proceeded as follows:

First, the aerial view (see fig. 77), encompassing the landscape and the entire earthwork as it springs out from the shore, balloons toward the picture plane, and then curls back inward toward the center of the piece. Next the viewpoint swings around in a counterclockwise direction and begins to close in on the *Jetty* (fig. 78). Through a series of further rotations, with the viewpoint of the photographs dropping ever closer to the ground plane (fig. 79), the specific materiality of the *Jetty* begins to assert itself at the expense of its more abstract identity as a spiral form. The final image is an extreme close-up view of salt crystals (fig. 80). This is where Smithson's sequence of photographs stops—the *Spiral Jetty* is at the limits of the Morellian microscope. We can imagine that if the photographer came any closer either the image would fall out of focus or the camera lens would scrape up against the salt. The double-counterclockwise rotation (once through the air and once along the surface of the *Jetty*) set up by the sequence seems to have reached its forensic endpoint; it has stopped, braked by the chaotic tangle of forms. Having taken an almost Icarian fall from the general to the particular, we seem to have gone as low as we can go.

Smithson's sequence of photographs seems to follow a Morellian progression. Peering into the "spiral ear," ever closer, Smithson presents us at last with a detail that stops or grounds our search. But, just as Wind's critique of forensic connoisseurship destabilized Morelli's telltale detail, so must this journey down the material labyrinth of Smithson's aural scale ring hollow. For if we look more closely at the salt crystals in Smithson's final "detail" (see fig. 80), we find that they, too, carry echoes. Consider the following statement that Smithson made about salt crystals in the "Spiral Jetty" essay: "Each cubic salt crystal echoes the Spiral Jetty in terms of the crystal's molecular lattice. Growth in a crystal advances around a dislocation point, in the manner of a screw." Smithson's claim about the molecular structure of salt, which demonstrates that he is still fully engaged with the spiral-dislocation model of crystal deposition discussed in Chapter 2, suggests

that his photographic series might as well have continued down below the current detail. Something like the electron micrograph that we have already seen in figure 18, in fact, would occupy the next position in the photographic sequence, showing us the *Jetty* at the next order of magnification (fig. 81).[21]

This extension of the sequence accomplished, we find that we have fallen through the detail only to reencounter an aerial view. The salt crystal—on the one hand an index of specificity and certainty, is actually being ghosted by its own abstract diagram. At the level of the detail, perhaps the last frontier of instantaneous presence, the *Jetty* slips back into an aerial detachment. The very notion of the resistant material detail (as that which differs from, and thus grounds, or resists, the overview) becomes inoperable. Smithson actually says as much when he claims that the *Jetty* retains the same spiral form regardless of the position from which it is viewed: "The Spiral Jetty could be considered one layer within the spiraling crystal lattice, magnified trillions of times. . . . Here is a reinforcement and prolongation of spirals that reverberates up and down space and time." This is why it is significant that Smithson's final detail (see fig. 80) shows salt crystals deposited on a tumbleweed (and not, as one might expect, simply a closer view of the crystals on the rocks of the *Spiral Jetty*). The tumbleweed helps to reinforce the suggestion of "a prolongation of spirals," because, were it set in motion, the salt crystals clinging to it would be propelled along a spiral path. The tumbleweed (which Smithson was careful to identify in his caption) helps destabilize the center of the spiral by suggesting that the viewer can "tumble" further into the work.[22]

This instability applies at the aerial, or "upper," end of the photographic series as well. Consider the hills behind the *Jetty* in figure 77; they align in such a way that the far band (the Promontory Range) reaches around behind the near band (Rozel Point). Within the context of the other photographs, in which the spiral arms of the *Jetty* often appear as recessing horizons (see fig. 79), these overlapping bands of mountains separated by water strongly suggest the arms of some even larger spiral, one that is itself presumably embraced by another, and so on.

Smithson even extends this spiraling to the process of representing the *Jetty*: "For my film (a film is

Spiral Jetty, 1970.
Photo by Gianfranco Gorgoni.
Estate of Robert Smithson.

a spiral made up of frames) I would have myself filmed
from a helicopter (from the Greek *helix, helikos* meaning
spiral)." If the spiral form lurks in the broader landscape, the form of the piece as a whole, and in the structure of the salt molecules that encrust it, then the spiral
extends all the way down and all the way up the scale
of scale. Translated into temporal terms: the salt-crystal
detail cannot provide us with a single "instant" that
might consummate the work, because it, too, participates in the spiraling continuity of the *Spiral Jetty* and,
indeed, of the entire span of history itself. To look at a
"detail" of the *Spiral Jetty* is to peer into an abyss or
maelstrom of scale which, in its own helical trajectory,

Spiral Jetty, 1970.
Photo by Gianfranco Gorgoni.
Estate of Robert Smithson.

Spiral Jetty, 1970.
Photo by Gianfranco Gorgoni.
Estate of Robert Smithson.

Spiral Jetty, 1970.
Photo by Gianfranco Gorgoni.
Estate of Robert Smithson.

I. M. Dawson, electron micrographs (detail).
Reproduced in Charles William Bunn,
Crystals: Their Role in Nature and Science, 1964.

reiterates the form of the detail itself: "All is out of proportion. Scale inflates or deflates into uneasy dimensions. We wander between the towering and the bottomless. We are lost between the abyss within us and the boundless horizons outside us." Gary Shapiro has demonstrated that there is a "persistent direction in [Smithson's] work that leads from vertical structures to horizontal ones, in which a spiral is squashed or projected onto a plane." I would merely add that Smithson's constantly slipping sense of scale, one that incorporates both "the towering and the bottomless," allows him to inject his squashed spiral with a profound sense of verticality.[23]

From Gold to Salt: Historical Flavor

The salt crystal, then, serves as the ultimate key to Smithson's crtitique of the Golden Spike. It frustrates all those, from Morelli to Greenberg, who would seek to apply the historical Midas Touch to an isolable moment. As a substance invested with aural resonance (and, of course, with taste), it serves as the chemical basis of a critical synaesthesia that dismantles the optical fixations of the art market and of traditional historical thought. Indeed, the salt along the *Jetty* was central for Smithson from the beginning. The "Spiral Jetty" essay treats salt as the motivating concern for the entire project—its first paragraph is devoted to an uncharacteristically prosaic discussion of Smithson's search for an appropriate salt lake in which to produce the earthwork. He sketched out other salt works throughout this period, with titles like *Island of Salt Crystals in Red Water*. In his *Plan for Museum Concerning Spiral Jetty* (see fig. 68) he specifies that the rocks surrounding the spiral staircase be encrusted with salt. And the *Spiral Jetty* itself serves, if nothing else, as a saltworks. The sheltering arms of the spiral increase the concentration of brine in the water, allowing for a higher rate of crystal deposition. The color of the water within the coils of the *Jetty* is usually a darker red than the water surrounding the piece, which signals the increased rate of precipitation of salt.

With Smithson's intervention at the Great Salt Lake, salt replaces gold as the essential substance of history. It perfectly embodies, in its crystalline structure, Smithson's model of time as a depositional "continuance." And it is not only an abstraction but also an enaction of Smithson's additive model of history at the site. Salt—that is to say, history—accumulates along the rocks, materially embodying the *Spiral Jetty*'s durational extension. The crystals function as a continually revised appendix to Smithson's work, holding it in a perpetual condition of delay. For this reason, salt is the primary agent preventing the *Spiral Jetty* from attaining the state of completion that the Golden Spike represents. (It also corrosively precludes the *Jetty*'s conservation as an art object—as any sculpture conservator will attest, salts are the primary threat to the integrity of a stone artwork.) If gold embodies pure historical value, concentrated and distilled, salt participates in an entropic and supplemental historical economy: to "salt" the earth is to make barren or useless, just as to "salt" an account is to give artificial or excessive value to the items therein. Salt, like Smithson's history, is an additive.[24]

And yet, as I have already suggested, the very salt crystals that embody the principle of historical excess and remainder, the very salt crystals that function as a kind of radical materialist additive, also arrange for their own transcendence. As Smithson's telescoping/ microscoping series of photographs of the *Jetty* demonstrate, salt serves as the agent of vertical scaling in the piece, investing it with a profound unity across all magnifications. A bit of wordplay on the term "scale" itself helps to clarify Smithson's understanding of this paradoxical power of salt to serve as both a horizontal and a vertical agent. On the one hand, the salt assures that the *Spiral Jetty* is "covered with scale"—in the sense that "scale" is a noun referring to a crust, scab, or shell surrounding an object, but at the same time it functions as a principle of vertical motion or connection, as in the verb "to scale" (a mountain, a staircase, etc.). The idea of scale, as Smithson uses it, acknowledges excess, remainder, and supplement while also incorporating them within a larger vertical movement of transcendence. This play on scale accords with Smithson's own penchant for wordplay, which has its own saltiness—indeed, to "salt" a narrative is (in one now obsolete usage) to lend it a taste of piquant wit. Smithson's scaling has the power, ultimately, to dematerialize the material without ever denying it its essential materiality. The salt is base matter, to be sure, but in the *Spiral Jetty* it attains what Smithson called in another context "a transcendental state of matter."[25]

The *Spiral Jetty* functions as a structure that brings particulars under the aegis of a new kind of totalizing pattern, one that manifests itself not across the usual Euclidean space but rather across scale. There is a technical term for this operation—*recursive symmetry*. The concept did not become widely circulated until after 1975—when fractals first became popular—but Smithson had clearly developed his own version of it in 1970. Throughout this period, scientists and mathematicians were beginning to model recursive symmetries for the first time; perhaps the most familiar results of their efforts are fractal graphics, which display self-similarity across infinite magnifications. I do not wish to make too much of this comparison, but it is worth pointing out that Smithson spent the late sixties and early seventies engaging in many of the same pursuits that proto-chaos-theorists were also following: exploring complex, turbulent, or entropic systems and finding ways to conceptualize them within fields of endeavor that traditionally valued order. In fact, Smithson's work of the early seventies could provide a virtual prospectus of the kind of phenomena that Benoit Mandelbrot and others were beginning to describe for the first time: non-laminar flows (see fig. 47), irregular basin boundaries (*Broken Circle*, 1970, Emmen, Holland), and stochastic phenomena of all kinds. While Smithson's work has traditionally been understood as opposing order through disorder, Smithson seems ultimately to have been interested in finding a new kind of order within disorder. As cultural theorist N. Katherine Hayles has argued, "Chaos theory does not undermine an omniscient view. Rather, it extends it beyond where even Newtonian mechanics could reach." This recursive symmetry is significant because it signals a form of completion and wholeness that cannot be attained in the everyday historical world of the Golden Spike. In his career-long engagement with mirroring and bilateral symmetry (see Chapter 2), Smithson coded it as a sign of the inevitable fragmentation of time in the limited world of historical perception. Here, at the *Spiral Jetty*, the salt allows a glimpse of a new, eternal symmetry that might finally heal the asymmetries of human history. A salt is, by definition, a substance created out of this kind of stabilizing resolution. Produced by the reaction of an acid and a base, salts form a stable union of a positive and a negative ion. The two chemical components of common salt, sodium and

chlorine, are violently reactive alone, but achieve an immutable permanence in salt. Salt embodies the impulse of matter to achieve an inert configuration, its energies in a state of equilibrium.[26]

Derrida has spoken about the concept of "seasoning," arguing that it operates within the realm of sublimation and dialectics. He points out that the French term *relever* can be translated as "to redeem," "to preserve," and "to season"—one adds seasoning to a food in order to change it but also to heighten the food's original flavor, to give it, as Derrida says, *"still more of its own taste."*[27] The salt acts to "season" the *Spiral Jetty*. It is an additive, supplementing the *Jetty* with concrete "historical flavor" but at the same time a preservative, maintaining its internal impulse toward a larger spiral resonance. Seasoning both negates and preserves (hence sublimates, in Hegel's formulation) the original object. This is the role of salt in the *Spiral Jetty* and historicity in Smithson's work as a whole.

Smithson was discussing his work explicitly as a form of dialectical resolution during these years. In a 1970 interview on his current work, he claimed that "all of the things internally have that aspect, they are all involved with the unification of the duplicity, the dual aspect is reconciled within the pieces, and reflects a greater scale of the dialectic."[28] Drawing upon not only Lenin but also Nabokov and other writers, Smithson understood the spiral's association with dialectical synthesis. In one of his notebooks, as part of a list he compiled under the heading "A Metamorphosis of the Spiral," he transcribed the following quote from Nabokov's *Speak, Memory: A Memoir*. "If we consider the simplest spiral, three stages may [be] distinguished in it, corresponding to those of the triad. We can call 'thetic' the small curve or arc that initiates the convolution centrally; 'antithetic' the larger arc that faces the first in the process of continuing it; and 'synthetic' the still ampler arc that continues the second while following the first along the outer side."[29]

If the *Spiral Jetty* can be said to operate within the realm of Hegelian dialectics, it can also be understood within the category of the aesthetic. Smithson's salt crystals, for example, approach the aesthetic category of the "concrete universal," inasmuch as they manage to solve the classical aesthetic problem of representing a whole without distorting the particulars of which it is composed. To borrow a phrase from literary critic Terry Eagleton's *Ideology of the Aesthetic*, we might say that the *Spiral Jetty* "represents on the one hand a liberatory concern with concrete particularity, and on the other hand a specious form of universalism." To suggest that Smithson's project operates in the realm of classical aesthetics is to counter, or at least revise, the many claims that have been made for its participation in a postmodern "anti-aesthetic." Art historian Hal Foster, in the introduction to the famous collection of essays by that same name, defines as anti-aesthetic art that resists "the idea that . . . art can now effect a world at once (inter)subjective, concrete and universal—a symbolic totality." But by this definition Smithson's work, with its concern for commensurate parts and wholes, seems resolutely *aesthetic*. The *Spiral Jetty*, in its reconciliation of general and particular, fulfills what Eagleton calls "the mystery of the aesthetic object," meaning that "each of its sensuous parts, while appearing wholly autonomous, incarnates the 'law' of the totality." We have, at the *Spiral Jetty*, the world in a grain of salt.[30]

Smithson's aesthetics of history have specific implications for its stance toward its monumental neighbor, the Golden Spike. The *Jetty*, with its emphasis on extension, duration, labor, and materiality, offers up a history of the transcontinental railroad that is more sympathetic to Chinese workers than to robber barons. Yet Smithson's historical intervention in Utah is more complicated than a transfer of historical ownership from one group to another. Indeed, by setting its own matter into such profound historical resonance, the *Spiral Jetty* prevents any group from seizing or claiming history. The *Jetty* lifts history into scales beyond the reach of historical narrative, insisting upon its material preservation of history but nevertheless refusing to allow it to be grasped. The *Jetty* is sympathetic to the claims of difference, specificity, materiality, and historicity that the protesters were making known at the centennial re-driving of the Golden Spike. But it does not propose to take this plenary field of work and time and make it grounds for some simply oppositional history. Although the *Jetty* is made entirely of material, peripheral details, it does not offer up those details as material for the construction of a new historical narrative. It offers no isolable points, parts, or products that can be selected for progressive narrative construction of a traditional ("trivial") history. Rather the *Spiral Jetty* pre-

serves peripheral histories by pulling them out of range of history itself. It redeems lost histories by incorporating them into the crystalline fractal of universal time, where they may resonate but do not, precisely, reside.

Conclusion: History from the Maelstrom

Scholars have often noted that the *Spiral Jetty* alludes obliquely to a Native American legend about cosmic whirlpools inhabiting the Great Salt Lake.[31] I would suggest, however, that a whirlpool legend of more immediate relevance to Smithson's project is Edgar Allan Poe's short story "A Descent into the Maelström." Smithson knew this text well and occasionally cited it in his writings.[32] The tale describes the "prodigious suction" of an abyssal whirlpool off the coast of Norway; it captures a man and his fishing boat, sending them spiraling down the vertical walls of an immeasurable funnel. The man survives the experience, which was, he attests, terrifying enough "to change these hairs from jetty black to white," and he relates his observations:

Looking about me upon the wide waste of liquid ebony on which we were thus borne, I perceived that our boat was not the only object in the embrace of the whirl. Both above and below us were visible fragments of vessels, large masses of building-timber and trunks of trees, with many smaller articles, such as pieces of house furniture, broken boxes, barrels and staves. . . . I now began to watch, with a strange interest, the numerous things that floated in our company. . . . "This fir-tree," I found myself at one time saying, "will certainly be the next thing that takes the awful plunge and disappears,"—and then I was disappointed to find that the wreck of a Dutch merchant ship overtook it and went down before.[33]

The presence in the whirlpool of the Dutch merchant ship (in Poe's Knickerbocker New York a structure with unmistakable connotations of pastness) suggests that the fluid dynamics of the descent into the maelstrom have distinctly historical connotations—or, rather, ahistorical ones, for the maelstrom functions to confound historical time. The old man's watch stops at precisely the moment that his boat begins slipping into the currents of the whirlpool. And the confusion of objects within the funnel suggests a breakdown of stable periodization. The Dutch ship coincides improbably with the narrator's boat. Poe also seems careful to provide what we might call a thermodynamic coding of the whirlpool's other objects, which range from raw materials to spent wreckage (the above quote lumps together various entropic stages of wood, from tree trunks to lumber to furniture to "broken boxes"). The shifting velocities and overlapping trajectories of this flotsam suggest a massive historical blender, in which the material evidence of history is swept inexorably into the immeasurable depths, becoming completely absorbed by the maelstrom.

The *Spiral Jetty* opens a similar historical abyss in the Great Salt Lake. In its pretensions to plenary historicism it performs its own "prodigious suction," drawing into itself all historical matter within its expansive horizon. And the recursive symmetries under which it organizes that matter send historical practice into a vortical tailspin. Stable points of reference (like the Golden Spike) are unfixed. Historical matter, unfettered from its evidentiary connection to particular events and formations, glides along its helical trajectory into a transcendent unity.

The ultimate question that we are forced to ask, then, is whether history can—or should—be performed upon the *Spiral Jetty* itself. Has Smithson, in pulling the bottom out from under history, produced a work that renders its own historicization impossible? Trapped (in Smithson's words) "between the towering and the bottomless," the historian seems thwarted in her attempts to locate secure events or objects from which to construct her "trivial histories." Indeed the position of the historian vis-à-vis the *Spiral Jetty* is as precarious as that of Poe's boatman vis-à-vis the maelstrom itself.

And yet Poe's tale does not entirely preclude history; indeed, a certain form of history is the condition of possibility of the tale itself. As a narrative, the tale requires that the narrator survive his descent into the maelstrom and report back upon his observations. "I alone am escaped to tell thee"—this biblical trope of a narrative snatched from oblivion animates many of Poe's stories. In "A Descent into the Maelström," it hinges on certain machinations of the narrator while trapped inside the whirlpool. He notices that objects of a certain shape (cylindrical, in this case) seem to be moving more slowly down the walls of the whirlpool: "A cylinder, swimming in [the] vortex, offered more resistance to its suction, and was drawn in with greater difficulty than any equally bulky body." By lashing him-self to a water-cask, the narrator is thus able to delay his descent long enough so that he rises again to the surface of the sea when the maelstrom subsides, and so he lives to describe the strange admixture of historical wreckage that he observed circling the mouth of eternity. In Poe's story, then, the possibility of history depends on the selection of the proper vehicle—one designed to accommodate the vortical slippage of its environment even as it resists its ultimate pull.

In this book I have likewise designed (or borrowed) critical-historical vehicles that both acknowledge and resist the eternalizing pull of Smithson's abyssal productions. The aim has been to navigate the perpetual slippage of history that Smithson's work suggests without slipping out of history altogether. For as much as Smithson's work may desire to attain the entropic transcendence of the historical flotsam from which it is built, the specific shapes and traces of history yet remain inscribed within it. Smithson's crystalline centrifuges—whether the churning sandbox in the Passaic essay (see Chapter 3), the "political whirlpool" of the Yucatán project (see Chapter 4), or the *Jetty* itself—ingest historical matter and send it spiraling toward its entropic end. But until that distant day when the final crystallization of history actually does occur (if, indeed, it is to occur), tales can still be spun out of Smithson's maelstroms. The historical matter on the verge of disappearing into the *Spiral Jetty* must ultimately be thrown back on the shores of the historical world. There, reconfigured by its trip into Smithson's vortical symmetries, it offers up new ways of telling the histories that Smithson's work engages.

Smithson, in the last analysis, recognized this. There is a famous scene in the *Spiral Jetty* film in which the artist, viewed from a helicopter above, stumbles along the length of the *Jetty* until he reaches its inner endpoint. He stands at the edge for a few moments, hesitating over the water as if waiting to be taken up into the recursive spiral himself and to enter some final transcendent crystallization of time and matter. But then (this salty apotheosis not having occurred) he turns, in a gesture both tragic and funny, to walk slowly back out of the spiral toward the shore. It is at this moment of return that Smithson's work, like Poe's, renews the possibility and the necessity of history.

INTRODUCTION

1 For the *Spiral Jetty* project files see Robert Smithson and Nancy Holt papers, 1905–1987, Archives of American Art, Smithsonian Institution, Washington, D.C. (hereafter Smithson Papers). Smithson discussed Mono Lake in terms of both Twain and tufa in an interview with Dennis Wheeler in 1969. See "Four Conversations Between Dennis Wheeler and Robert Smithson," in Jack Flam, ed., *Robert Smithson: The Collected Writings* (Berkeley: University of California Press, 1996), 222 (hereafter *Writings*). Smithson mentions Poe in "A Sedimentation of the Mind: Earth Projects," in *Writings*, 108. For the terms *open space* and *general conceptual matter* as they have been applied to Smithson's work, see Henry Sayre, "Open Space: Landscape and the Postmodern Sublime," in *Object of Performance: The American Avant-Garde Since 1970* (Chicago: University of Chicago Press, 1989); Mark Rosenthal, "Some Attitudes of Earth Art: From Competition to Adoration," in *Art in the Land: A Critical Anthology of Environmental Art*, ed. Alan Sonfist (New York: Dutton, 1983), 62.

2 Smithson, "Some Void Thoughts on Museums," in *Writings*, 41.

3 For semiotic interpretations of Smithson's work see especially Craig Owens, "Earthwords," in *Beyond Recognition: Representation, Power, and Culture* (Berkeley: University of California Press, 1992), 40–51 (see also note 7 below). For Smithson and the picturesque see Yve-Alain Bois, "A Picturesque Stroll Around *Clara-Clara*," trans. John Shepley, *October* 29 (Summer 1984): 32–62; Ron Graziani, "Robert Smithson's Picturable Situation: Blasted Landscapes from the 1960s," *Critical Inquiry* 20 (Spring 1994): 419–51.

4 I'm indebted here to Fredric Jameson's description of the contemporary view of diachrony: "So it is that depth forms (if any exist, like prehistoric monsters) tend to be projected up upon the surface in the anamorphic flatness of a scarcely recognizable afterimage, lighting up on the board in the form of a logical paradox or a textual paralogism." Jameson, "Antinomies of Postmodernity," in *The Jameson Reader* (London: Blackwell, 2000), 235.

5 Smithson, 1970 interview with Paul Toner, in *Writings*, 240–41. Smithson is likely referring here to George Kubler's argument that biographical art history makes it "easy to overlook the continuous nature of artistic traditions." See Kubler, *The Shape of Time: Remarks on the History of Things* (New Haven: Yale University Press, 1962), 6–7. Dominick La Capra, *Rethinking Intellectual History* (Ithaca: Cornell University Press, 1983), 32; the work of Michael Ann Holly, who speaks of the "past's role in the act of construction" of its own histories, is also relevant here. Michael Ann Holly, *Past Looking: Historical Imagination and the Rhetoric of the Image* (Ithaca: Cornell University Press, 1996), 14.

6 Fredric Jameson, *The Seeds of Time* (New York: Columbia University Press, 1994), xiv.

7 Some of the key texts that interpret Smithson's work as post- or anti-modernist include Craig Owens, "Earthwords," and "The Allegorical Impulse: Toward a Theory of Postmodernism," in *Beyond Recognition*, 40–51, 52–69; Rosalind Krauss, "The Double Negative: A New Syntax for Sculpture," in *Passages in Modern Sculpture* (New York: Viking, 1977); Ann M. Reynolds, "Robert Smithson: Learning from New Jersey and Elsewhere," Ph.D. diss., City University of New York, 1993 (published in 2003 by MIT Press); Caroline A. Jones, "Post-Studio/Postmodern: Robert Smithson and the Technological Sublime," in *The Machine in the Studio: Constructing the Postwar American Artist* (Chicago: University of Chicago Press, 1996), 268–343; Jessica Prinz, "Words *En Abime*: Smithson's Labyrinth of Signs," in *Art Discourse/Discourse in Art* (New Brunswick, N.J.: Rutgers University Press, 1991), 79–123; Marjorie Perloff, "The Demise of 'And': Reflections on Robert Smithson's Mirrors," *Critical Quarterly* 32, no. 3 (1990): 81–101; and Gary Shapiro, *Earthwards: Robert Smithson and Art After Babel* (Berkeley: University of California Press, 1995).

8 Alan Liu, "Local Transcendence: Cultural Criticism, Postmodernism, and the Romanticism of Detail," *Representations* 32 (Fall 1990): 104.

9 Typical of this approach was the 1976 bicentennial exhibition at the Museum of Modern Art, which took the American landscape as the guarantor of a transhistorical artistic communion, ultimately arguing that abstract expressionism was a natural outgrowth of luminism. See Kynaston McShine, ed., *The Natural Paradise: Painting in America, 1800–1950* (New York: Museum of Modern Art, 1976). There were pressing reasons for producing this kind of history at the time; indeed the emergence of American art as a field of study in the sixties and seventies was arguably dependent upon progressive historicism. A fledgling field that needed a vocabulary with which to justify the relevance of its inquiry, it borrowed from the prestige of postwar American art by positing itself as its necessary historical origin.

10 See Gary Shapiro's critique of John Beardsley's work in "Entropy and Dialectic: The Signatures of Robert Smithson," *Arts Magazine* 62, no. 10 (June 1988): 99; Pamela M. Lee, "'Ultramoderne': Or, How George Kubler Stole the Time in Sixties Art," *Grey Room* 2 (Winter 2001): 54; Theodor Adorno, *Aesthetic Theory* (Minneapolis: University of Minnesota Press, 1997), 19.

11 For these models, see Jacques Lacan, "The Unconscious and Repetition," in *The Four Fundamental Concepts of Psychoanalysis*, trans. Alan Sheridan (New York: Norton, 1978), 17–64; Walter Benjamin, "Theses on the Philosophy of History," in *Illuminations*, ed. Hannah Arendt, trans. Hary Zohn (New York: Schocken, 1968), 257–58; Georges Bataille, "The Notion of Expenditure," in *Visions of Excess: Selected Writings 1927–1939*, ed. and trans. Allan Stoekl (Minneapolis: University of Minnesota Press, 1985), 116–29.

12 W.J.T. Mitchell, "Interdisciplinarity and Visual Culture," *Art Bulletin* 77 (December 1995): 541.

13 For an introduction to current memory discourse see Natalie

Zemon Davis and Randolph Starn, eds., *Memory and Counter-Memory*, special issue, *Representations* 26 (Spring 1989). For an early and important application of the idea of traumatic repetition to art-historical analysis see Hal Foster, "Who's Afraid of the Neo-Avant-Garde?" in *The Return of the Real: The Avant-Garde at the End of the Century* (Cambridge: MIT Press, 1996), 1–33.

14 Peter Osborne, quoted in Alex Coles, "Introduction," *The Optic of Walter Benjamin, de-, dis-, ex-* 3 (1999): 8. For Benjamin's vocabulary of revolutionary historicism see "Theses," 255, 262, 263, and passim.

15 Owens, "The Allegorical Impulse," identifies Smithson as a key artist within an allegorical postmodernism prefigured by Benjamin's writings. The classic introduction to Benjamin's understanding of history is Susan Buck-Morss, *The Dialectics of Seeing: Walter Benjamin and the Arcades Project* (Cambridge: MIT Press, 1989). Two more recent studies, both of which focus specifically on art and art history, include Eduardo Cadava, *Words of Light: Theses on the Photography of History* (Princeton, N.J.: Princeton University Press, 1997), and Coles, *The Optic of Walter Benjamin.*

16 See Yve-Alain Bois and Rosalind Krauss, *Formless: A User's Guide* (Cambridge: MIT Press, 1997), 43–86.

17 Smithson, "Fragments of a Conversation"; "A Sedimentation of the Mind: Earth Projects"; "The Eliminator"; "A Museum of Language in the Vicinity of Art"; "Quasi-Infinities and the Waning of Space"; interview with P. A. Norvell; all in *Writings*, 190, 112, 327, 88, 34, 194.

18 See Rosalind Krauss, "Entropy," in *Formless: A User's Guide*, 73–78. P. W. Bridgman, *The Nature of Thermodynamics* (New York: Harper, 1961), 175. This passage was underlined in Smithson's copy of the book (Smithson Papers).

19 Smithson to Martin Friedman, n.d., Smithson Papers, reel 3834, frame 49. Smithson, "Can Man Survive?" in *Writings*, 368.

CHAPTER 1. HISTORY IN SMITHSON'S RELIGIOUS PAINTINGS

1   Robert Smithson to Nancy Holt, undated (probably 1959), in Robert Smithson and Nancy Holt papers, 1905–1987, reel 3832, frame 742, Archives of American Art, Smithsonian Institution, Washington, D.C. (hereafter Smithson Papers); Smithson, interview with Paul Cummings for the Archives of American Art, in Jack Flam, ed., *Robert Smithson: The Collected Writings* (Berkeley: University of California Press, 1996), 271, 283 (hereafter *Writings*). For a good biographical summary see Per. J. Boym, ed., *Robert Smithson Retrospective: Works 1955–1973* (Oslo: National Museum of Contemporary Art, 1999), 282–93. For Sandler's review see *Art News* 58, no. 6 (October 1959): 18.

2   See McDarrah's photographs of Ted Joans's birthday party on July 25, 1959, several of which feature Smithson. Fred W. McDarrah and Gloria S. McDarrah, *Beat Generation: Glory Days in Greenwich Village* (New York: Schirmer Books, 1996), 95–98; there is also a photo taken at one of Smithson's own loft parties in McDarrah's *The Artist's World in Pictures*

(New York: Dutton, 1961). For Smithson's other perambulations through the Greenwich Village Beat scene see the Cummings interview in *Writings*, 274–76.

3   Robert Smithson to George B. Lester, May 1, 1961, Robert Smithson letters to George B. Lester, 1960–1963, Archives of American Art, Smithsonian Institution, Washington, D.C. (hereafter Lester Letters).

4   Smithson to Lester, April 7, 1961, Lester Letters.

5   Smithson had been raised a Roman Catholic and seems to have been especially encouraged in this regard by his aunt, Julia Duke, who lived with the Smithsons throughout Robert's childhood and whom he described as a "second mother" in a letter to Lester (May 1, 1961, Lester Letters). For a summary of Smithson's family ties to Eastern Orthodox as well as Roman Catholicism see Caroline A. Jones, *The Machine in the Studio: Constructing the Postwar American Artist* (Chicago: University of Chicago Press, 1996), 280–81.

6   The small catalogue for the exhibition at the Diane Brown Gallery, which includes an essay by Peter Halley, remains an essential source of information and reproductions: *Robert Smithson: The Early Work, 1959–1962* (New York: Diane Brown Gallery, 1985), unpaged. The other key sources on Smithson's early work include Eugenie Tsai, "Reconstructing Robert Smithson," Ph.D. diss., Columbia University, 1995, 58–97; Tsai, *Robert Smithson Unearthed: Drawings, Collages, Writings* (New York: Columbia University Press, 1991); Jones, *Machine in the Studio*, 278–303. Both Tsai and Jones have interpreted Smithson's early work in an antimodernist vein. Tsai argues that the unruly multiplicity of Smithson's early drawings, collages, and writings, along with their failure to provide any obvious indication of Smithson's future direction, serve to unravel any Kantian/Greenbergian narrative of modernist progress that might be applied to Smithson's development. Jones, whose psychoanalytic account was the first to offer an explanation of Smithson's unlikely transition from anguished figuration to crystalline abstraction, also defined the early work as an antimodernist instrument. For Jones, the writhing gods, men, and monsters of the early images would be eventually sublimated into Smithson's landscape practice, where they would lurk as a libidinal subtext of the "technological sublime" and would perpetually derail all attempts at modernist closure. On the problem of Smithson's own partial renunciation of his early work, see Jones, "Robert Smithson's Suppressed "Pre-Conscious" Works: Intentionality and Art Historical (Re)Construction," in *Memory & Oblivion: Proceedings of the XXIXth International Congress of the History of Art* (Dordrecht: Kluwer Academic Publishers, 1999): 937–47. See also Paul Wood, "Dialectical Transformations: Robert Smithson's Early Work," *Arts Magazine* 63, no. 7 (March 1989): 34–39.

7   For the use of "interest" in this context see Jones, *Machine in the Studio*, 280–81; Tsai, *Robert Smithson Unearthed*, 14–16; and Halley, *Robert Smithson* (unpaged).

8 Smithson to Lester, May 17, 1961, Lester Letters. Lester had argued that a religious show would not be diverse enough.

9 Smithson to Lester, undated, Lester Letters.

10 Smithson to Lester, May 1, 1961, Lester Letters.

11 Smithson to Lester, May 17, 1961, Lester Letters.

12 On Kerouac see Allen Ginsberg, "A Definition of the Beat Generation," *Friction* 1 (Winter 1982): 50–52. Quoted in Boym, *Robert Smithson Retrospective*, 18. Key Eckhardt texts in Smithson's library include *Meister Eckhardt: A Modern Translation*, trans. Raymond Bernard Blakney (New York: Harper Torchbooks, 1941), and the Eckhardt texts anthologized in H. A. Reinhold, ed., *The Soul Afire: Revelations of the Mystics* (New York: Meridian, 1960). The religious works by Chesterton included *The Catholic Church and Conversion* (New York: Macmillan, 1961), *St. Francis of Assisi* (New York: Doubleday, 1957), and *The Everlasting Man* (New York: Doubleday, 1955). His books on mysticism by Evelyn Underhill included *The Mystics of the Church* (New York: Schocken, 1964), *Mysticism: A Study in the Nature and Development of Man's Spiritual Consciousness* (New York: Dutton, 1961), *Practical Mysticism* (New York: Dutton, 1943), *Essentials of Mysticism* (New York: Dutton, 1960), and *Worship* (New York: Harper Torchbooks, 1957). For "antidemocratic intelligentsia" see Smithson, "Frederick Law Olmsted and the Dialectical Landscape," in *Writings*, 161. Smithson's own comments about his interests in Anglo-Catholicism are from the interview with Paul Cummings in *Writings*, 282–84. Dan Graham discusses Smithson's conservatism of these years in an interview with Eugenie Tsai in *Robert Smithson: Drawings from the Estate*, exh. cat. (Westfälisches Landesmuseum für Kunst und Kulturgeschichte Münster, 1989), 8–18.

13 G. K. Chesterton, *William Blake* (London: Duckworth & Co., 1910), 144.

14 Thanks to Kristin Schwain for informing me about the ritual significance of the bell, and to Jeffrey Hamburger for pointing out the aggressive motion of the hand.

15 Smithson, "The Iconography of Desolation," in *Writings*, 322 (emphasis in original).

16 Ibid., 320.

17 Smithson to Lester, undated, Lester Letters. See also ibid., 321.

18 Smithson to Lester, undated, Lester Letters.

19 Halley, *Robert Smithson: The Early Work*, unpaged; Smithson had been interested in drawing since high school, when he had briefly entertained the idea of becoming an illustrator (interview with Paul Cummings, in *Writings*, 276).

20 Smithson to Lester, undated, Lester Letters.

21 Smithson to Lester, undated, Lester Letters.

22 Smithson to Lester, undated, Lester Letters.

23 Smithson to Lester, undated, Lester Letters.

24 See Michael Fried, *Three American Painters* (Cambridge, Mass.: Fogg Art Museum, 1965), 14; Michael Leja, "Jackson Pollock: Representing the Unconscious," in *Reading American Art*, ed. Marianne Doezema and Elizabeth Milroy (New Haven: Yale University Press, 1998), 455–59.

25 Smithson to Lester, undated, Lester Letters. Smithson's admiration for Blake has been occasionally mentioned in the literature but not yet examined in detail. Smithson himself described his paintings of the early sixties as cosmological images somewhere between Blake and Bosch (interview with Paul Cummings in *Writings*, 289). Contemporary reviewers also described Smithson's connections to Blake. See Boym, "Sensuous Ethos," in Boym, *Robert Smithson Retrospective*, 44n.9. Alan Brilliant, a close friend of Smithson, recalled seeing Blake's drawings with him at a show at the Museum of Modern Art in 1956 (Tsai, "Reconstructing Robert Smithson," 94).

26 William Blake, "Ruth.—A Drawing," in *The Complete Writings of William Blake*, ed. Geoffrey Keynes (New York: Random House, 1957), 585. For a good discussion of Blake's relationship to neoclassical theories of line see Morris Eaves, *William Blake's Theory of Art* (Princeton, N.J.: Princeton University Press, 1982), 9–44.

27 Blake, "A Vision of the Last Judgment," in Keynes, *Complete Writings*, 605.

28 Blake, "The Ghost of Abel," in Keynes, *Complete Writings*, 779.

29 Caroline Jones has also addressed Smithson's use of boundaries in her discussion of Smithson's "dialectics of the cartouche." See Jones, *Machine in the Studio*, 294–95.

30 Chesterton, *William Blake*, 161.

31 For Smithson's interest in natural history see the interview with Paul Cummings in *Writings*, 279, and Ann M. Reynolds, "Reproducing Nature: The Museum of Natural History as Nonsite," *October* 45 (Summer 1988): 109–27. Smithson's copy of the Buchsbaum text is in the Smithson Papers (Ralph Buchsbaum, *Animals Without Backbones: An Introduction to the Invertebrates* [Chicago: University of Chicago Press, 1948]).

32 The phrase "Sea of Time and Space" appears in Blake's "Jerusalem," plate 49, in Keynes, *Complete Writings*, 614.

33 Blake, "The Bard, from Gray," in Keynes, *Complete Writings*, 576 (emphasis in original); "A Vision of the Last Judgment," in Keynes, *Complete Writings*, 614; Smithson, "Iconography of Desolation," in *Writings*, 323.

34 Smithson to Nancy Holt, dated "Monday 24" (probably July 24, 1961), Smithson Papers, reel 3832, frames 744–45; Smithson, "The Iconography of Desolation," in *Writings*, 321. Smithson is referring here to Bernard Berenson's diaries of art-travel through North Africa, Sicily, and the rest of Italy: Bernard Berenson, *The Passionate Sightseer* (New York: Simon and Schuster, 1960).

35 Smithson, interview with Paul Cummings, in *Writings*, 278–79. Other crashes are probably also at work in this collage. Smithson's close friend Danny Donahue had been killed in a motorcycle accident in 1959.

36 Smithson to Lester, undated, Lester Letters.

37 Tsai, *Robert Smithson Unearthed*, 19; Smithson to Lester, two undated letters, Lester Letters.

38 Chesterton, *William Blake*, 137, 166, 167.

39 Smithson to Lester, undated, Lester Letters; Smithson, "The Iconography of Desolation," in *Writings*, 320.

40 Smithson to Lester, undated, Lester Letters; Smithson to Nancy Holt, dated "Rome Friday July 29 1961 A.D.," Smithson Papers, reel 3832, frame 785.

41 Smithson, interview with Paul Cummings, in *Writings*, 286, 287.

42 Henry James, "A Roman Holiday," quoted in Robert Spoo, "Joyce's Attitudes Toward History: Rome, 1906–07," *Journal of Modern Literature* 14, no. 4 (Spring 1988): 482.

43 Smithson, "The Iconography of Desolation," in *Writings*, 324. The precise dating of this essay has not been established. The typescript at the Archives of American Art is labeled "1961," while in the *Writings* it is dated as "c. 1962." Based on the progression of Smithson's attitudes in his letters to Lester, I would place the essay in the autumn or winter of 1961, after Smithson's show in Rome had ended and after he had returned to New York. His letter to Lester of September 22, 1961, for example, is very similar to the second half of "The Iconography of Desolation" in its vocabulary and ironic tone.

44 Ibid.

45 Ibid., 326 (ellipsis in original).

46 Ibid., 324–25.

47 Smithson, "The Spiral Jetty," in *Writings*, 150; Smithson, "The Iconography of Desolation," typescript, Smithson Papers.

48 Thomas Pynchon, "Entropy," in *Slow Learner* (Boston: Little, Brown, 1984), 98.

49 Smithson to Lester, 22 September 1961, Lester Letters; "What Really Spoils Michelangelo's Sculpture" and "Ultramoderne," in *Writings*, 348, 63.

50 Smithson to Lester, May 1, 1961, Lester Letters. For Greenberg's take on Noland see "Louis and Noland," in *The Collected Essays and Criticism*, vol. 4, ed. John O'Brian (Chicago: University of Chicago Press, 1993), 94–100.

51 Clement Greenberg, "The Case for Abstract Art," in O'Brian, *Collected Essays*, 80–81.

52 Greenberg, "Sculpture in Our Time," in ibid., 60.

53 I am indebted to Ann Reynolds's trenchant discussion of Smithson's refutation of Greenberg's model of opticality. See Ann Reynolds, "Robert Smithson: Learning from New Jersey and Elsewhere," Ph.D. diss., City University of New York, 1993, 45–89.

54 Here I part company with Caroline Jones, who argues that "it was only after the publication of Fried's essay in June of 1967 that Smithson began to identify . . . his own emerging antimodernist position" (Jones, *Machine in the Studio*, 315). But although Fried certainly galvanized certain latent themes in Smithson's work, Smithson had already worked through the issues Fried raised by the time "Art and Objecthood" was published. Few discussions of Fried's article can match the complexity and eloquence of the article itself, so one should first consult the original. It is reprinted in Gregory Battcock, ed., *Minimal Art: A Critical Anthology* (Berkeley: University of Cali-

fornia Press, 1995), 116–47. For some of the most influential discussions of the article see Hal Foster, "The Crux of Minimalism," in *The Return of the Real* (Cambridge: MIT Press, 1996), 35–70; Douglas Crimp, "Pictures," in *Art After Modernism: Rethinking Representation*, ed. Brian Wallis (New York: New Museum of Contemporary Art, 1984), 175–88. Indispensable for a historical understanding of Fried's impact on later art history is a discussion between Fried, Rosalind Krauss, and Benjamin Buchloh: "Theories of Art After Minimalism and Pop," in *Discussions in Contemporary Culture*, vol. 1, ed. Hal Foster (Seattle: Bay Press, 1987), 52–87.

55 Smithson, "The Iconography of Desolation," in *Writings*, 320, 323.

56 Fried, "Art and Objecthood," in Battcock, *Minimal Art*, 145 (emphasis in original).

57 Smithson, "Letter to the Editor," in *Writings*, 67, 66; Michael Fried, *Art and Objecthood: Essays and Reviews* (Chicago: University of Chicago Press, 1998), 52, 73. Fried also notes that "he alone among contemporary artist-writers seems to have been aware of the implications for the question of linguistic meaning of my assault on literalism" (73–74). Note that Fried still gives himself critical priority on the question of literalism, characterizing Smithson's ideas as a response to his own. For further analysis of the critical dialogue between Smithson and Fried, see Amy Newman, *Challenging Art: "Artforum" 1962–1974* (New York: Soho Press, 2000), 11–12, 256, 290, 506; Robert Linsley, "Mirror Travel in the Yucatan: Robert Smithson, Michael Fried, and the New Critical Drama," *res* 37 (Spring 2000): 7–30.

58 Smithson, "Letter to the Editor, in *Writings*, 67.

59 See Smithson, "The Spiral Jetty" and "The Iconography of Desolation," in *Writings*, 143, 325.

CHAPTER 2. THE DEPOSITION OF TIME

1 John Shearman, *Pontormo's Altarpiece in S. Felicità*, 51st Charlton Lecture delivered at the University of Newcastle upon Tyne (Westerham, Kent: Westerham Press, 1971), 14; Arnold Hauser, *Mannerism: The Crisis of the Renaissance and the Origin of Modern Art* (London: Routledge & Kegan Paul, 1965), 182; Daniel B. Rowland, *Mannerism: Style and Mood* (New Haven: Yale University Press, 1964), 18.

2 Leo Steinberg, "Pontormo's Capponi Chapel," *The Art Bulletin* 56, no. 3 (September 1974): 394. For a discussion of the quandary over the title of the painting see Steinberg, 385n2. Smithson himself would have known the painting as a Deposition (his several books on Mannerism referred to it as such).

3 Giuliano Brigante, *Italian Mannerism* (Edition Leipzig, 1962), 22; Steinberg, "Pontormo's Capponi Chapel," 394. Steinberg's broader argument is that the painting functions as a kind of rotational hinge within the larger architectural space of the Capponi Chapel. The figures are, he argues, frozen at the end of the process of turning the body of Christ around and outward toward the painting depicting God at the other side of the chapel.

4 Rowland, *Mannerism*, 12 (underlining Smithson's). For

Smithson's understanding of the relationship between Mannerism and modern painting see Ann M. Reynolds, "Robert Smithson: Learning from New Jersey and Elsewhere," Ph.D. diss., City University of New York, 1993, 75–78.

5 Smithson, press release for his second one-man exhibition at the Dwan gallery, 1968. Quoted in Reynolds, "Robert Smithson," 141.

6 Smithson, "Towards the Development of an Air Terminal Site," in Jack Flam, ed., *Robert Smithson: The Collected Writings* (Berkeley: University of California Press, 1996), 53 (hereafter *Writings*).

7 Smithson, quoted in Robert Hobbs, *Robert Smithson: Sculpture* (Ithaca: Cornell University Press, 1981), 64. Hobbs does not give a citation for this quote, but a letter exists with similar (though not exact) wording (Smithson to "Lollie," n.d., Robert Smithson and Nancy Holt papers, 1905–1987, reel 3832, frames 747–49, Archives of American Art, Smithsonian Institution, Washington, D.C. [hereafter Smithson Papers]).

8 See Smithson, "Donald Judd"; "Entropy and the New Monuments"; "The Crystal Land"; "Towards the Development of an Air Terminal Site," in *Writings*, 4–6, 10–23, 7–9, 52–60.

9 Smithson, interview with Paul Cummings, in *Writings*, 287.

10 Smithson to Martin Friedman, n.d., Smithson Papers, reel 3834, frame 49.

11 Charles Bunn, *Crystals: Their Role in Nature and Science* (New York: Academic Press, 1964), 45.

12 Ajit Ram Verma and P. Krishna, *Polymorphism and Polytypism in Crystals* (New York: Wiley, 1966), 207. See also Harold Hilton, *Mathematical Crystallography and the Theory of Groups of Movements* (1903; New York: Dover, 1963), esp. 92, 150; Smithson, "The Spiral Jetty," in *Writings*, 147.

13 Smithson, interview with Paul Cummings, in *Writings*, 294.

14 Mary Ann Doane, *The Emergence of Cinematic Time* (Cambridge: Harvard University Press, 2002), 9.

15 Smithson Papers; Smithson, "Spiral Wreckage," Smithson Papers, reel 3834, frame 55. See also Smithson's annotations in his copy of P. W. Bridgman, *The Nature of Thermodynamics* (New York: Harper, 1961), 174–75.

16 Smithson, "Spiral Wreckage."

17 Bunn, *Crystals*, 192.

18 Max Jammer, *Concepts of Space: The History of Theories of Space in Physics* (Cambridge: Harvard University Press, 1960), 131.

19 Previous discussions of Smithson's interest in enantiomorphism have tended to interpret it in strictly deconstructionist terms, and have focused on its implications for Smithson's critique of modernist models of vision. For notable examples see Reynolds, "Robert Smithson," 67–89; Rosalind Krauss, "Entropy," in Yve-Alain Bois and Rosalind Krauss, *Formless: A User's Guide* (Cambridge: MIT Press, 1997), 78; Gary Shapiro, *Earthwards: Robert Smithson and Art After Babel* (Berkeley: University of California Press, 1995), 68.

20 Immanuel Kant, *Prolegomena to Any Future Metaphysics*, quoted in Martin Gardner, *The Ambidextrous Universe* (London: Penguin, 1967).

21 Smithson, "Pointless Vanishing Points"; "Incidents of Mirror-Travel in the Yucatan"; "Minus Twelve"; interview with Paul Toner; in *Writings*, 359, 131, 115, 240. For a Lacanian analysis of the structure and visual effects of the *Chambers* see Timothy Martin, "De-architecturisation and the Architectural Unconscious: A Tour of Robert Smithson's Chambers and Hotels," *de-, dis-, ex-* 2 (1998): 89–114.

22 Smithson, "Quasi Infinities and the Waning of Space"; "The Shape of the Future and Memory"; "Incidents of Mirror-Travel in the Yucatan"; in *Writings*, 34, 332, 131. Smithson frequently cited (or invented variations upon) his favorite Nabokov quote: "The future is but the obsolete in reverse." The quote, which Smithson underlined along with a few others in his copy of the short story "Lance," concerns the tendency of writers to imagine the future in terms of the past, rendering the two time fields interchangeable: "Now if one is perfectly honest with oneself, there is nothing extraordinary in the tendency to give to the manners and clothes of a distant day (which happens to be placed in the future) an old-fashioned tinge, a badly pressed, badly groomed, dusty something, since the terms 'out of date,' 'not of our age,' and so on are in the long run the only ones in which we are able to imagine and express a strangeness no amount of research can foresee. The future is but the obsolete in reverse." Vladimir Nabokov, "Lance," in *Nabokov's Dozen: A Collection of Thirteen Stories* (New York: Doubleday, 1958), 202.

23 See Jacques Derrida, "Différance," in *Speech and Phenomena and Other Essays on Husserl's Theory of Signs*, trans. David B. Allison (Evanston: Northwestern University Press, 1973), 129–60. Smithson was almost certainly unaware of Derrida's work. I am aware of only one text by Derrida in Smithson's library. This was Derrida's "Structure, Sign, and Play in the Discourse of the Human Sciences," which was reprinted in Richard Macksey, ed., *The Structuralist Controversy* (Baltimore: Johns Hopkins University Press, 1972). Although Smithson owned the book, there is no evidence that he ever read the essay; even if he had, he could not have done so until it was published, in 1972, near the end of his life. I have come across no reference to Derrida in any of his writings, drafts of writings, or interviews. On my notion of the "enantiomorphic hinge," cf. Gilles Deleuze, *The Fold: Leibniz and the Baroque*, trans. Tom Conley (Minneapolis: University of Minnesota Press, 1995), and Derrida's discussion of "The Hinge [La Brisure]," in *Of Grammatology*, corrected ed., trans. Gayatri Chakravorty Spivak (Baltimore: Johns Hopkins University Press, 1998), 65–73.

24 Mark C. Taylor, "System . . . Structure . . . Difference . . . Other," in *Deconstruction in Context: Literature and Philosophy* (Chicago: University of Chicago Press, 1986), 3, 24.

25 Smithson, "A Sedimentation of the Mind: Earth Projects," in *Writings*, 110. Smithson owned two books by Husserl: *Ideas: General Introduction to Pure Phenomenology*, trans. R. Boyce Gibson (New York: Humanities Press, 1967), and *The Phenomenology of Internal Time Consciousness*, ed. Martin

Heidegger, trans. James O. Churchill (Bloomington: Indiana University Press), 1966. He also seems to have gleaned much of his information about Husserl from Marvin Farber's *Aims of Phenomenology: The Motives, Methods, and Impact of Husserl's Thought* (New York: Harper & Row, 1966). Smithson mentions Husserl's work explicitly in one of his drafts of the 1967 essay "The Monuments of Passaic": "The duality between urban and suburban seems especially acute in New York City, so much so that one's consciousness of time becomes dual. This seems to relate to what Husserl refers to as 'the phenomenology of internal time-consciousness'" (emphasis Smithson's). Smithson, draft of "The Monuments of Passaic," Smithson Papers, unprocessed collection.

26 Möbius, *Der barycentrische Calcul* (Leipzig, 1827), cited in Linda Dalrymple Henderson, *The Fourth Dimension and Non-Euclidean Geometry in Modern Art* (Princeton, N.J.: Princeton University Press, 1983), 7n13.

27 Martin Gardner, *The Ambidextrous Universe* (New York: Basic Books, 1964), 169. Other books in Smithson's library that Henderson identifies as influential for the propagation of ideas about the fourth dimension in postwar American art include Edward Kasner and James Newman, eds., *Mathematics and the Imagination* (New York: Simon and Schuster, 1965); Robert Marks, ed., *Space, Time, and the New Mathematics* (New York: Bantam Books, 1964) (Smithson's copy is inscribed "Daniel Graham"). Linda Henderson, *The Fourth Dimension and Non-Euclidean Geometry in Modern Art*, new ed. (Cambridge: MIT Press, forthcoming 2004). The cutout of the "Romantic" crystal ended up in Smithson's photostat *Grave Mounds with Object* of around 1966. It is reproduced in Robert Sobieszek, *Robert Smithson: Photo Works* (Los Angeles: Los Angeles County Museum of Art, 1993), 20.

28 Ann Reynolds has definitively established Smithson's interest in alternating perspective figures (although she interprets Smithson's use of these images from a deconstructive rather than a synthetic standpoint). See Reynolds, "Robert Smithson," 25–32. For the four-dimensional implications of reversing figures see Rudy Rucker, *The Fourth Dimension* (Boston: Houghton Mifflin, 1984), 46. As Rucker explains, "The sort of twinkling rearrangement that takes place [when alternating perspective figures reverse] is equivalent to a rotation through the fourth dimension."

29 For a discussion see Thomas Crow, "Art Criticism in the Age of Incommensurate Values: On the Thirtieth Anniversary of *Artforum*," in *Modern Art in the Common Culture* (New Haven: Yale University Press, 1996), 85–93. For more on Smithson's collaboration with TAMS on the airport project see Mark Linder, "Sitely Windows: Robert Smithson's Architectural Criticism," *Assemblage* 39 (August 1999); Suzaan Boettger, *Earthworks: Art and the Landscape of the Sixties* (Berkeley: University of California Press, 2002), 52–69; Carlton Evans, "Site/Non-sight: Robert Smithson's Dialectics of Vision," Ph.D. diss., Stanford University, forthcoming, ch. 3.

30 Smithson, "Towards the Development of an Air Terminal Site," in *Writings*, 58, 52, 53.

31 Ibid., 53.

32 J. W. Dunne, *An Experiment with Time* (London: Faber and Faber, 1952), 117.

33 P. D. Ouspensky, *Tertium Organum: The Third Canon of Thought*, trans. Nicholas Bessaraboff and Claude Bragdon (New York: Knopf, 1950), 100, 102 (emphasis in original).

34 Smithson, "Towards the Development of an Air Terminal Site," in *Writings*, 52 (emphasis mine).

35 Smithson, draft of "Quasi-Infinities and the Waning of Space," Smithson Papers, reel 3834, frame 375; Ouspensky was discussed in Smithson's texts by Max Jammer and Martin Gardner; Smithson, draft of "The Monuments of Passaic," 7, Smithson Papers, reel 3834, frame 1186.

36 C. H. Hinton, quoted in Dunne, *An Experiment with Time*, 113. The term *block universe* derives from Herman Weyl, who used it in his *Philosophy of Mathematics and Natural Science* (Princeton, N.J.: Princeton University Press, 1949).

37 Smithson, "Towards the Development of an Air Terminal Site," in *Writings*, 52, 53. This is similar to what Roland Barthes calls the *coenesthesis* of the jet pilot, wherein "an excess of speed turns into repose." Roland Barthes, "The Jet-Man," in *Mythologies*, trans. Annette Lavers (New York: Noonday, 1972), 71.

38 Smithson, "Towards the Development of an Air Terminal Site," in *Writings*, 53 (emphasis in original).

39 Ibid., 58.

40 Smithson's copy of Bunn, *Crystals*, Smithson Papers. For the link between the crystalline form in *Proposal for a Monument at Antarctica* and Smithson's well-known sculptural installation *Plunge*, see Hobbs, *Robert Smithson: Sculpture*, 72.

41 Linda D. Henderson, "Mysticism, Romanticism, and the Fourth Dimension," in *The Spiritual in Art: Abstract Painting 1890–1985*, exh. cat., Los Angeles County Museum of Art (New York: Abbeville, 1986), 219–37; Evelyn Underhill, *Mysticism: A Study in the Nature and Development of Man's Spiritual Consciousness* (New York: Dutton, 1961), 259 (Smithson Papers); *St. Augustine, Confessions*, trans. R. S. Pine-Coffin (New York: Penguin, 1961), 261.

42 Smithson, "Towards the Development of an Air Terminal Site," in *Writings*, 60; Smithson refers to Malevich in two of his published essays of this period. In "Entropy and the New Monuments," he claims that the new art constitutes a re-creation of Malevich's non-objective world (*Writings*, 14). Malevich's book of the same title (*Non-Objective World*) is not in Smithson's library at the Archives of American Art, but Smithson twice cites it in "A Sedimentation of the Mind: Earth Projects" (*Writings*, 103–4, 109). It would be interesting to trace Smithson's relationship to Malevich; especially suggestive would be a comparison between Smithson's "Alogons" and Malevich's theories of "alogical realism." See Henderson, "Transcending the Present: The Fourth Dimension in the

Philosophy of Ouspensky and in Russian Futurism and Suprematism," in *Fourth Dimension* (1st ed.), 238–99. There are also many intriguing similarities between Smith and Smithson. Both grew up Catholic in New Jersey, both studied at the Art Student's League in New York City, and neither man went to college but both became known as broad-ranging, articulate, and humorous autodidacts sought out for their bar conversation. They shared admiration for Alexander Graham Bell and Buckminster Fuller, and, most importantly, adopted crystallography as a morphological and ontological principle. There were, of course, major differences, notably Smith's humanism; see Robert Storr, *Tony Smith: Architect Painter Sculptor* (New York: Museum of Modern Art, 1998). Smithson admired Smith greatly; for his comments on his work see *Writings*, 49, 58–60, 66, 96, 102–3, 106, 340.

43 Smithson, "Entropy and the New Monuments," in *Writings*, 12–14. Smithson's interpretation was not particularly well received by the artists mentioned in the article. In fact, his relationship with the artists now known as minimalists, who felt that he was misrepresenting their work, was strained at the time. In the February 1967 issue of *Arts Magazine* Donald Judd contributed a single-sentence letter to the editor that read "Smithson isn't my spokesman." The sentence became a slogan—"Robert Smithson is not my spokesman"—and was printed on buttons that the artists wore to exhibitions. See James Sampson Meyer, "The Genealogy of Minimalism: Carl Andre, Dan Flavin, Donald Judd, Sol LeWitt and Robert Morris," Ph.D. diss., Johns Hopkins University, 1995, 300. On Smithson's difficulty fitting in with the minimalists at this time see "Interview with Dan Graham by Eugenie Tsai," in *Robert Smithson: Drawings from the Estate*, exh. cat. (Münster: Westfälisches Landesmuseum für Kunst und Kulturgeschichte, 1989), 8–22. The lesson to take from all this is that "Entropy and the New Monuments" reveals more about Smithson's evolving aesthetic agenda than it does about the other artists' concerns.

44 Smithson, "Donald Judd," in *Writings*, 6.

CHAPTER 3. FORGETTING PASSAIC

1 Smithson, "A Tour of the Monuments of Passaic, New Jersey," in Jack Flam, ed., *Robert Smithson: The Collected Writings* (Berkeley: University of California Press, 1996), 68–74 (hereafter *Writings*). The date of Smithson's tour is misquoted in the first printing of *Writings* as September 20, 1967. Smithson's field notes confirm the date as the 30th, and it is on this date that the *New York Times* printed the art reviews that Smithson mentions reading on the bus in his travelogue. Smithson's "advertisement" for the Passaic tours is "See the Monuments of Passaic New Jersey," in *Writings*, 356 (ellipsis in original). Smithson later led at least one group of friends along his tour route in Passaic. He took artists Claes Oldenburg and Allan Kaprow on a tour in January of 1968, according to Nancy Holt in an interview with Ann M. Reynolds. See Reynolds, "Robert Smithson: Learning from New Jersey and

Elsewhere," Ph.D. diss., City University of New York, 1993, 175. Even several years later, Smithson appears to have been offering Passaic tours to fellow artists, as suggested by the letter dated January 4, 1970, to Smithson from British artist Hamish Fulton, proposing that Smithson meet him in Passaic for a joint tour project (Robert Smithson and Nancy Holt papers, 1905–1987, reel 3833, frame 57, Archives of American Art, Smithsonian Institution, Washington, D.C. [hereafter Smithson Papers]).

2 Smithson's appointment books give a good indication of the frequency of these trips, and they also occasionally mention the names of the artists and friends that accompanied him (Smithson Papers). Smithson's "Nonsites" are well known for questioning the efficacy and transparency of the representational strategies of the landscape tradition. (The *Franklin Nonsite* shown in figure 31, for example, conflates perspectival structure, mapping, and specimen display into a single unstable "reference" to the city of Franklin, New Jersey.) The best overview of the Site/Nonsites and other sculptural works that resulted from these expeditions is in Robert Hobbs, *Robert Smithson: Sculpture* (Ithaca: Cornell University Press, 1981), 88–122. For background on the specific New Jersey sites visited by Smithson see William R. Klink, "Robert Smithson: New Jersey Artist of the Earth," *New Jersey History* 99, nos. 3–4 (1981): 183–92.

3 For the Passaic project's critique of art-world pieties see Reynolds, "Robert Smithson," 110–79; Suzaan Boettger, *Earthworks: Art and the Landscape of the Sixties* (Berkeley: University of California Press, 2002), 45–69. On Smithson's use of photography see Craig Owens, "Photography *en abyme*," in *Beyond Recognition: Representation, Power, and Culture* (Berkeley: University of California Press, 1992), 27–28; Robert Sobieszek, *Robert Smithson: Photo Works* (Los Angeles: Los Angeles County Museum of Art, 1993), 30–32 and passim. For a recent discussion of the Passaic project in the context of architecture and urbanism see Sébastien Marot, *Sub-Urbanism and the Art of Memory*, trans. Brian Holmes (London: Architectural Association, 2003), 36–55. On the idea of *terrain vague* see Ignasi de Sola-Morales Rubio, "Terrain Vague," in *Anyplace*, ed. Cynthia Davidson (Cambridge: MIT Press, 1995).

4 The original negatives and Instamatic snapshots from Smithson's Passaic tour are now held by the Estate of Robert Smithson and the Archives of American Art, respectively. Small contact prints of all of the negatives, showing the scope and sequence of Smithson's photographic activities on the tour, have been published in Sobieszek, *Robert Smithson: Photo Works*, 90–93.

5 Smithson, "Fragments of a Conversation"; "The Monuments of Passaic"; in *Writings*, 190, 72.

6 Smithson, "The Monuments of Passaic," in *Writings*, 70 (ellipses Smithson's).

7 See Citizens' Improvement Association of Passaic City, *Passaic City, New Jersey, and Its Advantages as a Place of Residence and as a Manufacturing Centre* (Citizens' Improvement Asso-

ciation, 1886); Michael Ebner, "Strikes and Society: Civil Behavior in Passaic, 1875–1926," *New Jersey History* 97, no. 1 (1979): 7–24; David J. Goldberg, *A Tale of Three Cities: Labor Organization and Protest in Paterson, Passaic, and Lawrence, 1916–1921* (New Brunswick, N.J.: Rutgers University Press, 1989).

8   For concise accounts of Passaic at around the time of Smithson's tour see "Passaic Debating Uncertain Future," *New York Times*, Jul 8, 1968, 41; Michael Ebner, "The Future of River City: Passaic, New Jersey's Contemporary Urban Political History," *Urbanism Past & Present*, no. 3 (1976–77): 16–20. For the industrial profile of mid-century Passaic see James Bryon Kenyon, *Industrial Localization and Metropolitan Growth: The Paterson-Passaic District*, Research Paper no. 67, University of Chicago Department of Geography (Chicago: University of Chicago, 1960). On the retail patterns in this area of New Jersey: Lizabeth Cohen, "From Town Center to Shopping Center: The Reconfiguration of Community Marketplaces in Postwar America," *The American Historical Review* 101, no. 4 (October 1996): 1050–81. On the pollution of the Passaic River: Norman F. Brydon, *The Passaic River: Past, Present, Future* (New Brunswick: Rutgers University Press, 1974), 270–317.

9   A concise chronological biography can be found in Per. J. Boym, ed., *Robert Smithson Retrospective: Works 1955–1973* (Oslo: National Museum of Contemporary Art, 1999), 282–93. As is well known, another essential piece of historical context for the Passaic project is William Carlos Williams's five-part historical poem *Paterson*. Smithson revered Williams, who had actually served as Smithson's pediatrician when he was growing up in Rutherford. Although Smithson does not allude directly to Williams in the Passaic essay itself, in a later interview he pointed out that his Passaic travelogue "could be conceived of as a kind of appendix" to Williams's modernist landmark. *Paterson* had an obvious impact on Smithson's own writing at all levels, particularly on his tendency to equate language and thought with geological processes. Smithson's famous assertion that "One's mind and the earth are in a constant state of erosion, mental rivers wear away abstract banks, brain waves undermine cliffs of thought, ideas decompose into stones of unknowing" is not much of a leap from *Paterson*, where "red basalt, boot-long, / tumbles from the core of his mind, / a rubble-bank disintegrating beneath a / tropic downpour." A notable similarity between *Paterson* and "Passaic" is the citational brand of history applied by both Williams and Smithson; both incorporate undigested source material throughout their texts. Smithson discusses *Paterson* in his interview with Gianni Pettena, in *Writings*, 298, and in his interview with Paul Cummings, in *Writings*, 285. His Patersonian quote about the "stones of unknowing" is in his 1968 essay "A Sedimentation of the Mind: Earth Projects," in *Writings*, 100. For the Williams quote see *Paterson*, rev. ed., prepared by Christopher MacGowan (New York: New Directions, 1992), 47. See also John Beck, "Prolapsed Metropolis: The Entropic New Jersey of

William Carlos Williams and Robert Smithson," *Borderlines: Studies in American Culture* 5, no. 3 (1998): 240–52.

10 Eric Wm. Allison, "Historic Preservation in a Development-Dominated City: The Passage of New York City's Landmark Preservation Legislation," *Journal of Urban History* 22, no. 3 (March 1996): 350–76; Joseph B. Rose, "Landmarks Preservation in New York," *Public Interest*, no. 74 (Winter 1984): 132–45; Ada Louise Huxtable, "Downtown New York Begins to Undergo Radical Transformation," *The New York Times*, Mar 27, 1967, 35.

11 See the following articles in the *New York Times* for the basic outlines of the debate: Thomas W. Ennis, "'Villagers' Score Landmarks Move," Dec 10, 1965, 71; Thomas W. Ennis, "Landmarks Unit Cuts Up 'Village,'" Nov 24, 1966, 70; "'Villagers' Fight Landmark Ruling," Dec 22, 1966, 28; "'Village' Is Named a Single Landmark," Mar 17, 1967, 27; Maurice Carroll, "'Village' Is Named a Landmark," Apr 30, 1969, 44.

12 Alois Riegl, "The Modern Cult of Monuments: Its Character and Origin," trans. Kurt W. Forster and Diane Ghirardo, *Oppositions* 25 (Fall 1982): 32.

13 Smithson, "Ultramoderne," in *Writings*, 63–65. Because "Ultramoderne" is so short I will not cite specific page numbers from the article in these notes.

14 The Landmarks Preservation Act stipulated that only buildings thirty years and older would be considered for preservation. Although many of the buildings in "Ultramoderne" were just over that limit and therefore technically eligible, it was not until 1985, almost twenty years after Smithson's "Ultramoderne" article was published, that the group of twin-towered apartment buildings Smithson explored along Central Park West would be designated as landmarks.

15 See Le Corbusier, *Towards a New Architecture*, trans. Frederick Etchells (New York: Payson & Clarke, 1927). Joseph Masheck has also noted this connection. Masheck, who is one of the few commentators to have attached significance to Smithson's historical references, goes on to compare Smithson's *Fountain Monument* to the monumental forms in Fritz Lang's film *Metropolis* and to Charles Sheeler's River Rouge paintings. See Masheck, "Smithson's Earth: Spontaneous Retrievals," in *Historical Present: Essays of the 1970s* (Ann Arbor, Mich: UMI Research Press, 1984), 129. On industrial and "negative tourism" see Kenneth W. Maddox, *In Search of the Picturesque: Nineteenth Century Images of Industry Along the Hudson River Valley*, exh. cat. (Annandale-on-Hudson, N.Y.: Bard College, 1983); Dean MacCannell, *The Tourist: A New Theory of the Leisure Class* (Berkeley: University of California Press, 1999), 40.

16 Smithson, "The Monuments of Passaic," in *Writings*, 71–72.

17 Smithson, "A Guide to the Monuments of Passaic New Jersey," draft of "The Monuments of Passaic," Smithson Papers.

18 Ethel Schwartz, quoted in "Passaic Debating Uncertain Future."

19 Smithson, "The Monuments of Passaic," in *Writings*, 74. Passaic's passivity in the face of economic development was likely an important part of its entropic appeal for Smithson (I

will be discussing Smithson's own strategies of passivity in Chapter 4). However, Passaic did have historical monuments that some thought were worth protecting from the highway. Landscape architect Mitchell Rasor, in an article about his own revisitation of Smithson's monuments, has shown that the construction of Highway 21 through Passaic involved the eradication of most of a Civil War cemetery (the monument in figure 42 was probably located there, since the doomed cemetery was on Smithson's path through the city). See Mitchell Rasor, "Revisiting Hours: Robert Smithson's Passaic," http://www.mrld.net/passaic.pdf. Another preservationist battle, remarkably similar to Passaic's in its outlines if not its results, was brewing in nearby Paterson. A group of Paterson citizens had managed to halt the planned construction of Highway 80 through the Great Falls area in order to conserve the historic industrial structures there. Paterson's riverfront area would be listed on the National Register of Historic Places by 1970 and would even come to feature a "Historic Landmark Walking Tour." Smithson's own walking tour of Passaic stands in conspicuous, and possibly conscious, contrast to the situation upstream. See Sarah J. Gibson, "The Great Falls/S.U.M. Historic Landmark Walking Tour" (Paterson, N.J.: Paterson Museum, 1976); Adele Chatfield-Taylor, "A Proposal for Paterson," *Architectural Forum* 132, no. 1 (January/February 1970): 72–77.

20 The photographs from Bergen are reproduced in contact print form in Sobieszek, *Robert Smithson: Photo Works*. The location of this tour has not been previously attributed, but I have been able to determine that a pyramidal mausoleum that Smithson photographed repeatedly in this series was (and is still) located in the Flower Hill Cemetery in Bergen. On the camera as a mechanization of perspective see Jeff Wall, "Unity and Fragmentation in Manet," in Thierry de Duve et al., *Jeff Wall* (London: Phaidon, 1996), 78–89; Hubert Damisch, "Five Notes for a Phenomenology of the Photographic Image," in *Classic Essays on Photography*, ed. Alan Trachtenberg (New Haven: Yale University Press, 1980), 289.

21 Smithson, "A Museum of Language in the Vicinity of Art," in *Writings*, 91; John Perreault, "Nonsites in the News," *New York* 2, no. 8 (February 24, 1969): 46; Smithson, "A Sedimentation of the Mind: Earth Projects," in *Writings*, 112.

22 For photography as "gorgonization" see Eduardo Cadava, *Words of Light: Theses on the Photography of History* (Princeton, N.J.: Princeton University Press, 1997), 59. My thinking on casting has been influenced by Rosalind Krauss's discussion of Bruce Nauman's early cast sculptures, which she interprets as an entropic "cooling" of space. Krauss, "Entropy," in Yve-Alain Bois and Rosalind Krauss, *Formless: A User's Guide* (Cambridge: MIT Press, 1997), 215.

23 Although it is likely that Smithson knew de Vries's work through his comprehensive study of sixteenth- and seventeenth-century perspective, there is no concrete evidence that he ever engaged specifically with this image. For a useful discussion of Cartesian perspectivism, which Smithson's perspectives implicitly oppose, see Martin Jay, *Downcast Eyes: The Denigration of Vision in Twentieth-Century French Thought* (Berkeley: University of California Press, 1993), esp. chapter 2.

24 Smithson, "Pointless Vanishing Points," in *Writings*, 358.

25 Edmund Husserl, *The Phenomenology of Internal Time-Consciousness*, ed. Martin Heidegger, trans. James O. Churchill (Bloomington: Indiana University Press, 1966), 47; George Santayana, *Skepticism and Animal Faith* (New York: Dover, 1955), 151. The art historian George Kubler, one of Smithson's key influences, also made this analogy in a text in Smithson's library. Kubler points out that "historians have to decide the relation of figure to ground in their representations of duration. A historical personage, for instance, stands to the conditions limiting his actions much as a visible design drawn upon the page stands to its background. . . . By this token history is like sight." George Kubler, "Style and the Representation of Historical Time," *Aspen* 5–6 (Fall/Winter 1967): 14. More recently, historian Elizabeth Deeds Ermarth has argued that modern historicism (especially in its nineteenth-century zenith) relied upon precisely this kind of perspectival construction of time. Historicism produces an optical illusion by reorganizing the temporal field into a series of bounded objects (events) that inhabit a neutral, homogenous "historical space": "After the turn of the nineteenth century . . . the idea of history comes into its own, adopting the convention which treats historical time as a neutral medium much like the analogous neutral space first constructed by Renaissance realist painters. . . . Conceived according to a particular grammar of perspective, this 'human' or social time is the medium 'in' which the forms of modernity can unfold and evolve." Elizabeth Deeds Ermarth, review of Robert Newman, ed., *Centuries' Ends, Narrative Means*, *History and Theory* 37, no. 1 (February 1998): 103. See also Michael Ann Holly, *Past Looking: Historical Imagination and the Rhetoric of the Image* (Ithaca: Cornell University Press, 1996).

26 James Elkins, *The Poetics of Perspective* (Ithaca: Cornell University Press, 1994), 154–59. Smithson wrote of Stoer: "The eleven woodcuts contained in his slim treatise, *Geometria et Perspectiva* (1567), are modestly presented as examples of perspective, but they are, in fact, veritable geometrical landscapes in which the vegetable world is replaced by disquieting helixes, where polyhedrons and globes in unsteady equilibrium substitute for the human figure." Smithson Papers, Notebook III, undated (reel 3834, frame 80).

27 Clement Greenberg, "The Case for Abstract Art," in *The Collected Essays and Criticism*, vol. 4, ed. John O'Brian (Chicago: University of Chicago Press, 1993), 81. Of course Greenberg's equation of the presence of the art object with "a mouth repeating a single word" trips off a battery of poststructuralist alarms, for it is precisely the instantaneous self-presence of the voice that deconstruction has placed at the root of Western metaphysical idealism. The voice (as opposed to the written word)

is that which supposedly brings the subject and the object of speech together in a moment of perfect simultaneity and proximity, and which has the power to make of the referent an "ideal object." As Derrida explains, "An ideal object is an object whose showing may be repeated indefinitely, whose presence to *Zeigen* is indefinitely reiterable precisely because, freed from all mundane spatiality, it is a pure noema that I can express without having, at least apparently, to pass through the world." Derrida, *Speech and Phenomena and Other Essays on Husserl's Theory of Signs*, trans. David B. Allison (Evanston: Northwestern University Press, 1973), 75. Fried inherits this notion from Greenberg and recasts it in the epigraph to "Art and Objecthood," which had just been published when Smithson set out for Passaic. Fried quotes Perry Miller quoting Jonathan Edwards: "'It is certain with me that the world exists anew every moment; that the existence of things every moment ceases and is every moment renewed.' The abiding assurance is that 'we every moment see the same proof of a God as we should have seen if we had seen Him create the world at first.'" Fried, "Art and Objecthood," in *Minimal Art: A Critical Anthology*, ed. Gregory Battcock (Berkeley: University of California Press, 1995), 116.

28 Jorge Luis Borges, "Funes the Memorious," in *Labyrinths*, trans. James E. Irby (New York: New Directions, 1964), 59–66; Marcel Proust, *Within a Budding Grove*, vol. 2 of *In Search of Lost Time*, trans. C. K. Scott Moncrieff and Terence Kilmartin, rev. D. J. Enright (New York: Random House, Modern Library Edition, 1992), 67.

29 Wall, "Unity and Fragmentation in Manet," 81.

30 Smithson, "Art Through the Camera's Eye"; "Incidents of Mirror-Travel in the Yucatan"; in *Writings*, 373, 120; Jill Bennett, "Stigmata and Sense Memory: St. Francis and the Affective Image," *Art History* 24, no. 1 (March 2001): 1–16. The underlined passage by Saint John of the Cross was from an excerpt in Smithson's copy of H. A. Reinhold, ed., *The Soul Afire: Revelations of the Mystics* (New York: Meridian, 1960), 76. Regarding "stigmatic" photography, cf. Roland Barthes's slightly different formulation of the "punctum" in his *Camera Lucida: Reflections on Photography*, trans. Richard Howard (New York: Hill and Wang, 1981), esp. 25–27.

31 T. S. Eliot, "Four Quartets," in *Complete Poems and Plays 1909–1950* (New York: Harcourt and Brace, 1934), 142.

32 Smithson, "Monuments of Passaic," in *Writings*, 73.

33 See Passaic Valley Citizens Planning Association, "Parking in Passaic's Central Business District: A Report Submitted to the Citizen's Committee on Parking and Traffic," (October 1955); "Center of Passaic Will Lose Tracks," *New York Times*, Jun 30, 1962, 21; "Middle of Passaic Loses Its Railroad in 2-City Ceremony," *New York Times*, Apr 3, 1963, 49. For residents of Passaic, the loss of the tracks was momentous. Many felt that they had lost a vital link—not only to the other cities served by the railroad but also to Passaic's own historical past. For a memoirist's reflections on the railroad and the park-

ing lot superseding it see Bob Rosenthal, *Wonderful Passaic: Memories and Recollections* (San Jose, Calif.: Writer's Showcase, 2000), 56–62. For a detailed view of the "railroad problem" in Passaic see Columbia University School of Architecture, Planning and Housing Division, "A Development Program for the Fourth Ward Area of Passaic with a Note on Regional Needs," 1949.

34 Wallace Haddon, quoted in "Passaic Debating Uncertain Future," 41; Ebner, "The Future of River City," 16–20. By the late sixties Passaic was seen as a case study in urbanism for its particularly acute ethnic fragmentation. See Francine F. Rabinovitz, *City Politics and Planning* (New York: Atherton Press, 1969), 73–77.

35 Smithson, "The Monuments of Passaic," in *Writings*, 74.

36 R. J. Blin-Stoyle et al., *Turning Points in Physics* (New York: Harper Torchbooks, 1961), 50; Smithson, "Monuments of Passaic," in *Writings*, 71.

37 For Smithson's donation see the acknowledgment of receipt by the fund, and related materials, in the Smithson Papers, correspondence files. For violence in Passaic see Martin Gansberg, "Passaic Quiet as Negro Officials Warn Youth Gangs to 'Cool It,'" *New York Times*, Jul 31, 1967, 18. The most destructive rioting was still to come, particularly during the summer of 1969, when a weeklong series of disturbances broke out over slum rents in Puerto Rican neighborhoods. See Sylvan Fox, "Passaic Violence Enters 5th Night," *New York Times*, Aug 8, 1969, 42; and Martin Gansberg, "Passaic Assesses Costs of Rioting," *New York Times*, Aug 17, 1969, 49. The *Sand-Box Monument*'s entropic commentary on difference applies not only to the history of race relations in Passaic, but also to its history of immigration. The sandbox, along with the leaky fountain monument (fig. 33), were both located in a park near Passaic Stadium. This park, like the *Parking Lot Monument*, was a recent addition to the landscape of Passaic: it had been dedicated as Taras Shevchenko Park in June of 1964. Shevchenko was a nineteenth-century Ukrainian poet and artist of picturesque landscapes. Known as the "Bard of Ukraine," he was a national hero for the large contingent of Ukrainian immigrants in Passaic. Lawrence Alloway identifies Shevchenko Park as the location of the sandbox in "Robert Smithson's Development," *Artforum* 11, no. 3 (November 1972): 57. On the dedication of the park see the website for the Ukrainian American Veterans Post in Passaic: http://www.uavets.org/Post17/Post17.html. On Shevchenko see Pavlo Zaitsev, *Taras Shevchenko: A Life* (Toronto: University of Toronto Press, 1988).

CHAPTER 4. SMITHSON AND STEPHENS IN YUCATÁN
Epigraph: Smithson, "What Is a Museum?" in Jack Flam, ed., *Robert Smithson: The Collected Writings* (Berkeley: University of California Press, 1996), 47 (hereafter *Writings*).

1 John Lloyd Stephens, *Incidents of Travel in Central America, Chiapas, and Yucatán*, vol. 1 (New York: Harper and Brothers,

1841), 1; Smithson, appointment book for 1969, in Robert Smithson and Nancy Holt papers, reel 3832, frames 531–2, 542, 544, Archives of American Art, Smithsonian Institution, Washington, D.C. (hereafter Smithson Papers). Smithson referred to "The Yucatan" (with the definite article) throughout his essay to designate the entire Yucatán Peninsula and its outlying areas. This may have been the most convenient way to denominate the entire area of Maya influence, which comprised several Mexican states as well as Belize, Guatemala, and Honduras, but the usage is incorrect and I have elected not to repeat it here except when quoting Smithson directly. I have likewise restored the accent in the final syllable.

2 Smithson, "Four Conversations between Dennis Wheeler and Robert Smithson," in *Writings*, 231. Most of the existing discussions of Smithson's Yucatán project mention Stephens only briefly, if at all, as an uncomplicated object of Smithson's various parodic-allegorical inversions. The exception is the chapter "The Displacement of History: Robert Smithson's Time Travel in the Yucatán" in Rebecca Ann Butterfield, "Colonizing the Past: Archaic References and the Archaeological Paradigm in Contemporary American Earth Art," Ph.D. diss., University of Pennsylvania, 1998, 14–83. Butterfield's chapter focuses on Smithson's employment of archaeological themes and strategies (burial, fieldwork, etc.), while mine concentrates on the motif of historical indifference (and its associated visual analogies) that each traveler predicates upon the landscape and its inhabitants. Other than Butterfield, the only texts that devote themselves primarily to Smithson's Yucatán project are Marjorie Perloff, "The Demise of 'And': Reflections on Robert Smithson's Mirrors," *Critical Quarterly* 32, no. 3 (1990): 81–101, and Robert Linsley, "Mirror Travel in the Yucatán: Robert Smithson, Michael Fried, and the New Critical Drama," *res* 37 (Spring 2000): 7–30. Brief discussions of the project in longer works include Gary Shapiro, *Earthwards: Robert Smithson and Art After Babel* (Berkeley: University of California Press, 1995), 98–104; Henry Sayre, *Object of Performance: The American Avant-Garde Since 1970* (Chicago: University of Chicago Press, 1989), 222–26; Robert Hobbs, *Robert Smithson: Sculpture* (Ithaca: Cornell University Press, 1981), 151–65; Ronald Graziani, "(De)terminating the Political Enframement in the Art by Robert Smithson," Ph.D. diss., University of California, Los Angeles, 1992, 139–43.

3 Victor Wolfgang Von Hagen, *Maya Explorer: John Lloyd Stephens and the Lost Cities of Central America and Yucatán* (Norman: University of Oklahoma Press, 1947), xiii. Van Wyck Brooks, in his *World of Washington Irving* (New York: Dutton, 1944), 491–99, discusses Stephens's reputation in New York and his influence among the *literati*. Melville, in *Redburn*, wrote about his own boyhood awe of Stephens, and Poe was very closely involved with Stephens's work, having published reviews of three of his four travel books. The hieroglyphics which appear on the fictional island of Tsalal in Poe's *Narrative of Arthur Gordon Pym*, for example, were inspired by Stephens's

ruminations on the glyphs he found at Sinai. Poe's glyphs, in a circular coincidence of which Smithson was probably not aware, then went on to inspire Smithson's work (see Smithson's reference to Tsalal in "A Sedimentation of the Mind: Earth Projects," in *Writings*, 108). For Poe's reviews of Stephens, see: review of *Incidents of Travel in Egypt, Arabia Petraea, and the Holy Land*, by John Lloyd Stephens, *The New York Review* 1 (October 1837): 351–67; review of *Incidents of Travel in Greece, Turkey, Russia and Poland*, by John Lloyd Stephens, *New York Review* III (October 1838): 460–63, review of *Incidents of Travel in Central America, Chiapas, and Yucatán*, by John Lloyd Stephens, *Graham's Magazine* XIX (August 1841): 94.

4 The two publications are *Incidents of Travel in Central America, Chiapas, and Yucatán* (New York: Harper and Brothers, 1841) (hereafter cited as Stephens 1841), and *Incidents of Travel in Yucatán* (New York: Harper and Brothers, 1843) (hereafter cited as Stephens 1843). During the first expedition (1839–40) Stephens explored sites in the southern and western areas of Maya influence. The second expedition (1841–42) was restricted to the northern part of the peninsula. Since the second trip was conceived as an extension of the first (which had been cut short by malaria), I will be treating them as a single expedition for the purposes of this discussion. Catherwood also published his own folio edition of twenty-five lithographs: *Views of Ancient Monuments in Central America, Chiapas and Yucatán* (London, 1844). For a good summary of the issues and personalities involved in "rediscovery" in this period see Michael Coe, *Breaking the Maya Code* (New York: Thames and Hudson, 1992), 73–98.

5 Stephens 1841, 1: 117–18.

6 Ibid., 118. For the classic discussion of the ontological implications of camouflage see Roger Caillois, "Mimicry and Legendary Psychasthenia," trans. John Shepley, *October* 31 (Winter 1984): 17–32.

7 Stephens 1843, 1: 95.

8 Stephens 1841, 1: 98; Catherwood, *Views of Ancient Monuments*, 3.

9 R. Tripp Evans has discussed the detachment of indigenous figures from their architectural heritage more extensively in "Classical Frontiers: New World Antiquities in the American Imagination, 1820–1915," Ph.D. diss., Yale University, 1998, 60–82. See also Curtis Hinsley, "Hemispheric Hegemony in Early American Anthropology, 1841–1851: Reflections on John Lloyd Stephens and Henry Lewis Morgan," *Proceedings of the American Ethnological Society* (1985): 28–40. Although Hinsley does not discuss Catherwood's drawings, he focuses on Stephens's "imaginative detachment of the ruins from a population of degraded villages and marauding soldiers" (31), with particular sensitivity to the effects of the Central American civil war that was brewing around Stephens throughout the first expedition.

10 Stephens 1841, 1: 118.

11 Stephens 1843, 1: 111; Thomas Pynchon traces the history of

the concept of sloth in the United States in his essay "Sloth," in Pynchon et al., *Deadly Sins* (New York: William Morrow, 1993), 10–23.

12 Stephens 1843, 1: 118.

13 Johannes Fabian, *Time and the Other: How Anthropology Makes Its Object* (New York: Columbia University Press, 1983). Although the entire book takes the denial of coevalness as its theme, see page 31 for a concise discussion of the term; Stephens 1843, 1: 111.

14 For the "sovereign gaze" see Michel Foucault, *Discipline and Punish*, trans. Alan Sheridan (New York: Vintage Books, 1979), 195–228; and idem, "The Eye of Power," in *Power/ Knowledge: Selected Interviews and Other Writings 1972–1977*, ed. and trans. Colin Gordon (New York: Pantheon Books, 1980), 146–65; Alan Wallach, "Making a Picture of the View from Mount Holyoke," in *American Iconology*, ed. David Miller (New Haven: Yale University Press, 1993), 80–91; Kenneth John Myers, "On the Cultural Construction of Landscape Experience: Contact to 1830," in *American Iconology*, 74. The term *contact zone* is Mary Louise Pratt's and invokes "the spatial and temporal copresence of subjects previously separated by geographic and historical disjunctures." Mary Louise Pratt, *Imperial Eyes: Travel Writing and Transculturation* (London: Routledge, 1992), 7.

15 Stephens 1843, 1: 64. The strabismus operation was still in its experimental phase at this time; the first successful operation on a living patient occurred in Germany in 1839. For the early history of the operation and its practitioners see Daniel M. Albert, introduction to *Three Treatises on Strabismus* (Birmingham, Ala.: Gryphon Editions, Classics of Ophthalmology Library, 1987). The volume includes facsimiles of three American texts on the subject, all contemporaneous with the Stephens expedition: Alfred Charles Post, *Observations on the Cure of Strabismus* (New York: Charles C. Francis, 1841) (Post's book is illustrated with engravings by Nathaniel Currier; see fig. 52); John H. Dix, *Treatise on Strabismus, or Squinting, and the New Mode of Treatment* (Boston: D. Clapp, 1841); Frank H. Hamilton, *Monograph on Strabismus* (Buffalo: Jewett, Thomas & Co., 1845). See also Daniel M. Albert and Diane D. Edwards, eds., *The History of Ophthalmology* (London: Blackwell Science, 1996), 240, 259. Ironically, although Cabot made sure that the eyes of his subjects were physically aligned, his operations alone would not likely have improved the patients' vision. Even today, the surgery must be followed by an extensive program of visual training to ensure that the once "lazy" eye learns to work in concert with the functional eye. But postsurgical care not being among the priorities of their expedition, Stephens, Catherwood, and Cabot left town the day after the operations. It does not seem too farfetched to say that these eye operations were worth more to the establishment of ethnohistorical hierarchies in Stephens's narrative than they were to the visual health of the patients.

16 Stephens 1843, 1: 58; Dix, *Treatise on Strabismus*, 27–28;

Hamilton, *Monograph on Strabismus*, 11. Stephens did not seem to know that among the ancient Maya strabismus had been considered a mark of distinction. Its onset was encouraged in newborns by attaching small balls of wax to hair that dangled between the eyebrows. Robert J. Sharer, *The Ancient Maya*, 5th ed. (Stanford, Calif.: Stanford University Press, 1994), 482.

17 Jonathan Crary, *Techniques of the Observer: On Vision and Modernity in the Nineteenth Century* (Cambridge: MIT Press, 1990), 104, 131–32. It was in 1838 that Charles Wheatstone published his famous paper describing his invention, the stereoscope, and proving that binocular vision involved "two different perspective projections . . . being simultaneously presented to the mind." See Wheatstone, "Contributions to the Physiology of Vision—Part the First. On Some Remarkable, and Hitherto Unobserved, Phenomena of Binocular Vision," in *Brewster and Wheatstone on Vision*, ed. Nicholas J. Wade (London: Academic Press, Published for the Experimental Psychology Society, 1983), 65–93.

18 Although Stephens is mentioned in innumerable survey discussions of nineteenth-century travel literature and Mesoamerican archaeological history, most of them rely either on Stephens's own accounts or on the single existing (and largely hagiographic) monograph, Victor W. Von Hagen's 1947 biography, *Maya Explorer*. The most thorough critical analysis of Stephens is also the most recent: R. Tripp Evans, "Classical Frontiers." Other exclusive or near-exclusive treatments of which I am aware include David E. Johnson, "'Writing in the Dark': The Political Fictions of American Travel Writing," *American Literary History* 7 (Spring 1995): 1–27 (Johnson divides his discussion between Stephens and Paul Theroux); Richard Preston, "America's Egypt: John Lloyd Stephens and the Discovery of the Maya," *Princeton University Library Chronicle* 52, no. 3 (Spring 1992); and Curtis Hinsley, "Hemispheric Hegemony." Jean Frédéric Waldeck, a naturalized French citizen who had visited Uxmal and who had lived among the ruins of Palenque, was convinced that the ancient builders were "Hindoos," and went so far as to include elephants in his lithographs of the sculptural reliefs at Palenque. Jean Frédéric Waldeck, *Voyage pittoresque et archéologique dans de province d'Yucatán pendant les années 1834 et 1836* (Paris, 1838). Stephens states his case against Old World origination theories in Stephens 1841, 2: 436–57, and 1843, 2: 307–13. For a lively introduction to Old World and lost continent theories, including their perseverance through the twentieth century, see Robert Wauchope, *Lost Tribes and Sunken Continents: Myth and Method in the Study of American Indians* (Chicago: University of Chicago Press, 1962).

19 Brooks, *World of Washington Irving*, 494; Stephens 1841, 2: 453, 456.

20 Angela Miller, *The Empire of the Eye: Landscape Representation and American Cultural Politics, 1825–1875* (Ithaca: Cornell University Press, 1993), 34. For a useful discussion of the sal-

vage paradigm see James Clifford, Virginia Dominguez, and Trinh T. Minh-Ha, "Of Other Peoples: Beyond the 'Salvage' Paradigm," in *Discussions in Contemporary Culture I* (Seattle: Bay Press, 1987), 121–50.

21 Stephens 1841, 1: 115. He did end up purchasing the site, snickering at the credulity of the seller, for fifty dollars.

22 Ibid., 115–16.

23 Catherwood owned and operated a panorama rotunda which he had built in New York in 1838, immediately before embarking for Central America. Stephen Oettermann, *The Panorama: History of a Mass Medium*, trans. Deborah Lucas Schneider (New York: Zone Books, 1997), 317–23. For information on the fire see Victor W. Von Hagen, *Frederick Catherwood Architect* (New York: Oxford University Press,1950), 82–84. The painting in question was *Moonlight*, 1833–34. On the tenure of the Maya artifacts on Cruger's island and their eventual acquisition by the Museum of Natural History, see Phil Santora, "Trip to Yucatán on the Hudson," *New York Sunday News*, Sep 5, 1971, 12–14 (American Museum of Natural History, Special Collections Files); Herbert J. Spinden, "The Stephens Sculptures from Yucatán," *Natural History* 20 (Sept–Oct 1920): 179–387; Carl C. Dauterman, "The Strange Story of the Stephens Stones," *Natural History* 44 (December 1939): 288–96. On the collection as it was installed in 1944, see Harry L. Shapiro, "Middle American Culture on Review: Treasures from the Past Dramatically Exhibited in a New Hall of Mexican and Central American Archaeology," *Natural History* 53 (March 1944): 100–18. For Smithson's relationship to the American Museum of Natural History see Ann M. Reynolds, "Reproducing Nature: The Museum of Natural History as Nonsite," *October* 45 (Summer 1988): 109–27.

24 Dwan, Holt, and Smithson had been planning the trip for at least a year. A postcard from Virginia Dwan, postmarked February 20, 1968, from Mexico, reads in part: "Met some people here who had explored Mayan area, so have some ideas for *our* trip.—should plan it for no later than April (mid.)" Smithson Papers, unprocessed collection. Smithson's Dover copy was an unabridged republication of the original 1843 volumes (New York: Dover, 1963). Smithson Papers. The nineteenth-century frontispiece is on film in the Smithson Papers, reel 3833, frames 660–63.

25 Smithson, "Incidents of Mirror-Travel in the Yucatan," in *Writings*, 119.

26 By combining the information in Smithson's article with Virginia Dwan's later recollections, it is possible to reconstruct a rough outline of Smithson's travels through the area. On their journey from New York, Smithson, Holt, and Dwan stopped first in Florida, visiting Sanibel Island and then spending a day with Robert Rauschenberg at his home on nearby Captiva Island. They then flew from Florida to Mérida, near the north coast of the Yucatán Peninsula (where Stephens, Catherwood, and Cabot had performed their strabismus surgeries 128 years earlier). From there they drove south past Uxmal, then west to Campeche, and southwest to Palenque. They took a plane east from there to Bonampak and then another further east to the Usumacinta River, where they embarked on a downstream dugout trip, returning upstream again after reaching Yaxchilan. Then they looped through Villahermosa, Frontera, Ciudad del Carmen, and the aptly named Laguna de Terminos, where the "Incidents," at least so far as they were recorded in Smithson's article, ended. Virginia Dwan interviews with Charles F. Stuckey, March 21–June 7, 1984, transcript, pages 9:39–9:44, Archives of American Art, Smithsonian Institution; and Smithson, "Incidents of Mirror-Travel in the Yucatan," in *Writings*, 126–31.

27 Hal Foster discusses these and other methods of recoding tribal objects in "The 'Primitive' Unconscious of Modern Art," in *Art in Modern Culture: An Anthology of Critical Texts*, ed. Francis Frascina and Jonathan Harris (New York: Harper Collins, 1992), 203.

28 The term *infinite myopia* derives from Smithson's earlier, somewhat cryptic entry in the catalogue for the 1966 show *Art in Process* at Finch College: "Interpolation of the Enantiomorphic Chambers," in *Writings*, 39–40; Smithson, "Pointless Vanishing Points" (1967), in *Writings*, 359. For my understanding of and interest in the *Chambers* I am indebted to Ann Reynolds's detailed analysis in "Robert Smithson: Learning from New Jersey and Elsewhere," Ph.D. diss., City University of New York, 1993, 67–89. For a Lacanian analysis of the structure and visual effects of the *Chambers* see Timothy Martin, "De-architecturisation and the Architectural Unconscious: A Tour of Robert Smithson's Chambers and Hotels," *de-, dis-, ex-* 2 (1998): 89–114.

29 Stephens 1843, 1: 61; Smithson, "Incidents of Mirror-Travel in the Yucatan," in *Writings*, 130.

30 Smithson, ibid.

31 Reynolds, "Robert Smithson," 67–89; Shapiro, *Earthwards*, 68; Rosalind Krauss, "Entropy," in Yve-Alain Bois and Rosalind Krauss, *Formless: A User's Guide* (Cambridge: MIT Press, 1997), 78.

32 Smithson, "Incidents of Mirror-Travel in the Yucatan," in *Writings*, 131. See also Homi Bhabha, "Of Mimicry and Man: The Ambivalence of Colonial Discourse," in *The Location of Culture* (London: Routledge, 1994), 85–92.

33 Smithson, "Incidents of Mirror-Travel in the Yucatan," in *Writings*, 129.

34 For Smithson's celebrations of sloth see especially his essay "What Really Spoils Michelangelo's Sculpture," in *Writings*, 346–48. On Flaubert see Victor Brombert, "An Epic of Immobility," *Hudson Review* 19, no. 1 (Spring 1966): 24–43. Smithson cites this article in his footnotes to "The Artist as Site-Seer; or, a Dintorphic Essay," an unpublished text in *Writings*, 343. Smithson's copy of the *Hudson Review* issue is in the Smithson Papers. For an excellent discussion of the "geometric narratives" of Valery, Robbe-Grillet, Borges, and others, and their relation to spatiotemporal modeling, see George Slusser and

Danièle Chatelain, "Spacetime Geometries: Time Travel and the Modern Geometrical Narrative," *Science Fiction Studies* 22 (1995): 161–86. On the lyrical novel see Ralph Freedman, *The Lyrical Novel: Studies in Herman Hesse, André Gide, and Virginia Woolf* (Princeton, N.J.: Princeton University Press, 1963). Several passages in this book are underlined in Smithson's copy in the Smithson Papers. For indifference see Moira Roth, "The Aesthetic of Indifference," *Artforum* 16 (November 1977): 46–53.

35 Smithson, "Fragments of a Conversation," in *Writings*, 189; Anton Ehrenzweig, *The Hidden Order of Art: A Study in the Psychology of Artistic Imagination* (Berkeley: University of California Press, 1967), 20–21, 29, 42; Smithson, "Discussions with Heizer, Oppenheim, Smithson (1970)," in *Writings*, 249. Smithson frequently acknowledged Ehrenzweig as an influence on his conception of "primary process"—his "low-level" working method of seeing and experiencing the sites to which he traveled. Ehrenzweig's influence is particularly apparent in Smithson's essay "A Sedimentation of the Mind: Earth Projects," in *Writings*, 100–13, in which he developed many of his ideas about the Site/Nonsite dialectic and about the increasing role of expedition in his work: "At the low levels of consciousness the artist experiences undifferentiated or unbounded methods of procedure that break with the focused limits of rational technique" (102).

36 Ehrenzweig, *Hidden Order*, 33; Smithson, "Incidents of Mirror-Travel in the Yucatan," in *Writings*, 129–30.

37 Jacques Derrida, *Speech and Phenomena and Other Essays on Husserl's Theory of Signs*, trans. David B. Allison (Evanston: Northwestern University Press, 1973), 82.

38 Smithson, "Earth" (a group interview for the 1969 *Earthworks* show at Cornell), in *Writings*, 181; Smithson, draft of "Incidents of Mirror-Travel," Smithson Papers, reel 3834, frame 573; Smithson, "Incidents of Mirror-Travel in the Yucatan," 129 (emphasis in original).

39 Smithson, "Incidents of Mirror-Travel in the Yucatan," in *Writings*, 208, 133n1, 127, 124; Smithson, "Four Conversations Between Dennis Wheeler and Robert Smithson," in *Writings*, 215, 214. In his attempts to apply a philosophy of inaction to his landscape practice, Smithson was well aware of the discourse of the pastoral. Although his work might be argued to be anathema to the pastoral, he did adopt many of its traditional aspects, not least its emphasis on passive contemplation. To cite a passage that he underlined in one of his books, "The contemplator looks upon the world and man with the calm eye of one who has no design on them" (Sebastian de Grazia, *Of Time, Work, and Leisure* [New York: The Twentieth Century Fund, 1962], 17; Smithson's annotated copy: Smithson Papers). But Smithson takes this "calm eye" of contemplation several steps further, from calmness to stupor, from leisure to exhaustion.

40 Smithson, "Incidents of Mirror-Travel in the Yucatan," in *Writings*, 133n1, 127, 125.

41 Ibid., 125, 124, 125, 130. Stephens succumbed to malaria in 1855 while overseeing the construction of the Panama railroad. Von Hagen, *Maya Explorer*, 1947, 271–97. For a discussion of infection as an analogy for disintegration in the nineteenth century, see David C. Miller, "Infection and Imagination: The Atmospheric Analogy and the Problem of Romantic Culture in America," *Prospects* 13 (1988): 37–60. For the connotations of infection and degeneration historically predicated upon tropical landscapes, see Nancy Leys Stepan, *Picturing Tropical Nature* (Ithaca: Cornell University Press, 2001).

42 Smithson, "Quasi-Infinities and the Waning of Space," in *Writings*, 36.

43 Smithson, draft of "Incidents of Mirror-Travel in the Yucatan," Smithson Papers, reel 3834, frame 573; Samuel Beckett, *Proust* (New York: Grove Press, 1965). For Beckett's main discussion of involuntary memory see pages 17–21. There are other references to Beckett's book in Smithson's Yucatán essay, notably on page 127, where Smithson's phrases "The Caretaker of Dullness—habit—lurks everywhere" and "the futile and stupefying mazes" are both near-transcriptions of text that Smithson had underlined in Beckett's book. He also refers to "futile and stupefying habits" in his unpublished essay "An Aesthetics of Disappointment," in *Writings*, 334–35, and cites Beckett's book in "Quasi-Infinities," 37; Aristotle had distinguished in his *De Memoria et Reminiscentia* between remembering, which he classified as something which simply besets the lethargic and dull-witted, and recollection or reminiscence, which he privileged as active and productive. See Richard Sorabji, *Aristotle on Memory* (London: Duckworth, 1972), 47, and David Farrell Krell, *Of Memory, Reminiscence, and Writing* (Bloomington: Indiana University Press, 1990), 13–19.

44 J. G. Ballard, *The Crystal World* (New York: Farrar, Straus & Giroux, 1966), 73, 94–95.

45 Claude Lévi-Strauss, "Overture to *Le Cru et le Cuit*," *Yale French Studies* 36 (1967): 61. Smithson's copy: Smithson Papers.

46 Claude Lévi-Strauss, *The Savage Mind*, trans. George Weidenfeld and Nicolson Ltd. (Chicago: University of Chicago Press, 1966), 36, 263. Smithson reiterated his interest in Lévi-Strauss's timeless primitivity in an interview given in October of the year of his Yucatán trip (1969): "Lévi-Strauss describes the primitive mind as constantly involved in a world of timelessness, that's made up of all these moments." "Tempo Concreto: Interview with Robert Smithson by Achille Bonito Oliva," *Domus*, no. 481 (December 1969): 42–43. This interview is not included in *Writings*.

47 Smithson, "Incidents of Mirror-Travel in the Yucatan," in *Writings*, 119.

48 G. Charbonnier, ed., *Conversations with Claude Lévi-Strauss* (London: Jonathan Cape, 1969), 32–33. The entirety of Chapter 3, "Clocks and Steam Engines," is relevant in this regard.

49 "I would recommend that you read *The Savage Mind*. . . . It's a difficult book. This is probably the most difficult area, this whole idea of primal consciousness, primitive consciousness.

This is really what I'm interested in. I'm not interested in what Lévi-Strauss would call the hot cultures, with their mechanistic and electronic technologies which he calls hot. It's the cool kind of cold tribal technologies where there is a sort of understanding, consciousness." Smithson, "Four Conversations Between Dennis Wheeler and Robert Smithson," in *Writings*, 207 (ellipses in original).

50 Lévi-Strauss, *The Savage Mind*, 233–34.

51 Octavio Paz, *Claude Lévi-Strauss, An Introduction*, trans. J. S. Bernstein and Maxine Bernstein (Ithaca: Cornell University Press, 1970), 85. Although I have not been able to locate Paz's book in Smithson's library, Dennis Wheeler mentioned it in a 1970 letter to Smithson (Smithson Papers); Lévi-Strauss, in Charbonnier, *Conversations with Claude Lévi-Strauss*, 38. Smithson marked this passage in his copy of the book (Smithson Papers).

52 Jacques Derrida, *Writing and Difference*, trans. Alan Bass (Chicago: University of Chicago Press, 1978), 291, 292.

53 Smithson, "Ultramoderne," in *Writings*, 65.

54 Victor W. Von Hagen, *World of the Maya* (New York: Mentor, 1960), 11. Smithson mentions the book while discussing the objects inside his rental car ("Incidents of Mirror-Travel in the Yucatan," 120). The book is not, however, in the Smithson Papers; Paz, *Claude Lévi-Strauss: An Introduction*, 90.

55 Adam Gopnik, "Basic Stuff: Robert Smithson, Science, and Primitivism," *Arts Magazine* (March 1983): 74–80; Marshall McLuhan, Interview, *Playboy* 16 (March 1969): 59. Quoted in David Wyatt, "Hot and Cool in Anthropology: McLuhan and the Structuralists," *Journal of Popular Culture* V (Winter 1971): 552; Smithson, "The Monuments of Passaic," in *Writings*, 74.

56 Mircea Eliade, *Cosmos and History: The Myth of the Eternal Return*, trans. Willard R. Trask (New York: Harper Torchbooks, 1959), 42. Smithson's copy: Smithson Papers; Butterfield, "Colonizing the Past," 23–37, provides an excellent discussion of the logic behind Smithson's selection of certain gods to appear in his narrative.

57 Smithson, "Incidents of Mirror-Travel in the Yucatan," 120. The following excerpt is underlined in Smithson's copy of *Degrees*: "All the maps you have are of no use, all the work of discovery and surveying; you have to start off at random, like the first men on earth; you risk dying of hunger a few miles from the richest stores." Michel Butor, *Degrees* (New York: Simon & Schuster, 1961), 33. Smithson Papers. Smithson had also quoted this excerpt in his essay of a year earlier, "A Museum of Language in the Vicinity of Art," in *Writings*, 91.

58 Smithson, "Robert Smithson: Hotel Palenque, 1972," *Parkett* 43 (1995), unpaged insert. The *Parkett* insert is a transcription of Smithson's commentary and a reproduction of all of the slides from the lecture he gave at the University of Utah in 1972. The lecture is not included in *Writings*. The term *invincible idleness* is from Smithson's 1967 essay "Ultramoderne," in *Writings*, 63–65.

59 Smithson, "Hotel Palenque," n.p.

60 Henry Giniger, "Guatemala is a Battleground," *New York Times Magazine*, Jun 16, 1968, 14–24; Peter Nehemkis, *Latin America: Myth and Reality* (New York: Knopf, 1964).

61 Smithson, "Incidents of Mirror-Travel in the Yucatan," 119, 120.

62 Nehemkis, *Latin America: Myth and Reality*, 4; Richard Gott, "Intellectuals & Politics in Latin America," *TriQuarterly*, no. 15 (Spring 1969): 258, 260. Holt, quoted in Janet Kardon, "Robert Smithson's Unrealized Projects," undated, unpublished manuscript, Smithson Papers, 8; Smithson, "Incidents of Mirror-Travel in the Yucatan," 127.

63 Smithson, interview with Willoughby Sharp, 1968, transcribed in Suzaan Boettger, ed., "Degrees of Disorder," *Art in America* 86 (December 1998): 76. This interview is not published in *Writings*.

64 Lucy Lippard, "The Art Workers' Coalition: Not a History," *Studio International* 180, no. 27 (November 1970): 171–74. See also idem, "The Politics of the Primitive," in Hobbs, *Robert Smithson: Sculpture*, 36, where she writes: "He watched the AWC as a detached bystander, too aware of our powerlessness to join in, and amused by the spectacle of all of us 'idealists' scrapping with each other. He was probably as politically confused about the role of the artist as the rest of us, but he also probably enjoyed it more, since chaos moving toward entropy was his natural element."

65 Smithson, "Art and the Political Whirlpool or the Politics of Disgust (1970)," in *Writings*, 134. Originally published as part of a symposium in *Artforum*, 1970. Smithson, "The Monuments of Passaic," in *Writings*, 74.

66 Smithson, "A Refutation of Historical Humanism"; "An Aesthetics of Disappointment"; "Art and the Political Whirlpool"; "What Is a Museum?" in *Writings*, 337, 335, 134, 51.

CHAPTER 5. SPIRAL JETTY/GOLDEN SPIKE

1 Quoted in the Golden Spike Centennial Issue facsimile of the June 1869 *Travelers' Official Railway Guide*. Ann Arbor: UMI, 1969.

2 Martin Heidegger, *Being and Time*, trans. Joan Stambaugh (Albany: State University of New York Press, 1996), 417–18. For the punctual Now and its history see Heidegger, ibid., 417, and Jacques Derrida, *Speech and Phenomena and Other Essays on Husserl's Theory of Signs*, trans. David B. Allison (Evanston: Northwestern University Press, 1973), 61–62. Another tantalizing theoretical model for the function of the spike (which I will not follow here) is Jacques Lacan's notion of the "point de capiton," variously translated as a quilting point and an upholstery nail, which secures the subject into the symbolic field.

3 See Robert M. Utley and Francis A. Ketterson, Jr., *Golden Spike* (Washington: U.S. Government Printing Office, 1969).

4 The commission had been created by executive order in 1967. For details about the ceremony and the event schedules see Golden Spike Centennial Celebration Commission, *Final Report*, 1970 (typescript, Utah State Historical Society, MSS

A86). Independently organized annual reenactments of the driving of the Golden Spike had been going on since 1952, but the Golden Spike National Historic Site was not designated as a part of the National Park Service until 1965, and it was only then that the reenactment ceremonies came under the aegis of the National Park Service's historical section. The centennial archive is held at the Golden Spike National Historic Site, Nathan Mazer Papers. (Mazer was the executive director of field operations for the centennial commission.)

5   On the exclusion of the Chinese workers from Russell's photograph see Martha A. Sandweiss, *Print the Legend: Photography and the American West* (New Haven: Yale University Press, 2002), 160–61. On Volpe's speech see "The Forgotten Men at Gold Spike Ceremony," *San Francisco Chronicle*, 12 May 1969. Golden Spike National Historic Site, Nathan Mazer Papers.

6   "(They Were Called 'Crocker's Pets') Little Yellow Men: Driven to Achieve the Impossible," in *The Story of the Wedding of the Rails, 1869 to 1969*, Robert Smithson and Nancy Holt papers, 1905–1987, Archives of American Art, Smithsonian Institution, Washington, D.C. (hereafter Smithson Papers); the Winchester rifle advertisement appeared in *Trains: The Magazine of Railroading*, May 1969. Golden Spike National Historic Site, Nathan Mazer Papers.

7   Smithson arrived in Utah in March 1970 and built the *Jetty* during the month of April (appointment book for 1970, Smithson Papers). Smithson was likely aware of the centennial even before arriving in Utah, since the ceremony had been national news. The *New York Times* ran at least two articles: "Rail Fans' Pilgrimages to Promontory," Mar 23, 1969; "Rail Spanning of Nation in 1869 Is Observed," May 11, 1969.

8   Robert Smithson, "The Spiral Jetty," in Jack Flam, ed., *Robert Smithson: The Collected Writings* (Berkeley: University of California Press, 1996), 145 (hereafter *Writings*). The special centennial edition of the paper is in the Smithson Papers. Smithson also had a copy in his library of Barry Combs's *Westward to Promontory: Building the Union Pacific* (Palo Alto, Calif.: American West, 1969). Of Smithson and the Golden Spike Motel, Dwan noted: "The Golden Spike Motel, for example, that dumpy nowheresville kind of place with linoleum rugs and strange heaters high up on the wall. To Bob the Golden Spike was not just a dump, it was an adventure, a place of mystery, so strange and exciting one would swear he was in a science fiction world." Virginia Dwan, quoted in Robert Hobbs, *Robert Smithson: Sculpture* (Ithaca: Cornell University Press, 1981), 20. On Smithson's museum plans see Kynaston McShine, ed., *The Museum as Muse: Artists Reflect* (New York: Museum of Modern Art, 1999), 86–89.

9   Clement Greenberg, "The Case for Abstract Art," in *The Collected Essays and Criticism*, vol. 4, ed. John O'Brian (Chicago: University of Chicago Press, 1993), 81; Michael Fried, "Art and Objecthood," in *Minimal Art: A Critical Anthology*, ed. Gregory Battcock (Berkeley: University of California Press, 1995), 145; Robert Smithson to Enno Develing, ca. 1971, Smithson Papers, reel 3833, frame 366.

10   Smithson, "A Sedimentation of the Mind," in *Writings*, 111–12 (emphasis in original). See also his unpublished essay "Production for Production's Sake," written in 1972: "The 'object of art' becomes more a condition of a confused leisure class, and as a result the artist is separated from his own *work*," *Writings*, 378 (emphasis in original).

11   On the idea of the breakthrough see Katy Siegel, "Breakthrough: Time in the 1950s and 1960s," in *Tempus Fugit*, ed. Jan Schall (Kansas City, Mo.: Nelson-Atkins Museum of Art, 2000), 116–31; Fried, "Art and Objecthood," 137.

12   See Jean-François Lyotard, "Acinema," in *The Lyotard Reader*, ed. Andrew Benjamin (London: Basil Blackwell, 1989), 176; Georges Bataille, "The Notion of Expenditure," in *Visions of Excess: Selected Writings 1927–1939*, ed. and trans. Allan Stoekl (Minneapolis: University of Minnesota Press, 1985), 116–29; Jacques Derrida, "Given Time: The Time of the King," *Critical Inquiry* 18, no. 2 (Winter 1992): 170.

13   See Alexander Alberro, "Time and Conceptual Art," and Kathy O'Dell, "Time Clocks and Paradox: On Labor and Temporality in Performance Art," in Schall, *Tempus Fugit*.

14   Smithson, "The Spiral Jetty," in *Writings*, 146.

15   The best source of information on the specifics of the construction process, including revealing interviews with leaders of the construction team, is Hikmet Dogu, "An Intermittent Illusion: Local Reaction to Robert Smithson's *Spiral Jetty*," Master's thesis, Hunter College of the City University of New York, 1996. See also Lawrence Alloway, "Robert Smithson's Development," *Artforum* 11, no. 3 (November 1972): 53–61, and Mark Saal, "Construction Crew Took on 'Nutso' Project and Won," *Ogden Standard-Examiner* 23, Jun 1996, 6–7D.

16   Smithson, "The Spiral Jetty," in *Writings*, 147.

17   On Morelli see Edgar Wind, "Critique of Connoisseurship," in *Art and Anarchy* (New York: Knopf, 1965), 32–51; Carlo Ginzburg, "Clues: Roots of an Evidential Paradigm," in *Clues, Myths, and the Historical Method*, trans. John and Anne Tedeschi (Baltimore: Johns Hopkins University Press, 1989), 96–125.

18   Wind, ibid., 44.

19   Smithson, "The Spiral Jetty," 143, 145, 153. Smithson did not invent "Mark Crystal"; he was a land specialist in the Utah department of natural resources. Crystal handled the special use lease for the land that the *Jetty* occupies. For a letter to Smithson from Crystal see the Smithson Papers, reel 3833, frame 425. For a sustained treatment of Smithson's relationship to proper names (especially his own) see Gary Shapiro, *Earthwards: Robert Smithson and Art After Babel* (Berkeley: University of California Press, 1995), 191–233.

20   Gyorgy Kepes, ed., *Arts of the Environment* (New York: George Braziller, 1972), 222–32. All photographs were taken by Gianfranco Gorgoni in the summer of 1970 under Smithson's direction.

21   Smithson, "The Spiral Jetty," in *Writings*, 147.

22   Ibid.

23 Ibid., 148; Smithson, "A Cinematic Atopia," in *Writings*, 141.
    See also his interview with Dennis Wheeler, "Four Conversations
    Between Dennis Wheeler and Robert Smithson," in *Writings*,
    203–4, 211; Gary Shapiro, *Earthwards*, 223.

24 On the metaphorical history of salt see Ernest Jones, "The
    Symbolic Significance of Salt in Folklore and Superstition," in
    *Salt and the Alchemical Soul: Three Essays by Ernest Jones,
    C. G. Jung & James Hillman*, ed. Stanton Marlan (Woodstock,
    Conn.: Spring Publications, 1995), 47–100.

25 "Scale" derives from the old French *escaille*, meaning husk or
    shell, a term that evokes accretion and inorganic growth.
    Webster's New Collegiate Dictionary, s.v. "scale"; Smithson, "Can
    Man Survive?" in *Writings*, 368.

26 N. Katherine Hayles, *Chaos Bound: Orderly Disorder in Contem-
    porary Literature and Science* (Ithaca: Cornell University
    Press, 1990), 15. The classic "manifesto" of fractal theory as
    applied to natural systems is Benoit B. Mandelbrot, *The
    Fractal Geometry of Nature* (New York: W. H. Freeman, 1977).
    For the best generalist account of the development of
    chaos theory see James Gleick, *Chaos: The Making of a New
    Science* (New York: Penguin, 1997). See also Mark C. Taylor,
    "Figuring Complexity," in *The Picture in Question: Mark
    Tansey and the Ends of Representation* (Chicago: University of
    Chicago Press, 1999), 99–128.

27 Jacques Derrida, "What Is a 'Relevant' Translation?" *Critical
    Inquiry* (February 2001): 195 (emphasis in original).

28 Smithson, interview with Paul Toner, in *Writings*, 239.

29 From an unpublished list of references in one of Smithson's
    notebooks in the Smithson Papers, reel 3834, frame 122,
    which traces historical and literary meanings of the spiral.

30 Terry Eagleton, *The Ideology of the Aesthetic* (London: Blackwell,
    1990), 9, 25; Hal Foster, "Postmodernism: A Preface," in
    The Anti-Aesthetic: Essays on Postmodern Culture (Seattle: Bay
    Press, 1983), xv; William Blake, "Auguries of Innocence,"
    in *The Complete Writings of William Blake*, ed. Geoffrey Keynes
    (New York: Random House, 1957), 431.

31 See Hobbs, *Robert Smithson: Sculpture*, 196.

32 See Smithson's 1968 essay, "A Museum of Language in the
    Vicinity of Art," in *Writings*, 88–90, where he twice mentions
    Poe's story.

33 Edgar Allan Poe, "A Descent into the Maelström," in *The Com-
    plete Tales and Poems of Edgar Allan Poe* (New York: Vintage,
    1975), 127–40.

INDEX